Therapy and the
Postpartum Woman

Therapy and the Postpartum Woman

*Notes on Healing Postpartum
Depression for Clinicians and the
Women Who Seek Their Help*

KAREN KLEIMAN

Routledge
Taylor & Francis Group
New York   London

Routledge
Taylor & Francis Group
711 Third Avenue,
New York, NY 10017

Routledge
Taylor & Francis Group
27 Church Road,
Hove, East Sussex,
BN3 2FA, UK

First issued in paperback 2014

Routledge is an imprint of the Taylor and Francis Group, an informa business

© 2009 by Taylor & Francis Group, LLC

ISBN 978-0-415-98996-1 (hbk)
ISBN 978-1-138-87293-6 (pbk)

Library of Congress Cataloging-in-Publication Data

Kleiman, Karen R.
    Therapy and the postpartum woman : notes on healing postpartum depression for clinicians and the women who seek their help / Karen Kleiman.
        p. ; cm.
    Includes bibliographical references and index.
    ISBN 978-0-415-98996-1 (hardbound : alk. paper)
    1. Postpartum depression--Treatment. I. Title.
    [DNLM: 1. Depression, Postpartum--therapy. 2. Psychotherapy--methods. WQ 500 K63t 2008]

    RG852.K564 2008
    618.7'6--dc22   2008012586

Visit the Taylor & Francis Web site at
http://www.taylorandfrancis.com

and the Routledge Web site at
http://www.routledge.com

Contents

For my daughter, Melanie

The Author

Karen Kleiman, MSW, licensed clinical social worker, is the author of *This Isn't What I Expected: Overcoming Postpartum Depression* (with V. Raskin), *The Postpartum Husband: Practical Solutions for Living With Postpartum Depression,* and *What Am I Thinking? Having Another Baby After Postpartum Depression.* She has been working with women and their families for more than 20 years. A native of Saint Louis, Missouri, Karen has lived in the Philadelphia area since 1982 with her two children and her husband. In 1988 she founded The Postpartum Stress Center, where she provides treatment for prenatal and postpartum depression and anxiety.

Foreword

Postpartum depression is not a moral failure, an ethical dilemma, or a symptom of weakness. It is a medical condition that often begins long before the baby is delivered. It is a neuropsychiatric illness that affects every cell in a woman's brain and body, some more obviously than others. But women who develop it rarely see it as a true medical illness no less real or serious than postpartum thyroid disease. Unfortunately, the same lack of insight plagues partners and clinicians in all too many instances.

Postpartum depression robs a woman of what can be one of the most spectacular and truly unique experiences of her life. Even in parts of the world where famine, disease, and violence daily threaten people's very existence, the birth of a child is greeted as a miracle and a symbol that all may be better someday. But postpartum depression sucks the lifeblood out of a mother and can torment her with guilt over bringing a child into the world. Postpartum depression can make the most optimistic woman question her very existence. And for the other parent? The shock of seeing one's partner *not* fall in love with her baby can leave gaping holes not just in the relationship, but also in the partner himself or herself. Postpartum depression is an illness that touches the immediate family, the extended family, and the woman's friends.

Therapy and the Postpartum Woman: Notes on Healing Postpartum Depression for Clinicians and the Women Who Seek Their Help presents a brilliantly written guide that is distinguished by its recognition of the biological nature of postpartum depression while acknowledging that the term "postpartum depression" belies the complexity of perinatal mood disorders. Ms. Kleiman stresses that psychotherapy is not a substitute for medications when somatic treatments are necessary. Instead, she works from the premise that, when used judiciously, psychotherapy is an essential therapeutic tool that can facilitate complete recovery by addressing the unique challenges posed by perinatal mood disorders.

Ms. Kleiman presents a theoretical framework in which the therapist "mothers the mother" by acting as the "good" mother who "must achieve that equilibrium between absolute support and appropriate boundaries." Using compelling patient narratives, she demonstrates just how to achieve that balance in order to teach the patient how to develop confidence in her own skills as a mother. There is a treasure trove of "clinical pearls" in this eminently readable book, which even the most experienced clinician will be able to use right away. For those new to the field, and for patients and their loved ones, the book offers a wealth of information on the nature of postpartum depression as a medical illness and the psychosocial issues that arise when a woman is faced with caring for a baby. Ms. Kleiman describes how the medical community tends to minimize the complexity of these issues and uses a "one size fits all" approach to treating depression. Readers will learn to be more effective advocates for proper treatment of perinatal depression. Therapists will also learn how to draw from their own experiences to facilitate the human connection between therapist and patient at a time when women feel isolated by shame and insecurity. Together, the therapist and the patient can work toward discovering the innate resilience that has allowed women to raise children even in the most extreme circumstances. Ms. Kleiman has developed a humanistic approach to psychotherapy for postpartum mood disorders that gives recognition to psychodynamic theory, but then she uses many cognitive–behavioral techniques to reach well-defined goals.

Therapy and the Postpartum Woman is an elegantly written book that not only offers practical advice but also does so in a way that will touch the lives of both patients and therapists. It is destined to become a classic for those experiencing or treating perinatal mood disorders.

Shari I. Lusskin, MD
Director of Reproductive Psychiatry
New York University Langone Medical Center

Acknowledgments

As I put this book together, I was reminded how blessed I am to be surrounded by such loving and gifted colleagues. First, I thank Dr. Marcie Weiner, our clinical director, for her gentle understanding of all that drives me and for her years of devoted hard work and support. Much of what I do is because she makes it possible.

I am also indebted to Trish McGarrigle, who went in a flash from counseling intern to my enthusiastic advocate, advisor, and greatest fan, guiding me every single step of the way. Trish was there to fill in the blanks whenever my brain seemed to stop short. I am also eternally grateful to Liz Goldman, MD, for her medical expertise and great friendship. And to Pam Eitzen, for her creativity, generous spirit, and ability to capture the essence of what it is in my heart.

Thanks to Dawn Moot, my editor, who fielded my incessant procedural questions, giggling each time I told her it was the wrong side of my brain, and helped escort this book into its final stages; her enthusiasm for this project was evident from the very beginning. And to Judith Simon, my production editor, for meticulously perfecting my not-so-perfect attention to detail.

I am especially grateful to Shari Lusskin, MD, for her support of this project and her untiring commitment to postpartum women and their families. Thanks to all my colleagues who never fail to support my work and to all the passionate volunteers who tirelessly give their time, energy, and compassion to the postpartum community. Thanks to every single woman who has ever walked into my office and believed in me, the process, and herself. My deepest gratitude to those women who will find pieces of their own lives within the pages of this book. Thank you for your trust and your willingness to trust others.

For their sustaining support and patience throughout this project, and for trusting that one day I would indeed finish and be able to reunite with the rest of humanity, I sincerely thank my dearest friends, Jason Sutliff, Sharon Friedman, and Elana Kripke.

For their unwavering support and lifelong affection, I thank my mother, Miriam Raskin, who will always write better than I do, and my father, Larry Raskin. Their steadfast commitment to each other has inspired much of what I do and who I am, both at work and at home. I am grateful to my sister and friend, Laurie Morgan; my brother, Richard Raskin; and my aunt, Susan Spiegel, who surround me with enduring love and support on a regular basis.

And from the deepest spot in my heart, I thank my children, Jeff and Melanie, for believing in me and for understanding how important it is to believe in themselves. And special thanks to my husband, Bruce, who makes marriage look easy and who always makes me laugh and feel loved.

Preface

Ever since I can remember, I wanted to be a mother. When I was a young girl, my favorite pastime was playing house, and, of course, I was the perfect mother. I held my sweet doll tightly to my chest and promised her a lifetime of whatever she wanted. I leaned against the giant oak tree in the backyard and cradled her in my arms, rocking her back and forth. "I love you," I whispered and told her that she didn't have to be afraid of anything. I would always take care of her. Forever and ever.

I was a very good mother when I was a child.

I knew all the right things to do, and I said all the right words. I was able to fix any problem, and, in return, I was loved unconditionally. If anyone asked, I would stand up tall, head up, shoulders back, and boast, "When I grow up, I'm going to be a mommy."

Before I had children, I never gave much thought to what kind of mother I would truly be. It was something I presumed would unfold naturally. As my children grew, I watched myself morph from the always nurturing, selflessly devoted, idealized mother in my mind's eye to one who would hyperventilate instantaneously when my son was 10 minutes late getting home from school. I experienced the chaos, the flood of unexpected emotions, the feelings of betrayal and disbelief when my children didn't see me the way I saw myself. I lived through anxiety from which I never thought I could recover. I made mistakes, I overreacted, and, above all, I learned how to be a mother the way everyone learns—by doing it. However, I wasn't depressed. I've never known the agony of mothering a child without being able to breathe. That is something I learned from the women who have trusted me with their private stories.

One major premise of this book is based on the notion that a woman who gives birth to a baby and who suffers from depression at the same time is generally not in the mood for therapy, and she does not want to take medication, or make time for one more appointment, or take care of herself, for that matter. She's tired and restless; she's overwhelmed and can hardly find the time to do what she needs to do. She's sleep deprived, hormonally compromised, and trying desperately to come close to her idealized image of what a mother should look, sound, act, and feel like. She's finding it hard to concentrate. She's crying more than she usually does. Her nerves are shot, and every single thing that anyone says or does makes her angry, sad, irritable, or scared to death.

Then, just when she begins to believe that having a baby was really not a good idea after all, someone tells her she needs to get help. Someone is worried about her. It may be her husband; it may be her doctor or her mother. It may even be her own inner voice that knows something is terribly, terribly wrong.

In the early stages of feeling bad, her typical response to someone suggesting she see a therapist for the treatment of depression is something like, "Are you *kidding*?! I don't have time." But if she feels bad long enough or if her symptoms are scary enough, she will make that call. When she does, it's the clinician's job to know how difficult it is to make that call and know exactly what to say and do to help her feel better.

When depression sets in, the birth of a child becomes more than a rite of passage. Postpartum depression can create a conglomeration of conflicting emotions; it can cause a woman to challenge everything she has ever thought about herself and about her own childhood experience, as well as her identification with her own mother. It robs her peace of mind and it makes her feel as if she's lost touch with her very core. It fractures her soul.

Thus, when we speak about treatment for postpartum depression, we refer to more than which therapeutic intervention is most effective or which medication is compatible with breastfeeding. Clinicians who treat women with postpartum depression the same way they treat anyone else with depression may miss some critical differences that will affect the outcome and, ultimately, the client's well-being.

Postpartum depression emerges at a time in a woman's life when both the demands and stakes are high. In addition to the disturbing feelings and symptoms, there is one more complicating factor. There is a baby in the picture. This makes everything more dramatic, more precarious, and much more urgent.

Whether it's a woman's first bout of depression or one of many, experiencing these symptoms while she transitions into her role of mother can make her wonder if this is just what being a mother feels like. Too often, a woman is unaware she is suffering from a treatable condition. Rather, it is perceived as a character flaw, a defect in the vision of maternal perfection she held so close to her heart.

For this reason, it is insufficient to treat only the illness when treating postpartum depression. Handing out a prescription for antidepressants and telling her to come back in a few weeks for a follow-up may, in the short run, relieve some symptoms, but it fails to address her wounded self-esteem and belief that she will never be a good mother. In doing so, we abandon the heart of a mother who has been injured beyond belief at a time when she expected what everyone else expected: *that this would be the happiest time in her life.* It seems our society should stop insinuating that this is so. As exciting as this time is for many women and their families, it is also a time in their lives when many are at risk for emotional illness (Frank, Weihs, Minerva, & Lieberman, 1998). It would be prudent for women to prepare for the possibility of depression rather than expect maternal bliss and then be blindsided by the illness.

I would definitely be a downer at any baby shower. While everyone else would be chatting about cribs and changing tables, I'd be thinking to myself: *Does she have enough help at home? Is her marriage solid? Does she have a history of depression? Did she really want to leave her job? Will she get enough sleep?* This is because I worry most about women who are not prepared, who are at risk for depression, or who think it can't happen to them. It can and it does. When it does emerge, the very last thing that woman feels like doing is telling anyone about it.

Despite increased attention to the illness, women with postpartum depression are still hesitant to reveal to their healthcare practitioners how bad they are feeling. Fearing judgment or casual dismissal, they hold tight to their private worries and simply hope they will go away on their own.

Sometimes they do. Often, they do not.

The good news is that there has been a huge shift in current thinking about postpartum depression brought on by increased public awareness. Groundbreaking legislation for improved screening practices and treatment options has paved the way for women who are seeking treatment. Yet, despite these recent advances, there remains an enduring unknown. Can we make the assumption, after we screen, assess, and refer for treatment, that a given woman will get decidedly good treatment? Therapists have rallied in response to this awareness campaign and are now in position to treat women with postpartum depression, but they need more information. A great number of experienced as well as new clinicians are now expanding their practices to incorporate this area of specialty. Clinicians can read up on postpartum mood disorders and familiarize themselves with the associated symptoms and treatments, but they also need insight into the practical application and hands-on tools with which they can navigate the therapeutic territory.

Sharing the therapeutic space with a woman with postpartum depression is uniquely challenging for the clinician. The client may be resistant to or eager for help. She may be grateful or resentful. She may be bleary eyed and bone weary. She may be motivated for treatment or suspicious of anyone's ability to help her. Nevertheless, it's a journey the two embark on together. A journey that challenges the postpartum woman's sensibilities, awakens her traumatized soul, and ultimately transforms her. For me, I never take that for granted and am forever honored to be an integral part of this journey toward recovery and renewal of self. I work hard to make sure that each client feels safe when she comes into my office seeking comfort and answers. I know she feels it the first time we meet. This is not simply because I understand postpartum depression; it's because I do my best to understand how hard it is for her to be there.

There are many excellent books on postpartum depression. Many are written with the voice of an authoritative expert offering solid information on the nature of the illness and treatment options. Other books on postpartum depression are written by courageous women who share their personal dramatic accounts through vivid stories of despair and determination, culminating in the success that enabled them to tell their stories. My own previous works on the subject were self-help books written as guides for the postpartum woman and her family to help them find their way through the fog of depression. To date, there are no postpartum books that take the reader inside the private world of the therapeutic experience to give both the clinician and the woman in therapy a clear sense of what to expect from this work together.

Long before I began writing this book, I was asked by a writer for a popular magazine to describe my theoretical ideologies. What did I believe was making a difference? How *did* I treat women with postpartum depression? Good question, I thought, and certainly one for which I should have an answer. After wavering a bit with procrastinating charm, I filled in the space with something like "We use a combination of supportive psychotherapy and medication when indicated." That worked for the time being.

More recently, when trying to satisfy the demands of publishers and academic reviewers, I was again forced to contemplate the theoretical foundation of work that had always come naturally to me. A book about my good instincts was surely out of the question. I started reading the works of brilliant minds such as D. W. Winnicott and felt a light bulb come on in my head: *Oh, so that's what I do!* Further exploration into earlier psychoanalytic teachings gave credence to the intuitive principle that mothering a new mother made perfect sense and helped postpartum women heal. It's all about the connection. The therapy, the treatment, the healing, and whether she comes into our office in the first place all depends on whether she feels connected to the process and to the relationship. This concept is not a new one for practicing therapists. Still, our connection with the postpartum woman is unique in that it emulates the mother–child relationship. Specifically, it is based on a need-dependency schema set in motion by the symptoms of depression. The thrust of this book is to take a closer look at these unique needs, with apologies to Winnicott for my simplistic integration of his inspiring work.

During our postgraduate training classes, clinicians convene from across the country to gather around the conference table discussing how it *feels* to do this work. Rather than lecture to an auditorium full of students hoping to gain knowledge of relevant theories and effective interventions, we discuss how painful it can be to sit with a woman who has lost her baby after carrying him in her belly for 9 months. We talk about how hard it must be to have ambivalent feelings about your new baby after 3 years of expensive, time-consuming, gut-wrenching infertility treatments. Most importantly, we talk about the connection between the therapist and the mother in therapy.

A point I will make repeatedly is that the connection is the reason that what we do works.

Early in the book, it will be clear that my voice is speaking directly to therapists, addressing clinicians who work with postpartum women as "we." In chapter 4, when I discuss the characteristics of a postpartum depression (PPD) therapist, I will shift to singular tense, speaking directly to "you," the therapist, because my objective is to facilitate individual introspection. At times, I will specifically reference our practices at The Postpartum Stress Center. Please note that these reflect only our approach and not necessarily those that might best serve other clinicians. I will also refer to the client as the "postpartum woman" for brevity's sake, rather than imply that every postpartum woman is experiencing depression—but certainly the ones I refer to here are. I presume that postpartum women will also be reading these pages, and because the notion of therapy can feel disquieting to many, my hope is to make the experience of therapy less intimidating for them.

It may at times appear that I am glossing over certain aspects of the illness in favor of focusing on topics I believe have significant bearing on the personal and professional experience as a whole. Throughout these pages I provide a framework for thinking about the woman who suffers from PPD and offer concepts that help her treating clinician better understand the circumstances that have brought her into therapy. Understanding the illness and treatment options are one part of the healing process. Understanding the woman's experience of this illness is something quite different.

For this reason, you might find that certain topics are missing from this book. For instance, if clinicians are looking for an explanation of the hormonal influence on postpartum depression or whether Wellbutrin is safe to take during pregnancy, they'll need to find that information in another resource. To be sure, there are facts that exist in the literature regarding the treatment of postpartum depression that remain the foundation for much of the work we do. Clinicians are obliged to continually stay informed and revise practice guidelines in order to provide state-of-the-art treatment. Therefore, I am comfortable making the assumption that clinicians will find theories and evidence-based research elsewhere to support their clinical decisions and address questions that may arise. In writing this book, my intention is to provide a new framework for thinking. It is not a comprehensive handbook on the treatment of postpartum depression. It is a compilation of my most meaningful experiences and personal reflections complemented by professional strategies and relevant research. Mostly, it is a book that probes the private world of therapy through dynamic exploration of what works and what doesn't work on the path to healing postpartum depression. I stand firm in my conviction that none of the abstract theories can explain what it really feels like to sit in the room and share the same space with a woman who no longer knows who she is. It is another matter altogether. It is quite personal.

A few years ago, a great researcher and colleague, Kathy Wisner, MD, honored me with the gift of her wisdom when I was attending one of her presentations on perinatal mood disorders. I recall approaching her just prior to the lecture, handing her a copy of my then-new book, *What Am I Thinking?* Being ever so humbled by her awesome expertise, I said something unimpressive, like "I love listening to you speak. I hope you'll like a copy of my book." I always feel somewhat irrelevant when I'm in her presence, perhaps because she speaks of meta-analyses and supraphysiologic doses of various compounds about which I know very little. I continued to gush with praise like a star-struck adolescent and told her how much I've always learned from her lectures and how listening to her reminded me of how much I still do not know. She welcomed me with her unassuming grace and, though unmoved by my adulation, thanked me for the book. She told me how helpful my books have been to the postpartum community and that my work was just the right complement to her research.

Then she said something I cannot remember exactly, but I felt it inside my heart and have carried it with me ever since. She reminded me how important my work was and that, though she studied and reported on the statistics and the implications for treatment, it was I who was in the trenches with the mothers who suffered and who had a front-row view of what was happening and what needed to be done. It was a gracious observation coming from someone who has so tirelessly dedicated her energy to this field of study. But, most importantly, it is this very perspective to which she referred that set the stage for this book. After all, I've always said I've learned everything I know from the women who seek my help.

I believe that women with postpartum depression have never been in a better position to get excellent help. Clinicians are beginning to pay closer attention to the unique needs of this special population of women. The individuals I have had the pleasure of supervising are incredibly passionate about this work. They are eager to enhance their skills and willing to dig deep into their own personal life experiences to find the best paths for healing.

For these reasons, I have set a few parameters for this book:

To clinicians:
> Whether you are a novice or seasoned therapist new to this field or an advanced clinician seeking to refine your work, the information in this book promises to enlighten you and enhance your clinical experience as well as increase the likelihood that your client will feel better sooner.

To postpartum women:
> Whether you are currently in therapy, considering entering therapy, or wondering why in the world you would need therapy after having

a baby, this book will facilitate a better understanding of the process. It will also help you determine whether therapy would be helpful for you or not and, if you already have a therapist, whether you are getting as much out of your work together as you can.

This book is *not:*

- An all-inclusive, comprehensive resource manual for postpartum mood disorders
- A reference book to answer all of your questions about postpartum depression
- A substitute for clinical supervision
- A self-help book for the treatment of postpartum depression

This book *will:*

- Provide an inside view into the world of therapy with postpartum women
- Offer specific suggestions and clinical interventions that have proven successful in clinical practice
- Encourage you to look deep inside yourself regardless of which side of the therapy office you sit, so that you can get the most out of the experience
- Provide clinical information illustrated by case vignettes for further elucidation
- Address specific challenges that clinicians and clients must confront throughout their journey together
- Help instill confidence and increase understanding of how therapy works and why it might not within the postpartum setting
- Augment the therapeutic process to increase the probability that both the treating clinician and the woman in therapy will benefit and learn from the mutually rewarding experience

A postpartum woman who seeks treatment needs to feel safe and understood. When she does, she can be free to tap into her own healing resources. The difference between a successful therapeutic experience and an unsuccessful one is solely determined by the connection between this woman and her therapist. *Therapy and the Postpartum Woman* is a companion tool for clinician and client, one that I hope will enlighten and embrace the process of therapy for them both.

Karen Kleiman, MSW

PART 1

The Framework: Women, Babies, and Therapy

CHAPTER 1

Masquerade
Clinical Profile

We will have to give up the hope that, if we try hard, we somehow will always do right by our children. The connection is imperfect. We will sometimes do wrong.

Judith Viorst
Necessary Losses

Postpartum depression is not always what it looks like. Women who are severely ill can present well and look good. Really good. At first glance, they can look good physically with every hair in place, and they can look good clinically, responding to our questions with deliberate precision. Unremitting symptoms of depression might be lurking behind the camouflage that things are fine. If clinicians aren't carefully reading between the lines at all times, they might miss that. Other times, symptoms that shriek with alarming intensity might be a sign of a transient emotional state that has less clinical urgency. To reconcile this apparent discrepancy, I emphasize the most basic lesson that shapes the work of a postpartum therapist: Do not assume, if she looks good, that she is fine; do not underestimate the enormous power a postpartum woman achieves by maintaining the illusion of control.

Early in my career, I received a phone call that was not unlike those I was used to getting on any given day. "I need your help," her voice said, shaky with a familiar desperation, begging for immediate attention. "I've never felt this bad. Something's really wrong."

Regardless of how many times I hear the impassioned pleas, hearing them never gets easier. I always feel the palpable terror. The words may vary with each voice, but the panic is the same. It's the feeling that accompanies the sheer loss of control and the descent into obscurity. "What *is* this? Who am I? *What is happening to me?*"

Megan was a 32-year-old mother of a 3-month-old daughter. Her frantic call reminded me of the ongoing challenge that clinicians face when treating the needs of postpartum women. It's not as though women with young babies can be expected to plan their crises according to our schedules. Ideally, I've always known that we should be prepared to see women who need to be seen without delay, but logistics of the practice and constraints of scheduling do not always make that possible. Still, there are some phone calls that scream such urgency that accommodations need to be made. Even the best training and the most impressive of organizational skills cannot substitute for good instincts. In this business, having good instincts can mean the difference between life and death.

Initial phone calls are a crucial part of establishing the therapeutic alliance. The challenge is whether we can *simultaneously* (1) review the relevant historical information, (2) assess the severity of the mother's needs, (3) ascertain whether there is a crisis situation, (4) determine the best course of intervention, (5) reassure and comfort her, (6) offer tools for preliminary symptom relief, (7) instill confidence that she will feel better so that we can reduce the secondary panic that sets in, (8) convey our expertise in this area so that she can trust the process and disclose the depth of her suffering, and (9) encourage her to follow up with the proposed action despite the fear, resistance, guilt, anxiety, confusion, despair, and overwhelming sense of hopelessness that misleadingly renders her unworthy of our professional attention and support.

And can we do all of this in 20 minutes or less, on the phone?

Megan told me she needed to come in that day. "My doctor gave me your number weeks ago; he knew I might feel this way. I was hoping I wouldn't, and then, when I started feeling so bad, I guess I hoped it would just get better on its own. But it's not." Megan's voice crumbled into tears. "I'm sorry," she whispered through her labored breath, as if she were imposing in some way.

I'm not certain why women feel the need to apologize when they cry. Perhaps, on some level, they fear (or know) that raw emotions can make others uncomfortable, forcing women to feel responsible for this burden. I hope, however, that skilled psychotherapists are able to tolerate this level of emotion and to be comfortable, albeit sensitized to some extent, with the pain their clients reveal to them.

If they are not, I wish they would find another profession.

"That's okay, Megan; it sounds like this is awful for you. Let me see what I can do to help."

Would that be enough to provide a trace of relief? Will I be able to pick the perfect words with just the right intonation to get across everything I need to say? As hard as it might be for her to make that first phone call (she did admit she carried the card for months before she came to terms with the extent of her suffering), actually making the call can bring enormous relief. By calling, it's as if a woman is saying, *I can't do this anymore. I need your help. Tell me what I need to do so I can feel better. I'm terrified. Tell me I will not always feel this way. Tell me I'm going to be okay.*

This is the voice of depression. These are the words that reach out from beneath the surface, gasping for air. This is the language that serves to protect women from themselves, when they can no longer breathe, when they are too tired to move, too weak to eat, and too hopeless to care. If they are lucky, they find the words to cry out for help when someone is there to listen.

A response to this call should include the following message: *I know what to do to help you feel better. No, you will not always feel this way. You don't have to suffer by yourself. I can tolerate whatever you are feeling and whatever you need to tell me. We will make a plan and get you on track to feeling like yourself again. You will get better.*

This is the beginning of the magic. It is how these women begin to get better. It is the initiation of therapeutic healing, a hint of relief, a splash of hope while they are drowning in despair. It is what connects them to the process.

The likely result is an initial reprieve, taking on any number of forms. It can be expressed: *Thank you. I feel better already that I called.* It can be implied: *Okay, I'd love to come in and make an appointment.* It can be tentative: *I'm not sure anything can help; I don't even know why I called.* Or it can be misdirected: *I'm not sure what to do for myself, can I call you in a couple of days?* Whatever the outward appearance, one thing is certain: No one makes this kind of phone call in the first place unless they are scared, desperate, symptomatic, or in a state of unfamiliar and quiet panic (unless, of course, she is a terribly compliant patient who is dutifully following the instructions of her concerned healthcare provider). It is our obligation to know that each woman who calls is asking for something that is hard (if not impossible) to ask for and important to get. She is not likely to reveal what this is at first. She is, however, certain to need it.

It is our job to figure out what that is.

Megan and I talked for a few minutes on the phone, and I asked if she felt she could wait until the end of the day, at which time I could stay later and see her. Or, did she need to go to an emergency room? She reassured me that she could wait but was grateful that I could squeeze her in that same day. When her appointment time rolled around, I was finishing a last-minute phone call and heard someone in the waiting room that I presumed to be her. I remember the waiting room when it was not filled with mothers who were struggling with mothering. I remember thinking, how do I make this small space pleasant enough for women who are feeling so lost? After all, a woman who gives birth to a baby does not plan to go to a therapist. Typically, this is not something a postpartum woman is motivated to do on her own for personal growth or spiritual edification. Under other circumstances not related to childbirth, women seeking therapy may do so with purposeful anticipation, along with some trepidation and an incentive for change.

But let's face it, when a woman has a baby (add sleep deprivation, mood swings, cracked nipples, 30 pounds she hopes belong to someone else, raging hormones, a screaming infant, and a husband who wonders where his wife went), making an appointment to see a therapist to talk about how guilty, anxious, nervous, remorseful, and inadequate she feels is not high on her priority list.

Thus, we conclude that few postpartum women are there by choice, which is not typically the case in the broader population of therapy clients. In the early years of my career, I pondered this notion of imposed therapy. I realized that many of the women calling were doing so only to comply with the request of their doctors or loved ones. This made me consider how important the superficial trimmings of a waiting room—the space that first greeted a reluctant postpartum woman in distress—might be.

The waiting area should be warm and inviting, but professional. It needs to suggest that we are experts while, at the same time, be unassuming and engaging. How do you do that in a room? The colors? Sage and beige—they work. The choice of furniture? Shabby chic is one good way to make sure nothing has to match. Magazine collection? I used to fill the rack with all kinds of intellectual materials so everyone would be impressed with my intellectual propensity. Now I only get *People* magazine because that's all everyone, including me, wants to read, anyway. Guilty pleasure, they tell me—better than chocolate. Soft classical music, lots of creative writings, educational materials on postpartum depression, and a disclaimer framed on the wall, though admittedly insufficient, for women who have suffered a loss and must sit amid the pregnant and postpartum energy.

The walls of each office are covered with wallpaper rich in deep warm colors and framed images portraying women in varying emotional states. I love the way the office makes me feel each day I walk in. Every time I open the door, I feel how good it feels to be there.

I walked into my waiting area to greet Megan. Our first phone call was only hours ago that morning, so her disquieting sentiments remained fresh in my mind. As hard as we try to resist the temptation, most therapists probably make some assumptions about what someone "sounds like" on the phone, what they may "look like" in person, and what we might expect to see when we first set eyes on them. *Will she be disorganized and symptomatic? Will she be demure and soft-spoken? Will she be resistant and hostile? Will she be dependent or demonstrative?*

On this day 20 years ago when I was embarking on the profession that would shape the rest of my life, Megan demonstrated that everything I thought

I knew up to that point would mean something completely different within the context of women and postpartum depression. It wasn't that becoming a mother was a dramatically new concept for me, either personally or professionally. Rather, it was this notion of becoming a mother while weakened by depressive thinking. The two don't mix well.

In its most simplistic connotations, motherhood is often synonymous with elation, joy, and anticipation shared by a couple on the sublime brink of parenthood. Take that dynamic force of life and love and overlap it with the hopelessness of depression and the heavy heart of a mother who is disconnected from her baby, and we are left with a raw, indescribable injury to a woman's spirit and soul.

I wasn't prepared for what I saw. Megan sat tall in the chair and stretched out her arm to firmly greet my welcoming hand. Her grip was strong and deliberate, something I regularly take notice of and often a fleeting sign of inner resourcefulness. Her auburn hair was cut short, very short, smoothed back with a peach colored band wrapped snuggly behind her ears. Her makeup was on, lipstick and all, button-down tailored shirt tucked neatly into her ironed jeans. Her fabric belt matched her headband, which I couldn't help but notice matched her manicured nails. I daresay she had spent more time putting herself together than I did on my best day. Megan smiled a warm, I'm-so-happy-to-be-here-and-meet-you smile and followed me into my office.

In the moments that followed, I marveled at how she looked and, equally important, *why* she looked that way. This was no feeble effort on her part. It took time, thought, effort, and attention to detail that belied her state of mind. Surely this was not a coincidence.

I am forever a student of postpartum depression: observing the cues, studying the subtleties, trying to comprehend what sometimes makes no sense. Though it still strikes me as peculiar and something I would not have the strength to carry off, I am beginning to understand why it's so important for women struggling with depression to look so good. There's an undeniable loss of control that is so hard to bear that it forces women to make a choice between two options: give up completely or fake it. When giving up isn't an option, creating an illusion of control becomes their sole driving force.

Megan was clearly being driven by such a force. As she spoke, I continued to be struck by how different she looked from what I expected after speaking to her briefly on the phone. She was so composed, almost rigid in her presentation. Her words, though spoken softly, were strong and poignant: "All I ever wanted was to have children. Ever since I can remember. I'm not so sure about that right now. I'm not so sure about anything. My sister wanted children, too. We used to talk about that, we used to play house together, both of us cradling our dolls against our breasts; she was mommy number one and I was mommy number two." Tears hugged her blushed cheeks as she continued. "She never got to have children. She couldn't stand the pain. She couldn't save herself." Megan lowered her head and sighed. Then held her breath and sat quietly.

"Megan, what happened?" I asked quietly.

"She couldn't take the pain anymore." She seemed to stop breathing, becoming one with the still silence in the room.

"What happened?" I am certain I was holding my breath as well.

"She found my father's gun. She knew exactly where it was. We all knew where it was. She was only 22 years old, sweet baby. It was 8 years ago. Seems like yesterday."

Megan again sighed deeply and slowly through her nose, held her breath and let it out slowly and deliberately while she closed her eyes. Story after story, she recalled their shared history of role playing and baby making, giggling with anticipation of the real-life mothers they would surely become one day.

The birth of Megan's daughter 3 months earlier seemed uneventful until a few weeks after she was born. Megan was well aware of her family's history of depression and her sister's lifelong fight with the illness that eventually took her life. Megan revealed that she had struggled herself with depression in the past but had not sought help because it was "never as bad as Jackie's depression."

No, I imagine nothing ever felt bad enough compared to that. Until now.

Megan introduced me to the woman she had turned into since the birth of her baby: her deep sadness, her persistent feelings of hopelessness and despair. She described her ongoing effort to make sense out of a childhood that was distinguished by years of profound loss, abandonment, and impaired relationships. Her history seemed marked by incredible pain, including a father who left without sufficient explanation, a sister who committed suicide, and a mother who, besieged by her own relentless grief, insisted that Megan maintain precise order and control, at all times, of the home, of her life, of her self.

She described how the birth of her baby brought her perilously close to these deep-rooted feelings. Instead of overflowing with the joy and exhilaration she had hoped this child would provide, she felt consumed by depressive feelings and thoughts that tortured her on a daily basis. It was as if her baby triggered the resurgence of memories that had carefully been tucked away. Not just the childbirth experience, but the baby herself. Each time she looked at her, she felt she was paying the price for her sister's life. The guilt was almost unendurable.

It was then that I came face to face with a dynamic with which I would become only too familiar. Emerging from the depths of a history that she had carefully tucked away with whatever coping skills had enabled her to move forward through the grief, Megan believed, or hoped, she was past the pain. She had become successful in her career and learned how to maintain meaningful relationships, including a loving partnership with her husband, whom she described as "my rock." She eventually cultivated a sense of control in her own life, finally feeling as though things were close to being the way she wanted them to be. Her tendency toward perfectionism was both a curse and a positive driving force, steering her down one successful path after another. For the most part, her predisposition for depression was at bay.

Then she had a baby.

Suddenly, she's up all night, clinging to the hope that she can sleep for at least one 4-hour stretch. She is so tired it hurts. Her body hurts. Her eyes hurt. All she wants to do is sleep, just to catch up, just to get a break, just to feel like herself again. She can't take a shower without her baby in the bathroom with her, in the carry seat, so there are days she goes without showering because she resents the fact that she doesn't get 20 minutes to herself. She is hormonally, biochemically, psychologically, and physiologically compromised. She is doing her best to deflect depressive thoughts. Nothing is in its place anymore. Nothing makes sense. Everything she worked so hard to achieve feels out of step. She's cleaning, she's washing, she's changing linens, she's wiping off the kitchen table for the fifth time today, she's avoiding phone calls, she's changing diapers, she's feeding and changing and feeding and changing. She is tortured by her thoughts: *What if I love her too much and she leaves me? What if I don't love her enough? What If I'm not doing this right? What if I can't be a good mother? What if my mother was right that I'll never be able to do this? What if my husband leaves me? What if I get sick like my sister and plummet into the depths of despair? What if I should never have had this baby?*

How does she reconcile the intense contradiction of feeling so out of control with the equally intense and very urgent need to maintain control?

One way is by looking good.

That can work for a while. But eventually, as the symptoms of depression invade the territory further, systems weaken and the pretense of control crashes around her. When this happens, women like Megan are left feeling raw and excruciatingly helpless. Everything they have ever used to protect themselves no longer works. There is no shield from the pain or escape from the suffering. Panic sets in and permeates the air.

Forty minutes into the fifty-minute hour I asked Megan again, "How bad are you feeling right now?" This question can work well to penetrate resistance, in spite of or perhaps because of its simplicity, though it may need to be repeated. When women have new babies, they are used to people asking them if this is the best time of their lives. They are used to others asking them if they are tired. They are even used to strangers who ask them how many other children they hope to have. But most are not asked, even by their healthcare providers, whether they are feeling bad or how bad they are feeling.

"Bad." Megan responded with observable relief from the confirmation of her awful state of being.

"How bad?" I pursued.

"Really bad." She looked down and stared at her crossed leg, which was swaying back and forth for rhythmic comfort. "This afternoon, in my left hand I had a fistful of sleeping pills. In my right hand, I held a note I had written to my daughter and my husband. Then I heard the voice of my sister in my head and in my heart. That's when I called you."

I worry so about these severely depressed women masquerading as happy, attractive mothers who have everything under control.

When clinicians, healthcare practitioners, and psychotherapists begin to sufficiently understand this pretense of perfection, perhaps they will be better able to assess the emotional state of the women they are treating. If we can challenge the cultural myth of the perfect mother, we can begin to understand why so many women continue to feel imprisoned by their secret thoughts and feelings of shame. Many women, probably most women, still listen to the sounds of society instructing them to strive for the ideal when it comes to being a mother. It may not be something they admit to openly, but its influence is pervasive. It's like elevator music. It is present and may not be terribly inspiring, but as long as it's not offensive, it blends into the background.

The message women are hearing may be subliminal, but it is clear. Good mothers are supposed to be nurturing, devoted, and self-sacrificing; they should put their children's needs before theirs at all times. Presumably, they can do all of this while they continue to accomplish their own goals and maintain their sense of identity. When subscribing to this message of unyielding devotion, many find themselves clinging to a slipping sense of control or micromanaging their lives and becoming hypervigilant about their babies. Women believe they will feel better if they function this way. After all, who doesn't feel better when things are put away and in their proper place? But for women who struggle with depression, the margin of error is quite small. The line between keeping things in control and behaving compulsively to keep things from falling apart is a very fine one, indeed. In the process, women often lose sight of what is motivating this constant struggle for excellence and perfection in the first place. Who do they do this for? For themselves? For society? For their mothers? For the Joneses next door? For their sanity? I suspect most women are not ready to give up these impossible standards. But they should.

The fear of failing makes them very sick.

One of our greatest responsibilities in our role as therapist to these women who try so desperately to keep pace with their own unrealistic expectations is to simply tell them they don't have to do that anymore. They can stop working so hard. They can learn from their mistakes. They can stop looking so good. They can make a mess. They can live with imperfection.

I told Megan we would do all of this another way. I told her it was okay for her to feel what she needed to feel and that I could help her feel more in control of her life again. But the paradox is she would have to give up some control in order to regain it. Her look of puzzlement led me to describe it this way: Suppose you have a water balloon in your hand. It wiggles and rolls in your palm while you try to maintain a grasp of it. Quickly, it falls off balance, and your instinct is to clutch it tightly to hold on. But in grabbing it, one of two things will occur; it will either burst or pop right out of your hand. Either way, you have essentially lost control. There is only one way to maintain control of the wobbly balloon. It is, quite simply, to let go. By slowly releasing your grip, the filled balloon will settle into the center of your palm and be in balance. The more you squeeze, the less this is likely.

Megan understood the squeezing. She knew that this is exactly why she was so tired all the time, so exhausted from working so hard, from thinking so hard, from trying so hard to pretend that everything was okay. Giving her permission to give that up and let that go was the first breath of air she had felt for months. She took a deep, long sigh, filling her lungs with new life.

I observed Megan carefully while she listened to the words that offered her freedom from herself, permission to release her tight hold. She looked down at her closed fists that only a short time ago had clutched an excess of pills that would have surely ended her life. Slowly, she opened her fingers and let her hands relax with her palms empty and free. She looked down at her empty hands. After interlocking her fingers and holding tight, she touched her mouth in prayer position. Her eyes were closed. Her breathing was slow and deliberate.

Letting go never felt so good.

CHAPTER 2

Everything Gets in the Way
Resistance

Most women with new babies are not interested in psychotherapy. This is not to say that they are unwilling to engage in the process of healing. It means it does not make sense or fit into their world right now and they simply have no time for it. Once we link new motherhood with therapy, we instantly pathologize what is conventionally believed to be a natural, instinctive, and blissful event. One woman confesses:

> Women have babies all the time; it's the most natural thing in the world. Why do I need to go to therapy just because I've had a baby? I never needed therapy before. Now I have a baby and everything turns upside down? I don't get it.

Associating feelings of depression with the birth of a baby and having those feelings validated by a therapist can drive a stake into the fragile heart of an already guilt-ridden mother. Not only does she feel terrible and not understand why she feels so bad, but also now she is being told that the process of childbirth has contributed to her illness. Some women hear this and internalize it as if "My baby is making me sick." Subsequently, this can generate feelings of resentment toward the baby or extreme guilt for not feeling the way they expected they would. Either way, it's a crushing disappointment—one that many women find unforgivable.

When feelings cut that deeply at a time when energy and inner resources are scarce, it's hard to examine it further or face it at all. That's why a woman's resistance to therapy can be equal to the repulsion she bears when confronting her own painful feelings. Appreciating this resistance to therapy is crucial when engaging a woman in the process or motivating her to seek help.

As we explore the concerns many postpartum women have that can present as resistance to therapy, note that this is an overview and much of what is discussed here will be examined in greater detail throughout the book.

"IT'S A WEAKNESS"

Women with postpartum depression want explanations, they want reasons. They yearn to tie it all up in a neat bundle. *Why did this happen to me? I love my baby so much; how can I feel so sad?* They want answers from healthcare practitioners that might, with other illnesses, come in the form of blood tests, x-rays, or other tangible verification of a diagnosis. Jennifer, the mother of a 4-month-old asked, "Can't you just test my hormones to see if they are out of whack? Maybe that's all that's wrong. Maybe I can take hormones and be fine." Many women share her frustration and wish it were that straightforward. But because the diagnosis of postpartum depression results from a combination of biologic, environmental, genetic, and hormonal factors, we inevitably disappoint our clients when we confess we have no such medical test to determine the presence of postpartum depression. Beyond the use of reliable screening tools that we have at our disposal, the diagnosis is typically made by a skilled clinician after a comprehensive assessment. This is why clinicians interested in this specialty feel more comfortable and competent when they have specialized training and supervision in this area.

"I really thought I could take care of this myself," Jennifer continued. "I hate depending on others to take care of things for me. Honestly, I feel pathetic." Strong word, I remember thinking. And what a shame that asking for help is so hard for some people.

I tried to turn it around and make sense out of it for her: "Jennifer, I know it feels like a weakness in your character because you're so used to doing everything for everyone else, but think about this. It's a lot easier to sit at home and feel awful and not do anything about it while your symptoms worsen. It actually takes great strength and determination to make the decision to do something about the way you are feeling and be proactive about taking care of yourself. That's hard to do when you feel this bad. The decision to seek help comes from strength, Jennifer, not weakness." She nodded to confirm that she heard what I was saying. Perhaps she didn't believe what I was saying applied to her quite yet, but she heard me, and she wanted to believe what I was saying was true. Reframing the decision to seek support as strength of character can help postpartum women refocus and proceed with greater conviction.

"IT'S TOO MUCH MONEY"

Therapy is expensive. There are no standardized fees, so depending on where one goes and who one sees, fees can range from the lowest co-pay to the "we-have-to-pay-that-much-each-time-we-come?" end of the continuum. Some therapists will slide their fees; some will not. Some accept insurance; others do not. There is no easy solution for this barrier to treatment. If that weren't bad enough, women as a rule tend to have difficulty justifying spending money on their mental health: "If I were just strong enough to take care of this, I wouldn't have to spend this money" or "Now that I'm not working and we are a one-income family, there is no way we can afford this." One of the things we might say to this woman is, "If your baby were sick or your husband were bleeding, you wouldn't be worried about how much money it costs. It's time to take care of *yourself*. It's important." If she feels bad enough, this may be less of an issue because there is less ambivalence about the necessity for treatment.

There is no denying that good therapy is costly, but keep in mind that the cost of not treating a major depression is much higher. Untreated postpartum depression can have severe consequences, not only for the mother, but also for her child and the entire family (Lusskin, Pundiak, & Habib, 2007). Knowing this, each call that comes in is treated as seriously as the next. In our practice at The Postpartum Stress Center, if someone presents as a financial hardship, we do our best to accommodate to secure an evaluation. We slide our fees and will not turn any woman away due to her inability to pay. Among ourselves, we refer to this as a BMWYC (bring me what you can) and will accept whatever she brings us as payment in full for that initial consultation. If we feel her needs will be better met in another facility where she can follow up consistently, we will make the necessary contacts to facilitate that shift after our first meeting together. This policy may or may not work for all clinicians or in every setting. It is, however, a guiding principle in our practice with postpartum women. Because of the very nature of this work and the urgency of the issue in sight, we make allowances that may not apply to a general psychotherapy practice not specializing in the treatment of postpartum mood disorders.

This is not to say that this approach is trouble free. Clinicians know that working out financial details can become a therapeutic issue. Asking for money or discussing the economic terms of this alliance can feel like an intrusion, something that someone else should be doing. I often think about how convenient it would be to have a separate staff member deal with the financial transactions, but as appealing as it sounds to hand the responsibility to someone else, the issue would not change. Whether or not there is another person asking for and managing the money, the clinician is the one who must help the client determine what significance this work holds and how much that is worth. For newer clinicians, it can feel completely contrary to the purpose at hand. But it's not. Attaching value to the time a woman spends in therapy is a worthy lesson, particularly if taking care of herself is something she is not used to doing.

When we talk about reducing the fee, there is a very fine line to consider. Are we making this service more obtainable or are we diminishing its value? When is it okay and important to reduce the fee to provide greater access to help, and when must we stand firm with our position that this service and attention to her well-being are indispensable and, essentially, priceless. Weighing this apparent contradiction needs to be done on a case-by-case basis. Clinicians must tease out those clients who genuinely need us to make financial adjustments from those who would just prefer us to—a skill that can be instinctive to many therapists but always requires fine-tuning.

"IT MEANS I'M CRAZY"

Recent sensationalism of headline-grabbing accounts involving women with postpartum depression and psychosis has inhibited many women from seeking out the help they need. Most of us can relate to having a thought or a worry and believing that, if we keep it to ourselves or don't admit it, it will disappear on its own or not be real. Though it doesn't always make sense, this kind of magical thinking can be the force behind much of what we do and don't do when we are afraid of something. Some women with postpartum depression are so frightened of their imposing symptoms they simply don't tell anyone. This is often the case if their symptoms involve scary thoughts or negative intrusive images. Fear of losing total control or becoming psychotic keeps women from letting others know what is going on. *What if I do something terrible? What if they take my baby away? What if I hurt my baby? What if I snap and lose my mind completely?*

When the horror of Andrea Yates's story unfolded, many journalists and media bystanders mistakenly presumed that at least this tragedy would encourage others with postpartum disorders to come forward and get the help they needed. Regrettably, this was not the case. More and more women became immobilized by the fear that they too could be driven to madness. The unbearable guilt silenced them even further.

For clarification purposes, postpartum depression and postpartum psychosis are very different illnesses. They are both on the continuum of postpartum mood disorders, but psychosis is *not* a severe depression. It is a separate illness. Women with postpartum depression do not *become* psychotic; they do not *snap* and lose touch with reality. They may *feel* as though they are going crazy, but they are not.

Many postpartum women with symptoms of depression fear being labeled or misunderstood. Confessing that something is wrong can feel like taking a step off a cliff, not knowing how far they will fall. Historically, women's fears and hesitation to disclose postpartum symptoms might have been well founded, as their expressions of ill health too often rested in the hands of inexperienced or misinformed healthcare practitioners. Sometimes these providers, well intentioned or not, either overreacted or casually dismissed the disclosure of symptoms, leading to further misunderstandings and insufficient intervention. Women are, therefore, disinclined to trust that their concerns will be managed with expertise and compassion. When all healthcare providers as well as therapists begin to incorporate the notions of expertise and compassion into their dealings with postpartum women, we can chip away at the barriers that prevent these women from seeking help.

"IT MEANS I'M NOT A GOOD MOTHER"

Mothers in therapy: To many postpartum women, this is an oxymoron. Jennifer described it this way:

> I've wanted this baby more than anything in the world and now I'm sick? Now, I need help? What kind of mother am I? Good mothers don't obsess about bad things happening to their babies. Good mothers don't wish they didn't have their babies. Good mothers don't admit they feel inadequate, fearful, and overwhelmed. Besides, look at those mothers over there in the grocery store and playground and the mall. Now those are good mothers! You don't see them wishing away their babies or fretting about how hard this is or regretting they ever got pregnant in the first place. If I'm thinking these thoughts and feeling these feelings, I am not a good mother. My baby would be better off without me.

What makes postpartum depression difficult to discern for both the clinician and the woman struggling with symptoms is the fact that it's hard to differentiate the symptoms of the illness from how she feels as a mother. Many women simply think this is what being a mother feels like; maybe being panicked, nervous, ambivalent, nauseous, or despondent is part of being a mother, they might think. Because symptoms of depression can overlap with feelings that nondepressed postpartum women feel, such as fatigue, early morning wakening (Chaudron, Szilagyi, Kitzman, Wadkins, & Conwell, 2004), emotional lability, and excessive worry, it's hard for women to know when a feeling is indeed part of adjustment to motherhood and when it may be disproportionate to what new mothers should expect to feel.

One of our jobs is to reassure our clients that when we treat the illness, the symptoms get better and they will no longer think and feel this way. This concept bears repeating. Women with postpartum depression have a hard time distinguishing their symptoms from who they are. They believe that being a mother just feels this bad. It's important to appreciate this as an initial therapeutic challenge and explain this to our client. This explanation will help her separate her symptoms from who she is as a person and lift some of the burden she carries with her into the therapy.

Here we see how women are hampered by the distorted thoughts associated with depression. Generally speaking, symptoms of depression such as fatigue, amotivation, apathy, and despair interfere with help-seeking behavior. When we factor in the experience of becoming a mother and the guilt of not doing it in the expected or desired way, immobilization sets in, thereby increasing the isolation and potentially worsening the symptoms.

Unfortunately, the stigma of mental illness persists, and when we attach motherhood to that, it can send a woman further into despair and decrease the likelihood that she will ask for help. However, there is reason for optimism that this will change as we continue to educate and enlighten those on both sides of this issue—those who are suffering and those who are in a position to intervene and treat the illness.

"IT MEANS I'M NOT PERFECT; I'M NOT IN CONTROL"

Women with babies like to be in control. At a time when so much is unpredictable and chaotic, postpartum women try desperately to maintain control or, at the very least, maintain the illusion that they are in control. It feels impossible to accept the fact that things are unmanageable, whether it's because they are sick or not. It is experienced as a complete malfunction. To the postpartum woman, the inability to do this all herself and do it right represents a total breakdown of all that is important to her. Seeking help is equated with failure.

Rarely do we maintain that a personality trait has a causal role in mental illness. But sometimes an association between a personality type and subsequent risk for emotional illness is clear. Time and time again, we see the relationship between women with a tendency toward perfectionism and postpartum depression. Perfectionists tend to be overly self-critical with unrealistically high standards, which may contribute to the development of depression (Hawley, Ho, Zuroff, & Blatt, 2006), not to mention the havoc perfectionism itself can induce in a home with a new baby. The need for control at this time is indisputable. This is true for all postpartum women, regardless of what events have paved the way or made them particularly vulnerable or whether they are suffering from depression or not. Postpartum women yearn to maintain control during a time in their lives when they are surrounded by clutter and disarray. Control leads to feelings of empowerment, which leads to self-esteem, which leads to optimal emotional health.

So when a woman has a baby, feels like she is losing control, and simultaneously experiences feelings of hopelessness, worthlessness, panic, and despair, she will do everything in her power to reclaim order, even if it means pretending she is fine. And pretending she is fine means not asking for or accepting help.

"I DON'T HAVE TIME"

This is true. Postpartum women don't have time. This may be the biggest factor that impedes recovery from the outset. Women with new babies, whether they are depressed or not, are overwhelmed, exhausted, and trying desperately to cope with unknown and random variables. Their heads are spinning as they attempt to incorporate previously simple tasks into their new family structure. Some of them fit nicely. Many do not. Women with postpartum depression are less able to navigate these challenges and find themselves easily overcome by the demands of simply getting through the day. Finding time to squeeze just one more thing in can feel impossible.

But time is a relative concept. Most of us know this to be true in our own lives. *I don't have time to exercise* is a good example, or *I don't have time to sit with my husband and relax or read a book.* Everyone works hard. Everyone does the best she can. Everyone has exactly the same amount of time in the day and in her life, yet some people do seem to have more time to get things done, don't they? Why is that? Are they more motivated? Better organized? More efficient? More compulsive? Less compulsive? Do they care more about certain things? Are they more focused or less exhausted? The interpretations are endless. But the fact remains that we all have precisely the same amount of time. If taking care of ourselves means we must do less of something else, that's a choice each of us is free to make. This is not to suggest that this is easy. But it's a choice, nonetheless.

Within this context, it is our job to help a postpartum woman choose the option of taking care of herself, instead of putting herself at the bottom of her list of things to take care of. We can rely on scores of clichés to help us make this point to our clients: *You can take better care of your children if you take care of yourself. Happy, healthy mothers have happy, healthy babies. Flight attendants remind parents to put the oxygen mask over their own mouths first so they can save their children.*

Lastly, when postpartum women say they do not have time to come to therapy, seek treatment, or get help, it is not just an excuse. It is a symptom. Asking for and accepting help is just another way of declaring, "I'm sick," and many women do not feel ready, or able, to accept that.

Sometimes, it can be as simple as giving them permission to do so.

CHAPTER 3

Don't Call It Therapy

Reframing

It is presumed that most therapists who are interested in pursuing private practice work have been trained with a clinical emphasis during their academic
preparation. This emphasis highlights the conceptual psychodynamic framework and time-honored therapeutic traditions that have proven to make a significant difference in the lives of clients who seek our assistance. We have learned
about transference, countertransference, resistance, therapeutic alliances, and
boundaries. Most of us (I am hopeful it is *all* of us) pay careful attention to these
concepts throughout the course of our daily work with each individual client.
Much has been written about the therapeutic relationship and how it potentially guides an individual into new realms of healthy functioning.

However, as we have noted, therapy is time consuming, costly, and quite
possibly the last thing a woman caring for an infant feels like doing. So while
we underscore the notion that a postpartum woman may not be interested in
therapy, we shift our focus to what she *does* want. Symptom relief. Pure and
simple. That's it. She does not want to talk about how feelings of abandonment might be contributing to her sense of inadequacy. Nor does she want to
explore how her impaired relationship with her mother might have impacted
her self-esteem. She wants to sleep, to think clearly, to feel less anxious, and
to stop crying all day. She wants to return to her previous level of functioning
so she can get on with the business in her life.

Not far below the surface of simply getting through the day, we discover
a longing to reclaim her lost self or who she was before she had her baby. Alison was 3 months postpartum when she asked, "Will I ever feel like myself

again? Will I ever feel normal?" This quest becomes an underlying objective for the postpartum woman starting therapy. It may evolve throughout the process, taking on new form as insight develops, but it remains her primary goal, nonetheless. She is not yet able to see the larger picture. For example, her attachment to the baby will develop as she continues to heal, and her "old self" will indeed be absorbed into her new emergent self. Can and should this be interpreted and shared with her at this early stage? Would she even believe us if we assured her it will happen in due time? I suggest saying the words to her, whether she is able to see the larger picture or not. This is one of many things we might need to reassure her of, long before she is equipped to accept its certainty.

So how do we reconcile those larger therapy issues that are apparent to us with her desire for a quick fix? We need to present it from a different perspective. I generally do not use the word "therapy" in a first contact with a client. Instead, I focus on her coming in to get relief and a better understanding of what is going on. I emphasize the here-and-now, reassuring her that regardless of what we call this process, we know what to do to help her feel better.

THE CRISIS

If we consider attaching the concept of trauma to the postpartum woman, we begin to understand the enormity of loss involved and the urgency to retrieve her lost sense of self. This trauma-loss scheme can apply to a broad range of responses—for example, the perceived failure to meet her ideal expectations or an obstetric complication resulting in injury to her newborn. Any way we look at it, once a postpartum woman reaches our office, there is some degree of trauma to her soul. Anna Freud suggests reserving the term trauma for situations in which there is evidence that the ego has been overwhelmed and is unable to perform its normal functions, relying on its usual defenses (Freud & Furst, 1967). It is beyond the scope of this book to explore the history of ego psychology and how it may, or may not, apply to the birth process, except to say that whether or not it fits any strict definition, women with depression do indeed identify this experience as a trauma. Clearly, the ego has been overwhelmed. For now, it should be understood that the postpartum woman is experiencing psychic injury of previously unknown proportion. Add to that any prior loss, childhood trauma, history of depression, and so forth, and we begin to see the potential extent of the crisis.

Weeks into her treatment, Alison created her own expression for this passage in her life. She called it a "new normal." Life indeed has been changed forever, a concept that is hard to grasp while being bombarded with symptoms that make it feel impossible to get through the day. Although we may need to hold tightly to the secret that things will never be exactly the same as they were, in time, our therapeutic journey will bring her to that point of understanding. Never the same and sometimes better. A new normal, to be sure.

For the time being, however, at this earliest stage in our alliance, it's back to basics: to achieve symptom relief, to encourage coping strategies, and to facilitate healing. This initial phase of treatment can be viewed as creating the sanctuary. Women must hear, feel, and know that they are:

* Safe
* Not being judged
* Free to speak candidly
* Not the only ones who have said these things
* Not always going to feel this way
* In a place that is familiar with what they are saying and what they are feeling
* Protected from ridicule, criticism, and disapproval
* Beginning the process of recovery and that they can expect relief from their symptoms
* Being guided by an expert who knows exactly what to do to help them feel better

These concepts characterize good psychotherapy practice, whether or not the client has postpartum depression, so what is different in this context? Remember that women with postpartum depression have experienced a trauma that may be unclear to them. They don't always understand why they are in our offices. Unlike the more common therapy scenario with clients who are motivated to call for that first appointment, a postpartum woman is likely to be calling because her doctor told her to call, or her husband is worried about her, or because she's so tired of feeling so bad for so long she doesn't know what else to do. What's missing here is expressed intent.

Distinguished psychiatrist Hilde Bruch, MD, writes: "[The therapeutic interview] is an encounter with a definite purpose, namely that something of positive value and constructive usefulness for the patient should come out of it" (1974). Ask a postpartum woman why she is there in a therapy office and a clinician is likely to hear: "So I can stop crying and take care of my baby." Often, that is her sole purpose.

Few postpartum women are explicitly seeking therapy, but some do see this crisis as an opportunity to initiate or resume psychotherapy. When that intention is presented or expressed, it is generally best to defer attention to specific issues until the postpartum crisis has been resolved, unless, of course, they are interfering with the current crisis. We have to put out the fire before we do anything else. Symptom relief is always first and foremost.

THE SANCTUARY

The therapy office can be viewed as a framework that embraces our first contact with the postpartum woman in crisis. It is a sanctuary with structure. As a young therapist eager to ease the pain of postpartum women in distress,

I was struck by the overt anguish that faced me. The disbelief, the shattered dreams, the panic, the despair, and the detachment from everything they believed in showed on their faces and colored their words. At the same time, I could hear and feel the powerlessness that surrounded this despair—the nakedness of it all—swollen vaginas, bleeding nipples, engorged breasts, perineal damage, surgical stitches, and postpartum hemorrhaging, to name just a few. Everything was out of control. I would think about how these women must have felt before they came to see me—before they had the phone number of someone who might understand.

When my second child was 2 months old, I discovered a lump in my left breast while nursing her. After a preponderance of misguided recommendations and just plain bad advice, I decided to have the lump removed while I continued to breastfeed. That my obstetrician and breast surgeon were nervous about the lump was clear to me, so my options felt limited. What wasn't so clear was what I would do with the other issues by which I felt bombarded. Who, besides me, cared that I was breastfeeding my 2-month-old? Or that I was recovering from a C-section? Or that I was worried I had breast cancer because it ran in my family?

After the surgery and relief that the lump was benign, I found myself nursing a hungry child who was blissfully unaware that her enthusiastic suck was yanking at my fresh incision, forcing me to hold my breath and grab onto the sides of the bed for dear life. I persevered—breastfeeding, counting to 10, and returning for unscheduled surgical visits with bulging abscesses that required immediate aspiration. "Okay, that's it," my surgeon finally said. "Stop breastfeeding."

I called my obstetrician and was told: "Bind your breasts, restrict your fluids, and take some aspirin." So I did.

My daughter, who went from being exclusively breastfed to a plastic nipple purchased randomly and hastily, adjusted beautifully. I, however, did not adjust as effortlessly, weighed down by swelling breasts as milk spilled out randomly and most inconveniently. Certain that my hormones joined in protest, I quickly found myself wedged into a corner from which I saw no escape. It was hard for me to put into words. Nothing was really wrong. I was healthy and greatly relieved. My daughter was fabulous and had not skipped a beat in the exchange, and she did not seem to miss her mother's milk. Still, I found myself wondering whom I could possibly talk to about feeling so overwhelmed. And, why, I wondered, was I even so overwhelmed?

This was the first time I became acutely aware of how easily and often the needs of a postpartum woman fall through the cracks. Even without depression in this picture, I was an example of a mother recovering from abdominal surgery, with a new medical complication requiring surgical attention, an infant, a toddler, an abrupt shift in feeding and postpartum agendas, and an overload of demands placed on top of a sleep-deprived self. If clinical depression were added to this picture, it's easy to see how a woman could feel defeated.

A postpartum woman needs refuge from the suffering. She needs a place to go where she can find support, guidance, reassurance, and clarity. She needs a place to go to remind her that being a mother is not always going to be easy, but it is definitely not always going to feel like this.

This is how the seeds of my work were planted. I envisioned a sanctuary where women could gather their scattered selves and sit in the midst of unconditional support and expert guidance. Most clinicians are familiar with the inspiring work of D. W. Winnicott, renowned pediatrician and psychoanalyst, and his concept of a holding environment (1965). The construct was originally a reference to the psychic and physical adaptation between the baby and the mother. Winnicott viewed this connection and the role of the "good-enough mother" as key to the baby's sense of control and well-being.

Similarly, creating this sensitive space, a composite of cerebral and emotional energies, is precisely what we do, or should do, in therapy with the postpartum woman. One of our first tasks in establishing a connection with our postpartum client is to create this space, the sanctuary, the holding environment—a space that ultimately says, *"We understand, we know what this is, and we know what to do to help you feel like yourself again."*

REDEFINE THE PROCESS

Remember:

> If we tell a postpartum woman she needs therapy, she may not come.
> If we suggest she may have issues to work out before she feels better, she
>   may find someone else to talk to.
> If we tell her she will be agreeing to a once-a-week commitment for an
>   unknown period of time, she may tell us she has more important
>   things to take care of right now or cannot afford to spend the money.

For some postpartum women, there is even a slight revulsion from anything that may foster more dependence. This notion is complicated by the ambivalent feelings of mutual dependence with the baby, as well as an overwhelming sense of responsibility. It can all feel like too much. If, on the other hand, we tell her that our sole objective is to get her feeling better as quickly as possible, she is more likely to feel cared for and enticed by the prospect. We understand her regressed state as a natural response to the depressive trauma. We do not need to identify this to her; we only need to act accordingly.

There is a certain specialness that surrounds a woman who has just given birth. There is often so much excitement that it circuitously entitles a woman to expect considerations and attentiveness. As a culture, we tend to shower her with adoring praise and honor her achievement. Yet, if she struggles or admits discontent, she is often cast aside, disregarded, or patronized in some way, evidence of our society's inability to reconcile this seemingly contradictory aspect of childbirth. Clinicians must break through this intolerance by letting our clients know that their feelings of unhappiness, ambivalence, rest-lessness, or rage will be acknowledged, tolerated, and accepted.

With all the obstacles, denial, and distractions, why *are* women willing to seek out specialized therapists to help them during this demanding time? Because

- They are exhausted and tired of doing it all themselves
- They are terrified and need to know they'll get better and be okay
- They truly want to feel better, more than anything else
- They've tried to feel better on their own and it's not working
- No one else is listening or understands how bad they really feel
- They are afraid if they don't, they will feel worse and never feel bet-ter again
- They are deeply frightened by their feelings and fear they will be unable to fulfill this awesome role

When we reframe the therapeutic setting from the outset into one that feels more acceptable to a postpartum woman in a hurry to return to function-ing, we simultaneously make the process more adaptable to her way of think-ing and offer frontline symptom relief. We tell her it's okay that she's feeling this bad and that she'll feel better again. We hold her, as best we can from afar, and let her know she is safe. Is this therapy? Some would say it's a start. Others would say it's not at all. Most would say it's a basic human connection.

I say that it's the key, the blueprint for everything that is to follow between us.

CHAPTER 4

Anatomy of a Postpartum Depression Therapist*

The first question I am usually asked is "Do you have children?" After answering in the affirmative, I am asked, "Did you have postpartum depression?" I am repeatedly struck by the hint of disappointment when I reveal I did not have postpartum depression. There seems to be a tendency for women with postpartum depression to seek out women with similar experiences. This is one of the reasons why support groups can be so comforting during this time. Since the desire to normalize their experience is strong, some women believe they would be most comfortable in the presence of a therapist who can say, "I've been there."

Even though there are many areas of therapeutic expertise where a clinician's personal recovery may be relevant to the treatment (for example, with eating disorders and substance abuse), there can be hazards inherent in this relationship between the client and the therapist who has recovered from postpartum depression. First and foremost, a clinician who has recovered from postpartum depression must take careful note of how her experience *will* (yes, this is a not a maybe—it is definite) affect her work with postpartum women in therapy. (The same holds true for male therapists who may have supported their wives through postpartum depression.) If this is the case, it is strongly recommended that you engage in excellent supervision during

---

* As mentioned in the introduction, this chapter will take a slightly different format as I felt a more personal tone would be appropriate for this topic. Because I am asking the clinician to explore personal issues, it felt most effective to address the reader as "you" in this chapter.

the first few years of practice, which is always recommended in any case, so you can establish crystal clear boundaries and determine what relevance your personal experience may hold.

Secondly, you cannot presume that what worked for you will work for your client. It is especially important for you to clean you own mental slate and see each client through objective eyes, filtering out any preconceived notions that might be lingering from your own treatment. Thirdly, you always need to be cautious when determining whether or not to disclose any information pertaining to a personal experience.

Do women with postpartum depression prefer a female therapist? For the most part, women say that they do. In our practice, women indeed express a desire to be cared for by other women during the prenatal and postpartum periods. Although the male therapist on our staff can keep up with the best of our discussions on breastfeeding, nipple soreness, and vaginal deliveries, his competence is most valuable adjunctively, providing support for partners. This desire to connect with a female therapist has many components, which we will explore in more detail later. This is not to suggest that male therapists are not effective with postpartum clients. Quite the contrary. I am only suggesting that, when asked, most women do report a preference for a female therapist. As uncomfortable as this might make us to say aloud, it happens to accurately reflect the trend and needs to be addressed. In our practice, we are clear about our stance that all of our therapists, whether they are unmarried, without children, or men, are excellent therapists and can successfully treat women with postpartum depression. The fact remains, however, that women will assert earnestly that they prefer to have a female therapist. It's a "mother thing," I presume, which will be examined later in the book.

For now, you should consider the following questions that we pose in our postgraduate training course, as if you were on a job interview. Think carefully about your answers:

- What are your areas of greatest professional strength and skill?
- What are your areas of professional weakness?
- What do you consider your most valuable personal asset?
- What do you consider your most vulnerable feature?
- Why are you interested in working with this population?
- What makes you especially qualified to do this work?
- How do you think you make women feel who come to see you for treatment?
- How would *you* feel if you came to see you?
- What worries you most about doing this work?
- What experiences in your life have contributed to this interest?
- What clinical circumstance feels most challenging to you at this point?
- Do I think you are a good therapist?
- If you have children, do I think you are a good mother?

- If you are in a relationship, do I think you're a good life partner?

Are your answers to these questions too personal? Will you be able to construct and maintain appropriate boundaries and protect your client as well as yourself? Are your answers not personal enough? Do you feel suitably connected to this group of women and able to share a part of yourself throughout the process?

The reason the answers to these questions are important is this: If you are not committed to this work or don't feel that you are sufficiently trained or motivated to help women with postpartum depression, clients will sense this the minute they talk to you on the phone or enter your office for the first time. When this happens, you risk losing the connection. Postpartum women are drenched with a neediness that is vastly incompatible with how they want to feel right now. Therefore:

If you are too sympathetic, you might reinforce their feelings of helplessness.
If you are insincere, they will not trust that you can help them.
If you're uneasy, their guard will stay up and you will get no information.
If you're too tentative, they won't waste their time.

So what are postpartum women looking for? Simply put, they are seeking *compassion, information, support, reassurance, validation, expertise,* and *guidance.* Your capacity to provide some of these without *all of these* will not sufficiently address the issue at hand, as these concepts are inextricably entwined. You cannot effectively validate without support. You cannot guide without compassion, you cannot reassure without adequate information, and so forth. You should take the necessary time to explore your own abilities and limitations in these areas. Women asking for help during this time of their lives will accept nothing less and should not be expected to. The philosophy behind these concepts should be evident:

Compassion: to show a special kindness and empathy to those who suffer
Information: to educate with appropriate materials, data, evidence-based healthcare knowledge, and choices
Support: to provide unconditional acceptance and encouragement
Reassurance: to restore confidence and reduce anxiety
Validation: to provide evidence that a position or feeling is authentic and real
Expertise: to speak with authority in this specialized field
Guidance: to lead the way toward recovery with a prescribed course of action

The process by which we impart these concepts involves a number of therapeutic strategies. Fundamentally, it comes down to one thing, as it always does when discussing central principles of therapy: the relationship.

It doesn't matter how many degrees you have or where you went to graduate school. If she doesn't feel comfortable sitting with you and looking you in the eyes, all our well-crafted words will fall upon deaf ears. So you need to ask yourself, "Do I feel equipped? Capable? Confident?"

One of the first questions I ask a prospective therapist who is interested in working at our center is "Are you a good therapist?" Often, she looks at me as if this is a trick question, hesitating with ambivalence. She may be thinking: *If I say yes, I'll appear vain or arrogant. If I say no, I'll appear unqualified. If I say I'm not sure, I'll appear indecisive.* But it's rather simple to me. I'm hoping I hear a "yes." After all, why would I want to hire her if she's not a good therapist? Now I understand that just because someone says she is good at something doesn't make her good at it. But I can guarantee you this: If she says that she does *not* think she's a good therapist or that she's not sure, I suspect, at the very least, that she'd need more supervision and a great deal more experience.

The same principle holds true when a woman is sitting in your office and asks if you know what to do to help her feel better. You can play therapist and ask her why it's important for her to know. Or you can deflect the question and grab onto another topic. Or you can wonder privately to yourself whether you should come right out and answer her question. Or you can just say, "Yes, I know steps we can take to help you start feeling better."

I think that's the nicest way to respond—and certainly the most therapeutic.

SELF-DISCLOSURE

When is it helpful to talk about yourself and your experiences, and when is it too much information?

In the practice of psychotherapy, a commonly held view is that the disclosure of personal information about the clinician to the client should be discouraged. Most of us who were clinically trained decades ago were taught to avoid accidental disclosure and maintain strict boundaries. Violations of this pact would be counterproductive at best and, at worst, detrimental to the therapeutic goal and/or relationship.

In this unique setting where the postpartum woman seeks validation and support, understanding self-disclosure is relevant for several reasons:

1. Many clinicians who come to specialize in this work develop this passion as a result of their own experience with postpartum depression.
2. Many women seeking help may have preconceived notions that the experience of motherhood, rather than a graduate degree, is a prerequisite for their therapist.
3. Women who have recently given birth, who may still be bleeding, lactating, and sleep deprived, or who need to talk about mastitis,

sore nipples, and stretch marks are more interested in your ability to be real and your ability to connect.

It is helpful, therefore, to look at how self-disclosure can be used in this particular therapeutic context. When used appropriately, revealing personal information can be beneficial in the following ways. It can:

- Enhance the alliance
- Promote trust
- Facilitate engagement
- Increase compliance

Boundaries are essential. What information are you sharing? What is too much information? Why are you saying it? To whom are you saying it? How severe are her symptoms? How will it impact her? What will it look like if you choose not to say it?

Let's look at some examples of how this can play out in a session. Usually, the question is clear, but a direct and honest answer is not:

"Do you have any children?"

We could invent all kinds of unhelpful responses: *Yes. No. I hope to one day. I'm pregnant now. I don't like children. I had two miscarriages. I'm gay. I'm going through infertility treatments. I'm not married. Actually, I have seven children. I'm planning to try when my psychiatrist gives me clearance.*

There is a direct deliberate reveal:

Yes, I have two children.

Or there is the indirect reveal:

My own experience of becoming a mother has been my greatest resource for this work.

The decision to disclose should always be based on two things:
- A therapist's active decision to do so
- Content in the best interest of the client

The following examples illustrate the key points:

Is the information relevant to the issue at hand?

I wouldn't tell a client that I was nervous about getting on the airplane for my trip to California in the morning. *However,* I would tell her, if she asked, that I too know what it feels like to feel anxious about having a sick child while waiting for the doctor to call back.

Is it information that the client can deal with?

I wouldn't tell a client who was scheduled for a C-section in a month that mine had complications that led to a longer hospitalization and countless worries about my baby. *However,* I would tell a client who asks me if a mother ever stops worrying about her children that having adult children, unfortunately, does not make you immune to worry.

Is it the right timing?
    I wouldn't tell a pregnant client about my failed epidural or my spinal that was too high and created the sensation that I wasn't breathing, requiring the anesthesiologist to do on-the-spot panic control. *However,* I would tell a pregnant client that I, like her, was ambivalent about going back to work, but some things become clearer after being home with the baby for a while.

What is the context within which the disclosure takes place?
    I wouldn't reveal my sadness to a client if I were still recovering from the loss of a loved one. *However,* I would reveal my sadness if a client's account of the loss of her child moved me to tears.

What is your comfort level?
    Depending on the circumstances, my comfort with a particular client and particular issue dictates whether I answer a question directly or not. Many times, I use stories from my own experience as metaphors for the healing process, such as "It's like when my daughter was trying to grab on to the water balloon and get control. The tighter she held on, the less control she had."

How much should you disclose if you've had postpartum depression?

This is a tough question, and it's different for each clinician. It depends on (1) how severe your symptoms were, (2) how well you recovered, (3) how far removed you feel from the sting of the experience, (4) how comfortable you are revealing any of that, (5) how relevant you think it would be to a particular client, and (6) how reliable you think your instincts are regarding your client's ability to use this information.

    Keep this in mind: No client ever has to know that you experienced postpartum depression. It is not automatically part of the equation. You can, and I often think it's better if you do, decide it is not pertinent to the treatment. The reason is this: Many women who have recovered feel the force of two opposing perspectives. To start with, you might feel united with your client and able to relate on an intimate level, but at the same time you may feel conspicuously raw and vulnerable. It's as if the illness fractured your confidence and forever put a trace of doubt in your heart. This hesitation of spirit can be managed and overcome with good clinical supervision. Without it, it can impede your work in the following ways:

1. You might inadvertently over-identify with your client and her experience.
2. You might have strong opinions about what works and what doesn't work that may or may not be relevant or helpful to your client.
3. You may lose valuable objectivity.
4. You may unintentionally influence the course or outcome of your work together.

Although these points are danger zones for the inexperienced therapist, they can, if understood properly, be used to your (and her) advantage. For instance, if your own doctor missed your diagnosis of postpartum depression or dismissed your concerns, you may be able to draw upon that personal experience to help empower your client to follow through and say what needs to be said. Similarly, if your husband made a lasting impression on your recovery by saying the perfect thing or by responding in a certain way, you may want to encourage your client's partner by making a direct reference to that specific behavior or response.

To reiterate: My best advice to any therapist who has recovered from postpartum depression and is now redirecting all of that energy and passion into this work is to be careful and make sure you have good supervision where you can sufficiently explore whatever emotions this work raises for you.

BREAKING THE RULES

I remember my first few graduate school classes on *how to be a good therapist* or something as vaguely intriguing as that. I recall being captivated by the notion that the therapist can sit back while the client proceeds to tell his or her life story. It never felt quite right to me, but being the dutiful and compliant student and intern, I learned with the best of them to remain an active but silent listener, though eager to pounce with my premature interpretations and opinions. It's hard in the early stages of learning to balance what you know and what you think you know with what should and what should not be said.

In college Psychology 101 and graduate clinical courses, we learned certain guidelines for therapy or, more specifically, codes of behavior. Most had therapeutic merit and have managed to evolve with the times to an extent. These techniques have historically been considered unwise, yet I must admit that I find myself dipping into each area with the appropriate amount of guilt because I was instructed to do the opposite:

1. Giving advice
2. Accepting a gift
3. Revealing personal information
4. Discussing irrelevant or superfluous topics
5. Initiating session material rather than responding to client's initiation

6. Overstepping boundaries
7. Touching a client
8. Pursuing an uninterested client if he or she disengages from treatment
9. Spending time on the phone discussing what could be discussed in a session

I confess that the lessons I prefer to follow and teach stray from conventional psychotherapeutic rhetoric. I wonder what my graduate supervisors would think of my current practice skills, as I glide between what makes a good therapist versus what makes a good person. And if these are not mutually exclusive concepts, shouldn't we focus on what feels right and important in relational terms rather than terms of technique and procedure? Isn't it true that most excellent therapists were good at these skills long before they were trained and that untrained people can actually do just as well, in some instances? Far too many of us know well-trained clinicians who have achieved a high degree of competence in their field, yet we would not refer our sister or our mother to them. What we know and how we do it provide the structure. But the good stuff comes from who we are.

THE RELATIONSHIP

Your life experience, your personality, your style of therapy, your training, your supervision, your compassionate spirit, and your reason for doing this work all combine to generate an energy that your client will either perceive as useful to her or not. Bear in mind that most postpartum women are not voluntarily entering therapy because of their deep desire to work on unresolved psychological issues. They are entering this process because they are paralyzed and need to function without delay. If they determine that this time spent with you is not useful in that way or will not eventually lead them to their perceived path of recovery, they will lock down the process, and neither of you will achieve the desired outcome.

If who you are really does make a difference in this healing process and ultimate recovery, what do you do with this information? What can you do about the fact that your work will be colored by your experiences? Should you keep your personal thoughts and values out of the therapy office? Does that make you less objective? Does it make you less effective as a therapist?

Good therapists have good values. That's why your clients trust you and believe in what you say. If you keep the essence of who you are out of the relationship, you will be cheating your client out of your best work. Leaving yourself out of the work creates a one-dimensional experience. The client will hear the words, but she won't feel the energy. She'll understand what is being said, but she may not believe it will make a difference. Your ability to understand who you are and what that means and your ability to be authentic rather than neutral or vacantly objective enable you to truly and completely connect with your clients. With years of trial and error, practice, risks, and mistakes, clinical wisdom emerges. Clinical wisdom involves the partnership between your clients and their experiences and you and your experiences. It's a human encounter, a collaborative effort between two people that, ideally, empowers you both.

CHAPTER 5

The Holding Environment

After weeks of successful treatment, Eileen came in for what would be her final session. She thanked her therapist for all the help and said sweetly, "Every time I came here it felt like a warm blanket was wrapped around me."

I remember when Eileen, a pediatrician on leave after the birth of her first baby, came to The Postpartum Stress Center for her initial visit with our clinical director, Dr. Weiner. I was passing through our waiting room on my way out of the office, when I saw her hunched over the clipboard of forms she was painstakingly trying to fill out. Across from her sat her father. "She's not doing so well," he smirked. "She gets that from her father." I smiled, introduced myself, and bent down to kneel next to Eileen since she had not made eye contact with me; her eyes remained fixed on the forms she was trying to fill out.

"You okay?" I asked.

"No. Not at all." She shook her head, visibly trembling, still unable to look me in the eyes and seemingly uninterested in her surroundings.

"Okay. See if you can fill out the forms. If you can't do it right now, that's okay, too. Dr. Weiner will be with you in a few minutes."

Her father and I talked for a short while. I reassured both of them that they were in good hands and that we would make sure she got on track to feeling better. He thanked me as I rose from the floor; she never looked up from the papers.

That was the last time I saw Eileen because she was treated by Dr. Weiner—until weeks later when she was leaving the office after her session. Realizing that she looked familiar but unable to place the face, I asked Dr. Weiner who she was after she had left.

"That's Eileen. You remember her? She was the one you sat on the floor with in the waiting room," she remarked, never missing an opportunity to draw attention to my uncommon practices.

How a client changes physically as she gets healthier can be startling. "Wow, she looks good," I remarked, commenting that she barely resembled the woman curled up in the corner shielding herself from the outside world.

"I know," Dr. Weiner replied. "She's doing fabulously. She said being here was like one big hug."

That's when we know what we are doing is working.

Creating a secure and welcoming climate in which clients feel safe to experience and express their feelings is one of the hallmarks of psychotherapy. D. W. Winnicott first brought to our attention the notion that therapy, as in the primary mother–infant relationship, provides a holding environment, an environment of unconditional acceptance, interest, and empathy for the client and what the client has to say (1963). If we look more closely at the parallel between therapist and client and mother and infant, it becomes particularly illuminating. In accordance with Winnicott's description of this holding environment, the mother's ability to meet the emotional needs of her infant is crucial to the infant's development of a healthy self and his ultimate individuation. She responds to his impulses, thereby protecting him and reducing initial anxiety. Likewise, our role as therapists to the postpartum woman can take on characteristics of Winnicott's "good-enough mother,"* who intuitively cares for both her baby's physical and later emotional needs, establishing the foundation of ego development (1953). By being so attuned to these specific needs, the mom creates what Winnicott refers to as an "optimal holding environment" (1963) for the healthy establishment of a separate being. This primary connection with the mother provides an early sense of control and comfort.

Likewise, for the postpartum woman in therapy, her primary experience must be one of unconditional acceptance, patience, and, perhaps most importantly, a sense that she will be cared for—the sanctuary.

Many people who have never experienced intense anxiety presume that it is an acute state of nervousness or exaggerated worry. This may be true for some. But for a majority of postpartum women, for whom anxiety is predominant, it is an emotional state that is as close to the edge of insanity as imaginable. In comparison, for infants deprived of security, Rodman refers to Winnicott's description of this unthinkable anxiety as a feeling of "falling forever" (Rodman, 2003). Falling forever is a poignant expression that characterizes a great deal of what postpartum women in despair describe to us: *I will never get better. I will go crazy. I will die. I am alone.*

---

* Here, and throughout the book, when reference is made to the therapist taking on a "mother" role, I am not limiting this to female therapists. Rather, I am referring to maternal qualities that should be present in all good therapy, regardless of the therapist's gender.

When we highlight a new mother's indefinable need to be cared for, we discern a deeper purpose to this holding environment at the core of our work. One study attributing psychoanalytic concepts to postpartum depression pointed out that women with postpartum depression exhibited regression along dimensions of affect tolerance and expression, as compared to the non-depressed control group. They concluded that a high level of postpartum distress was associated with regressive tendencies, with particular respect to affective development and emotional expression (Menos & Wilson, 1998).

This regression can magnify right before our eyes in early sessions. If we think about this regression in the terms of Winnicott, who claimed that "there is no such thing as an infant" (1960)—implying that, without a mother, an infant cannot exist, and stretch our analogy to extreme dimensions, we begin to realize the role of the therapist with the postpartum woman. As our client sits awkwardly in this state of imposed dependency, she finds herself reluctantly clinging to the desire for comfort (symptom relief) and nurturance (compassionate expertise). This is not to suggest that she has reverted to an infantile level of functioning. It does suggest, however, that in order for her to successfully reenter her mommy–baby world, which is often contaminated with negative thoughts and feelings that repel her, the postpartum woman must first sit with her ambivalence, anxiety, and symptoms of depression—forcing her to confront her simultaneous need for caretaking. When she acknowledges, on some level, this state of vulnerability, she enters the holding environment and allows us to care for her in a manner that is compatible with an optimal therapeutic outcome.

When therapists assume the role of the "good-enough mother," we pave the way for "primary maternal preoccupation" (Winnicott, 1956), which enables us to be available to our client physically, emotionally, and exclusively throughout our work together. Not unlike Winnicott's constructs, our role is to teach and demonstrate that any imperfection along the way (and there will be many), as well as her rebound from perceived failure, is a necessary component for developmental progress. This holds true whether it refers to her progress in therapy, in recovery, or as a mother. Learning that there will be disappointments along the way is a message that may sound patronizing or overly simplistic, but it is one we should reinforce, nonetheless. Just as a child learns to pick himself up from a fall and push ahead, our client might need to be reminded that it's okay to lose ground while she is cautiously moving forward in all aspects of her present state.

In this way, we become the *good mother*, certainly "good enough" in Winnicott's (1953) words, flaws and all, but we strive to be even better than that. Because we are *not* her mother, we are in a unique position of integrating our theoretical training, our good instincts, our own life experiences, and our objectivity. In combination, these components create the good mother poised to nurture, support, and heal the postpartum woman in crisis.

Years ago, while attending a conference on postpartum depression, I was inspired by a friend and colleague, Larry Blum, MD (2007), as he discussed his work with postpartum women. In one of the few articles on the psychodynamics of postpartum depression (2007), he described his views on dependency as one of three *principal emotional conflicts*:

> A recent mother, in order to do all the work and endure all the deprivations involved in caring for a newborn, needs to be taken care of. She must also cope with her own emotional reactions to the baby's needs and demands. The baby may arouse the mother's own unconscious needy wishes and stir up envy of the baby's advantageous position in having these wishes to be cared for and fed realized. If she can accept her dependent need and ensure that she is in fact taken care of, and if she can tolerate her baby's dependency and her reactions to it, she is unlikely to develop a postpartum depression. If she cannot, she may be at risk.

I think this makes perfect sense. Winnicott (1947) elaborates on this notion when he says:

> An analyst has to display all the patience and tolerance and reliability of a mother devoted to her infant, has to recognize the patient's wishes as needs, has to put aside other interests in order to be available and to be punctual, and objective, and has to seem to want to give what is really only given because of the patient's needs.

Surely this must be the basis for all good therapy—not only that which applies to postpartum women.

When Hannah came to see me, she was well into the first postpartum year after the birth of her second child. I had previously treated her, so, with mixed emotions, I welcomed her with a greeting that always sounds a bit awkward: "Hannah, it's good to see you."

"Yeah, yeah. I'm thrilled to be here too," she quipped with her usual sarcasm.

"Come in and tell me what's been going on with you." I guided her with a tilt of my head toward my office, recalling that she was not comfortable with too much touching, too soon.

"Everything is great." She started the session as if years had not passed since our last meeting. "It really is."

"I'm so glad to hear that," I replied, mirroring her desire to remain on the surface for now.

We sat.

"I guess you're wondering why I'm here." Hannah was a smart woman. She always claimed not to understand how "this therapy thing" worked and outwardly voiced protest while she mocked its faint appeal to her. She had decided to give up her career as a lawyer to stay home with her kids and help her husband run his business. It was a decision that worked well for both of them, although often she referred to him as her "third child." "I don't know how anything would ever get done without me doing it," she often proclaimed.

But today felt different. She looked different. In the couple of years that had passed, she looked thinner (she said this was good); she looked tired and sad. The lines in her face were too pronounced for someone so young, I thought to myself.

She sat waiting for me to take the lead. "You okay?" I asked.

"I guess not, or I wouldn't be here, huh?"

"Why *are* you here today, Hannah?"

"I don't know." She rolled her eyes. I waited for her to think it through a bit.

"Aren't you supposed to figure that out? Isn't that what I pay you for?" Her flip attitude was always drenched with old anger and unmet needs from a childhood she described as "fine" but unloving. "Nothing was ever good enough. My A minuses weren't good enough. The way I took care of my brothers wasn't good enough. My mother even told me once that since I wasn't as pretty as the other girls, I should spend more time dressing better so I would be sure to fit in."

But today Hannah had a sadness that overshadowed her usual cynical manner.

"Why are you here, Hannah?" I asked again.

"I'm tired." Her voice cracked while she fidgeted to regain composure.

She *looked* tired. I listened while she described the course of her declining energy: The kids have been sick. Jake was laid off; he has some good prospects, but he has been irritable and probably depressed. Her father-in-law died last year after a lingering illness. Her mother still wasn't speaking to her after "she freaked out when we didn't come for Thanksgiving because Liam was sick." Finally, her best friend was diagnosed with stage four metastatic breast cancer, so she's been cooking for her and taking care of her two children.

"You've been busy," I said, commenting on her degree of overload. "Of course you're tired. You're very good at taking care of everyone else, aren't you?"

"I guess."

"That's part of what makes you so wonderful. It's good, really. But, Hannah, who takes care of you?"

"No one," she replied after a pause. "Why would anyone take care of me? Oh, is that how it's supposed to work?" She grinned, acknowledging her life-long resistance to asking for or accepting help from others.

"Yeah, I think so. That's how it's supposed to work. If we're lucky in life and blessed to be surrounded by loving people, it works best if sometimes we take care of them and sometimes they take care of us. That's only fair, don't you think?"

She rolled her eyes in classic Hannah fashion. And there we sat in our familiar pose, with her defended against the very thing she came looking for and me watching her squirm with discomfort.

"So why *am* I here?" she asked.

"Good question." I smiled. Her eyes pleaded for me to help fill in the blanks.

"Who takes care of you?" I repeated. "Where do you go to get your good stuff?"

"Here ... I guess." She looked straight into my eyes.

"Maybe that's why you're here."

"Maybe." She surrendered ever so slightly.

The holding environment. Where a woman can feel safe. This is where the therapist acknowledges and honors all that is put forth into that space. Within a framework of mutual respect and unconditional acceptance, we listen, we watch, and we care for each client. Not unlike holding the infant with primal needs and impulses, we stay attuned to the new mother's most primitive emotions, what is scaring her, what is immobilizing her, and what is so deep that she can't even put it into words. When we hold on to and tolerate these emotions, managing them without judgment and without feeling as overwhelmed as she does, we can succeed in containing them. In doing so, we effectively care for her, which is a prerequisite for postpartum healing.

THE GOOD MOTHER

There is a voice that speaks through depression's symptoms. It is a voice that cries out for help, leading postpartum women to this holding environment. Once the transfer of energy has evolved from the initial presentation of symptoms to the point of engaged empathy, it takes us to our definitive role—that of the *good mother.* A passage from my first book, *This Isn't What I Expected,* coauthored with Dr. Valerie Raskin (Kleiman & Raskin, 1994), provides a nice introduction to this concept:

> Most women never completely outgrow the need for approval from their mothers. It seems that no matter how old we get or how grown up we like to think we are, most of us can admit that it always feels good to hear our mothers tell us we're doing a great job. Some women may never have heard that growing up, so they long for it now—their mother's expectations were so high that no matter how good a job they did, it was never enough. Other women may have been so overprotected and indulged that they have a hard time discriminating whether they have done something right or wrong. More than one woman has confessed to us that she secretly wishes her mother could look over her shoulder during the 3 a.m. feeding and sweetly whisper, "You must be so tired. You are doing such a wonderful job. I'm so proud of you. You are such a good mother."

Each time I offer professional training for clinicians, I read this passage toward the end of our training. It never fails to touch each of us personally; I suspect that is because each of us can identify with that yearning for maternal approval throughout our own lives and, perhaps, even now.

"This is who we become; if the relationship works well, we become the *good mother*," I tell the group. "Not just *good enough*. But good, really good." Unlike our personal experiences in our own flawed mothering practices, we have the time to think about what to say and exactly how to say it, and we have the opportunity to say it without emotional entanglement. My children might stake the claim that I made way too many mistakes while they were growing up, and they'd be right. My clients, however, see it differently.

One could argue that a good therapist should always take on qualities of a good mother. Others might argue that a good therapist should never take on qualities of a mother. I am a firm believer that a postpartum woman in therapy for depression needs a good mother figure. If she has one of her own, she'll know exactly what she needs from you. If she is longing for one to fill the hole in her soul, she may not know what she needs until you demonstrate it. If her relationship with her mother was impaired in some painful way, she will either recoil from or cling to what you bring to her. As all good mothers must do, we must achieve that equilibrium between absolute support and appropriate boundaries. It is a delicate balancing act.

Women in postpartum crisis come to therapy to reclaim a lost part of themselves. We can best promote healing by uniting with this struggle for self. As we have seen, this core connectedness is the hallmark of the recovery process. When the therapist assumes the role of the good mother, he or she is in the best position to connect with the postpartum client and facilitate recovery. This connection is the gateway to symptom relief, which provides an immediate benefit to the mother and a more enduring benefit to the mother–child relationship that may be at stake (Murray, 1992).

Furthermore, this connection, admittedly central to all therapeutic alliances, has particular relevance to a woman who is desperately trying to balance her self, her baby, and her depression. Sometimes, it is an abstract concept intermingled with academic theories and psychodynamic constructs.

At other times, it's just about being a good mother.

"I'm sorry I'm late." Hannah burst into my office weeks into treatment. "It's so hard to get out of the house with all this stuff you know. And Cameron, of course, decided to vomit all over himself right when we were rushing out the door, so I had to go change him and then we got stuck in the worst traffic ever." Hannah plunked herself down onto the couch, distributing her layers of clothes, toys, and assorted paraphernalia every which way. "This is hard," she mumbled under her breath.

"It *is* hard, sometimes, isn't it? I think you're doing a great job."

"You do?"

"I do. Look at Cameron's face. Look how happy he is right now, watching you get yourself settled. He's just watching you, loving you."

Hannah smiled, enjoying the moment and the praise.

How do we ever know if we're doing a good job? Any therapist who is a mother herself can relate to that only too familiar isolation of mothering in a vacuum. How do I know if what I am doing is right? Or good? Or healthy? Where is the instruction manual? It used to be Dr. Spock. Now it's the Internet.

I watch carefully, as I had for weeks. "You're a good mother, Hannah," I declare quietly.

"I am?" she asked doubtfully, seeking further reassurance.

"Yes. Look how well you respond to him. Watch how he speaks to you with his eyes. See how you're holding him? Did you notice you were caressing him while you were focused on talking to me? You haven't skipped a beat. I think it's so natural for you that you hardly notice how well you are doing. I know it's been hard for you, but your attachment is strong and your instincts are good."

Hannah had indeed worked hard to get to this point, after months of depressive symptoms had interfered with her desire to attach to her son the way she had hoped. She was proud of how far she had come. Still, every once in a while she remained unsure.

"So yesterday he woke up screaming and you know Cameron rarely cries like that. I wasn't sure what was wrong and didn't know what to do. I was thinking of calling the doctor, but then I felt silly. But I was nervous, so I called and they told me to bring him in. They checked him out and said he was fine, probably teething, but he didn't have an ear infection, which is what I was thinking might be going on. Do you think that's okay that I took him in? Is it okay?"

Is it okay? Her question speaks volumes:

Is it okay that I am still unsure about how to read his signals?
Is it okay that I still get so nervous?
Is it okay that I still need the doctor to tell me that everything is okay?
Can I still be a good mother if I'm still insecure about things?
Is it okay for me to depend on others to help me know how my baby is doing?
Is it okay that I still need so much reassurance and support?

"It's all okay. You're doing great."

"Thanks. That's nice. So you think I'm a good mother, huh? That's good, coming from an expert, don't you think?" She smiled.

I returned the smile. I was proud of how far she had come. She was exuding confidence, yet still checking in for a nod of approval.

"Yes, it's good. You're doing great. You're a very good mother."

CHAPTER 6

Making a Diagnosis

"If I could just get some sleep, everything would be okay."
"All mothers worry like this. Of course I'm worried every time I put the baby down to sleep. Anything can happen. How could I possibly not worry?"
"I should never have had this baby. I don't think I can do this."
"I cannot feel like this for one more day. Not one more day."

Postpartum support group members

When is it postpartum depression and when is it something else?

During the first few weeks after giving birth, it is common for women to experience moodiness that is associated with hormonal changes as well as the stress of caring for an infant. Further complicating the diagnostic landscape is the very real concern that there are common experiences for nondepressed and depressed postpartum women, such as mood lability, changes in weight, sleep disruption, fatigue, and changes in libido. Because we expect there to be a degree of emotional upheaval during this time in a woman's life, it's difficult for her and her healthcare practitioner to differentiate between what we expect and what is troublesome enough to warrant attention and treatment.

Postpartum depression is generally accepted as an umbrella term to describe a number of psychiatric illnesses occurring after childbirth. However, such a comprehensive view can be over simplistic and lead to confusion in both the professional and lay communities. Despite greater awareness, there is still some question about discrete diagnostic categories. Expert opinion varies with respect to whether these disorders present alone or on a continuum. This chapter will touch on some of the most notable diagnostic categories as they relate to the postpartum period, with acknowledgment that each warrants greater detail and attention beyond the scope of this book.

- *Postpartum depression* is a syndrome best defined on a continuum of postpartum mood disorders ranging from mild to severe, arising during the first postpartum year. At least 10–20% of mothers will suffer from postpartum depression (Kumar & Robson, 1984), defined officially as a major depressive episode that has an onset within 4 weeks postpartum, according to the fourth edition of the *Diagnostic and Statistical Manual of Mental Disorders* (DSM-IV) (American Psychiatric Association, 2004). This, however, appears inadequate for most clinicians, whose practices are filled with women presenting with depressive symptoms well beyond this 4-week marker and who continue to be at risk well into the first postpartum year. Even though later-onset episodes fail to meet the 4-week specification, they seem to have the same features as those who fall within the 4-week time frame. Common symptoms can include excessive weepiness, insomnia, fatigue, agitation, pervasive feelings of sadness and hopelessness, irritability, suicidal thoughts, intrusive thoughts, panic, impaired concentration, guilt, and low energy.
- *Baby blues* is not postpartum depression. It is a transient, nonpathological state of emotional lability that requires no treatment (Beck, 2006). The blues are experienced by up to 85% of new mothers (Pitt, 1968), tend to peak between the third and fifth postpartum day, and usually last for hours to days. If symptoms are observed for less than 2 weeks, then a diagnosis of "baby blues" is appropriate (Epperson, 1999). In most cases it resolves spontaneously within the first 2–3 postpartum weeks and appears to be related to the hormonal fluctuations associated with childbirth. Common symptoms can include tearfulness, mood lability, fatigue, anxiety, irritability, and feelings of being overwhelmed.
- *Adjustment disorder,* as it applies to the postpartum period, has been referred to as postpartum stress syndrome by Kleiman and Raskin (1994). It usually resolves without treatment but can cause ongoing difficulties for the mother. It can create a mild disturbance in her ability to adapt to the demands of this life transition. Postpartum adjustment disorder responds well to reassurance and short-term, supportive therapy. The DSM-IV (American Psychiatric Association, 2004) definition of an adjustment disorder relates to difficulty occurring within 6 months of a specified event. The incidence of postpartum adjustment disorder is unclear because many women struggling with adjustment symptoms do not seek treatment. Common

symptoms can include marked stress reactions, low threshold for frustration, anger, irritability, and transient moodiness.

- *Postpartum psychosis,* also called puerperal psychosis, is associated with bipolar disorder and is relatively rare. This disorder affects approximately 0.1% (1 in 1,000) postpartum women (Gaynes et al., 2005). It is important to repeat that postpartum psychosis is distinct from postpartum depression. This distinction becomes crucial during initial assessment, not only diagnostically, but also to help interpret the symptoms to the woman with severe depressive symptoms who fears she is on the brink of madness. This feeling is too often reinforced by distortions in the media, who mislabel postpartum psychosis as postpartum depression and cause much unnecessary anxiety.

    Postpartum psychosis most often appears within the first few weeks after childbirth and puts the woman at significant risk for infanticide and suicide. There can be instances when severe postpartum depression is accompanied by psychotic symptoms, which can occur later in the postpartum period. Common symptoms of psychosis can include delusions, detachment from reality, bizarre thinking and behavior, severe distractibility, and confusion and auditory and visual hallucinations. Mood symptoms may be additionally present but are not the cardinal symptom of a psychotic illness. (Psychosis will be discussed in greater detail in chapter 28.)

- *Anxiety* is a hallmark symptom of postpartum depression. Postpartum depression is an agitated depression marked by excessive and predominant anxiety. In addition to the depressive symptoms, many postpartum women are surprised by the extent to which they feel anxious. Most often, depressive symptoms and anxiety symptoms occur simultaneously. Some women experience *generalized anxiety disorder* (GAD), complaining of constant worries and often physical manifestations such as nausea, gastrointestinal disturbances, or sleep problems. Another form of anxiety common for postpartum women is *panic,* characterized by unexpected "out of nowhere" waves of dread and feelings of terror. Women with panic attacks typically describe intense physical symptoms such as palpitations, chills, numbness, or the feeling that they are detached from their bodies. In severe cases they may feel like they are having a heart attack or dying. It is estimated that panic disorder affects up to 11% of mothers (Wisner, Peindl, & Hanusa, 1996).

- *Obsessive–compulsive disorder* (OCD) in the postpartum period is an anxiety disorder that is especially troubling for women. Although obsessive thinking is common with postpartum depression, some women experience obsessive thoughts to a much greater extent, often accompanied by severe anxiety and compulsive behaviors. When obsessions, with or without compulsions, interfere with a woman's ability to function, the diagnosis of postpartum OCD is given. Jenike (2004) projects that 3% of the general population has OCD, but statistics are not clear for postpartum OCD.

Many women fall into a category of OCD-like features rather than a full-blown postpartum OCD diagnosis. For example, some women who have postpartum depression with obsessional thinking get caught up in the obsessive calculations of timing naps and feedings. These efforts to maintain order may be either frustrating or soothing to the mother, who is desperately trying to gain a semblance of control. (Postpartum OCD will be discussed in greater detail in chapter 19.)

- *Posttraumatic stress disorder* (PTSD), as it relates to childbirth, has recently become the focus of long overdue attention. It is important to note that while some women may not meet diagnostic criteria for PTSD, we remain concerned about women who have had a birth-related experience that is perceived as traumatic—for example, an emergency delivery or obstetrical complication. Cheryl Beck (2004), author, researcher, and postpartum depression advocate, expresses it perfectly: *"Birth trauma is in the eye of the beholder."* Beck estimates that 1–6% of women experience some degree of postpartum stress after childbirth.

  Common symptoms can include exaggerated emotional and physical reactions to reminders of the trauma, feelings of detachment, and increased state of arousal (for example, hypervigilance or difficulty sleeping). Some women may experience flashback memories, panic, nightmares, or an avoidance of any trigger that may remind them of the scary experience.

- *Grief reaction:* Although we expect some degree of depressive symptoms to accompany any perinatal loss, such as miscarriage, stillbirth, abortion, or infant death, or other unexpected stressors related to childbirth, such as adoption, infertility, prematurity, prolonged bedrest, prenatal complications, multiple birth, birth defect, or disability, we must always keep in mind how susceptible a grieving mother is to clinical depression. Clinicians should pay particular attention to women who have a history of multiple losses or a history of depression. Often, a supportive environment where women can express their feelings of intense sadness and anger will lead to healing. Grief that is prolonged or complicated by an inability to function requires additional intervention.

- *A note on bipolar illness:* Careful screening for bipolar illness is essential. Strikingly, in a study of 30 new moms with a previous bipolar disorder diagnosis, 67% experienced a mood episode within 1 month after giving birth. Of the eight who had a prior history of postpartum depression, the recurrence rate was 100% (Freedman et al., 2002). Despite the small sample size, these findings are quite significant.

There is also evidence suggesting that women with bipolar disorder are at high risk for postpartum psychosis, with episodes following 25–50% of deliveries (Brockington, 1996; Jones & Craddock, 2001). This is an extremely high rate of illness that is much higher than the 0.1% statistic associated with psychosis in the general population (Jones, 2005). These combined statistics emphasize why screening for family history of bipolar illness is so vital, even with women who present with new-onset postpartum depression with no previous history.

Common symptoms can include mania (rapid speech, racing thoughts, decreased need for sleep, extreme agitation) or depression (low mood, despondency, irritability). Bipolar disorder can also present as a mixed episode, which features symptoms of both full-blown mania and depression, occurring either simultaneously or in rapid cycles.

- *Conditions can mimic depressive symptoms.* In particular, thyroid disorder can be exacerbated during the postpartum period. Therefore, it's important to rule out dysfunction in this area by making a referral for a physical and appropriate blood work. Additionally, the clinician needs to be alert to any other concomitant medical condition or potential factor, such as birth control pills, other prescriptions, over-the-counter medications, or herbal supplements that may complicate the diagnostic picture.

ADDITIONAL NOTES OF IMPORTANCE

- Postpartum depression can occur after the birth of any child, not just the first (American College of Obstetrics and Gynecology, 1999).
- At least 33% of women who have had postpartum depression have a recurrence of symptoms after a subsequent delivery (Epperson, 1999).
- After the initial episode, women who have had postpartum depression are at risk for both postpartum and nonpostpartum relapses of depression (Cooper & Murray, 1997).
- The symptoms of postpartum depression can be relieved and diminished within 1–6 months. But sometimes depression can become chronic. Without effective treatment, postpartum depression may continue for as long as 1–2 years (O'Hara, 1987).

Learning to distinguish the baby blues from mild postpartum depression or postpartum psychosis from severe postpartum depression is best accomplished and refined after years of exposure to women with postpartum mood disorders. But clinicians don't always have years of experience upon which to draw.

Assessments are often made in crisis, and rapid judgments must be made. This is one of the primary reasons postpartum specialists should ideally work within a multidisciplinary model, in particular, with psychiatric support.

Depending on point of reference and particular clinical practice, a clinician may, or may not, need to make a formal diagnosis unless one is working with insurance companies that require one to do so. If this is the case, remember that the postpartum specifier refers to a 4-week postpartum cutoff (American Psychiatric Association, 2004). After this time frame, clinicians need to apply other appropriate diagnoses such as adjustment disorder, dysthymia, or major depressive episode, to name a few.

Here are some key points to keep in mind when first making a diagnosis:

1. She may not be revealing everything yet.
2. Until certain that every question has been asked, don't hesitate to rely on a cheat sheet of assessment questions as a guide.
3. Don't forget to ask the questions that are hard to ask.
4. Don't forget to ask the same question again later in another way if there are any concerns about her response.
5. It is always helpful to have a support person accompany the client for additional information and perspective. This may not be possible or preferable, if she hesitates to disclose what she is worried about; however, strictly from a diagnostic standpoint, different perceptions of what's going on will typically shed more light in the long run.

IS POSTPARTUM DEPRESSION DIFFERENT FROM "REGULAR" DEPRESSION?

How *is* postpartum depression different from depression that is not related to childbirth? This is an excellent question and one that postpartum therapists need a good answer to, because clients will ask this.

As noted earlier, the "postpartum" specifier (American Psychiatric Association, 2004) limits the definition to a depressive episode that begins within 4 weeks of giving birth. This doesn't give us much room in which to move, and it does not play out that way in real life. There continues to be some debate about the restricted time of onset, and the literature supports the notion that postpartum depression can emerge beyond this 4-week time frame. Stowe and Nemeroff (1995) report that 60% of patients have an onset of symptoms within the first 6 weeks postpartum and it is usually diagnosed within the first 3 months postpartum. Still, at our center, we have women who come to us at 5, 6, or 11 months postpartum for an initial evaluation. We might speculate that these women have been suffering symptoms for some time, but this has not been validated.

We've all heard the joke: *Is it possible to have postpartum depression after 21 years? She won't leave the house!!* What's not so funny is that postpartum depression can and does linger. Our clinical experience shows us that it can emerge any time during the first postpartum year, and, due to the excessive demands (physically, emotionally, biochemically, environmentally), many specialists extend the diagnostic period to the first 2 postpartum years.

Postpartum depression presents a similar symptom pattern to depression that occurs at other stages in life, leading many experts to define postpartum depression as the presence of a clinical depression within the postpartum period. In this way, postpartum depression is exactly like any other depression that is unrelated to childbirth. But there's more to it than that.

First, let's look at the symptoms of major depression, as put forth in the DSM-IV (American Psychiatric Association, 2004). Five or more of these symptoms must be present within a 2-week period:

1. Depressed mood most of the day
2. Markedly diminished interest or pleasure in all, or almost all, activities
3. Significant weight loss or weight gain or decrease or increase in appetite
4. Insomnia or hypersomnia
5. Psychomotor agitation or retardation
6. Fatigue or loss of energy
7. Feelings of worthlessness or excessive or inappropriate guilt
8. Diminished ability to think or concentrate, or indecisiveness, nearly every day (either by subjective account or as observed by others)
9. Recurrent thoughts of death

Consider the woman who is feeling five, or six, or all of the symptoms listed, as many postpartum clients will: It's hard for her to get out of bed, difficult to get herself ready for the day, and virtually impossible to think about anyone or anything else except how she feels. As her symptoms begin to define her, the feelings of sadness, fatigue, exhaustion, inadequacy, uncertainty, and perhaps suicide permeate her day. Under the best of circumstances, even with sufficient support and excellent healthcare, this is a distressing picture.

Now, imagine this same woman with an infant. Just the two of them. Overwhelmed by an immeasurable force that feels both euphoric and inconsolable, she looks into the eyes of a child she doesn't know. She questions everything. *How will I do this? Why did I have this baby? What is wrong with me? Can someone take the baby away? Can I go away?*

Imagine the strain, the pressure, the utter disbelief in her capacity to respond appropriately. Little things become big things, and big things become insurmountable. The inability to take care of herself makes it feel impossible to care for anyone else. When a woman does manage to care for her infant by going through the motions and dissociating somewhat from her core pain, she may be able to carry this off for a while. When her sheer survival depends on the success of her deception, she is left with shame and an empty heart.

This juxtaposition of one of life's greatest gifts and one of life's most unkind illnesses is what makes postpartum depression different from depression that is unrelated to childbirth. It's hard to put into words, but this is what we mean when we say that it's the same, but it's very, very different.

An analogy inspired by Valerie Raskin, MD (Kleiman & Raskin, 1994), elucidates it this way:

> Imagine two women going in for an operation, one to have a kidney removed, one to have a breast removed. In both cases, the women will experience many similar things; they will both undergo surgery procedures, pain, recovery, and the loss of a body part. But in addition to those challenges, the woman who loses her breast will experience additional feelings and changes related to sexuality, self-esteem, and self-identity. So in many ways, the two are exactly the same. But in this way, the two are very different.

DIAGNOSIS DIFFICULTY

In spite of greater attention to postpartum illnesses and a current trend toward increased education and funding for screening protocols, women continue to suffer. The overlap between symptoms of a major depressive episode and changes that are normally associated with having a new baby can impede identification of postpartum depression. Further complicating detection of postpartum depression is the myriad of variables that thwart the new mother's ability to bring it to her health provider's attention. Some of these variables include:

- Mother's denial
- Mother's inability to mobilize self
- Unsupportive spouse dismissing concerns
- Desire for quick fix
- Social/family pressure and expectations
- Cost
- Geographic isolation
- Failure of women to recognize symptoms of depression
- Symptoms resembling postpartum normal maternal adjustment so that she is tempted to ignore or wait it out
- Stigma of mental illness
- Perceived benefit of not treating, based on hope of spontaneous remission
- Somatic expression of symptoms masking clinical presentation of depression
- Typical symptoms of depression (fatigue, lack of motivation, apathy, despair) interfering with help-seeking behavior

Furthermore, the mother may:

- Not know that the obstetrician or another doctor can help
- Be afraid of potential stigma of being "labeled" as depressed
- Feel guilty and fear being judged a "bad mother"
- Fear having her baby taken away
- Feel like it is inappropriate to discuss self-care or mental health issues
- Have concerns about confidentiality
- Not feel comfortable disclosing feelings in general

It's important for clinicians who are treating women with postpartum depression to keep these barriers in mind. This may be why it has taken the client 3 months to seek treatment or why she has had the phone number to a recommended therapist in her kitchen for months before calling. It may be why she sits tentatively in a waiting room wondering if she should just sneak out before she is called in for an initial evaluation. The anxiety is high. The stakes are high. Clinicians are in the best position to help her if we have all of the information.

Some of it she will share with us as she leads the way. Some of it we have to know before she walks in our door.

CHAPTER 7

The Voice of Depression

There are experts who maintain that depression is associated with the way in which we think. Other experts say depression is a medical illness with biological triggers. If depression is an illness that results from negative thinking, clinicians should focus on belief sets and restructuring the way our clients think. If, on the other hand, negative thinking is the consequence or, more explicitly, a symptom of changes in the neurotransmitters, then we might intervene biochemically.

There are some of us who believe, in most cases, that it is a combination of biology and the way in which we think. Most clinicians I have worked with and spoken to agree that both of these theories have merit, depending on the individual and the particular set of circumstances. There is no single explanation that applies to everyone. Theoretical foundations are always useful and can guide a clinician through the therapeutic process. But when we observe women up close and personally, we often see something else, something that adds another dimension to the therapeutic landscape: Depression is not only an illness; it is an illness with a purpose.

When women get depressed after having a baby, they are faced with an array of symptoms for any number of reasons, resulting from any number of factors. We do not always know why one woman gets depressed and another one with a similar set of circumstances does not. This is why each woman we treat represents a unique constellation of her own history and present experience woven together in the fabric of her story. Therapists know this already. But when we listen carefully to these stories, we can hear common themes emerge, words that echo one another, and tears that look familiar. Postpartum women are weary. Many of the postpartum women I see in my office tell me they just can't do it all anymore.

Of course they aren't doing it all, but it feels to them as if they are. Schedules are squeezed, resources are low, and sleep is at a premium. One could speculate that a postpartum woman feels as if she is doing it all, even though she is not, because

- Perhaps she was "parentified" as a child and asked to do more than a child should have to do and she hasn't yet slowed down.
- Perhaps she has been trying for 30 years to gain her father's approval.
- Her husband travels weekly for business and she is on her own too much of the time.
- Perhaps there are social and environmental restrictions or problems that are increasing her load.
- Her fear of losing control is keeping everything in check.
- She is a single mother with four children and two jobs.
- She is driven by some internal force that keeps her spinning and working and cleaning and organizing and proving something to herself or to someone or no one, but it's never enough and it's never quite right.

Whatever the reason, postpartum women who seek support are tired and depleted. Many have strong caretaking tendencies and are most content when they are in control of their lives and their relationships. Those who appear to be at great risk are women who emerge from codependent scenarios where they have in the past, and to this day, assumed more than their share of responsibility for others. This tendency can be nature's doing, but usually it is a result of environmental circumstances that coerce the woman to action. Some of these women are good at expressing what they really need. Many of them are not. Those who are not tend to bury their feelings, needs, and desires so deeply that even they are unaware of how to access them. Many have been doing this for a very long time and are quite good at it. It is well known what happens to feelings when they are suppressed. Sometimes they disintegrate into oblivion, but, more often, they morph into some unwelcome beast roaring for attention.

Consider this postpartum woman who has spent a lifetime taking care of others or has, in other ways, disregarded her own well-being. Regardless of the historical details or how she got here, to the point of depression, *she has now shut down.* Her body has shut down; her mind and her spirit have shut down. In this way, the depression serves to speak on her behalf, saying ostensibly: *That's it. I'm done. I cannot do this anymore. I'm tired. I'm weak. I'm completely done. I need to sleep. I need others to take care of me. I cannot do this by myself, not for one more day.* This is the voice of depression. When I explain this to a client in these terms and use those exact words as if reading a script, she says, "Yes, that's it. That's me," as if to say: *Thank you for saying that for me, I don't know how to say that for myself.*

In this way, depression can be viewed as an agent for the self, a driving force that serves to protect the core being. It may be the only way her system knows how to respond when she's overwhelmed. When stress is so severe and she is forced to find a solution in order to maintain control of her emotions, the depression becomes an interim state of protection.

Women tell us that it is almost impossible to describe depression to someone who has never experienced it. Nancy Linnon (2003), a gifted writer and teacher, describes this in my favorite piece on postpartum depression, titled simply, "Postpartum":

> I call the midwife two weeks after having Jacob because I cry a lot, because I feel overwhelmed, because I'm scared. "All natural reactions to having a new baby in the house," she says, friends say, strangers say. "Keep an eye on it," the midwife warns, but keeping an eye on yourself getting depressed is like trying to watch your hair grow— you know it's happening, but it's impossible to see on a daily basis.

In the short run, symptoms of depression may guard a woman from the onslaught of duties that feel insurmountable. It gives her permission, as it were, not to do so much. In an ironic twist, depression can make her feel as if relief has somehow been imposed upon her, offering a reprieve: *Maybe I should go someplace where I can just rest and not have to do anything.* But in the long run, it will reinforce feelings of helplessness and guilt: *I'm not able to do what I am supposed to be doing.*

If symptoms get bad enough, one hopes that intervention takes place. Husbands and families mobilize, healthcare providers get involved, and, in an ideal scenario, a woman is scooped up and surrounded by loved ones who continue to care for her throughout her recovery. It doesn't always follow this idyllic model, but this is what we work toward.

The reason this concept of the voice of depression is relevant to treatment is that, ultimately, one of the goals of treatment is for the client to learn how to tune into this potential dynamic and intervene at an earlier point, before symptoms set in or as soon as they emerge. Any time she is overwhelmed or at risk for overload, she needs to learn how to:

- Listen to her bodily cues if she is overwhelmed or exhausted
- Stop pushing herself when she is depleted
- Dial down her expectations
- Keep perspective on what others need and want from her
- Express what she needs to those who are close to her
- Give herself permission to slow down, rest, relax, and do less
- Stop feeling guilty when she learns how to take care of herself and actually responds accordingly

- Recognize her own symptoms of depression so she can respond without delay
- Engage her partner in this process so he can join forces with her or initiate the necessary steps to get help

When a woman experiences the murky waters of a depressive episode after childbirth, she inevitably finds herself sinking beneath the surface and gasping for air. In my experience, regardless of her particular cluster of symptoms, the majority of postpartum depression episodes lead to a triad of emotions: *helplessness, fear/anxiety,* and *dependency.* It's an easy conclusion to make and one that is promptly reinforced by asking a woman who is suffering from postpartum depression: *Do you have times when you feel helpless? Afraid? Overly dependent on others?* The answer is a resounding "yes." This is not to say that other emotions aren't confounding the profile or that these three conflicts impact every woman with postpartum depression. But they dominate enough cases to warrant a specific set of direct therapeutic responses to these principal emotions.

VOICE OF DEPRESSION RESPONSE MODEL

At The Postpartum Stress Center, our *voice of depression response model* incorporates this concept of three primary emotional states that respond best to an associated set of therapeutic responses. In order for the postpartum woman to feel safe and cared for, she needs to know, on some level, that being helpless, fearful, and/or dependent is okay. At the most simplistic level, she needs to know these feelings are expected and will subside as treatment progresses. She also needs to hear she will not experience these emotions in a vacuum. We explain that she is free to feel as bad as she feels, understanding that, within the structure of the therapeutic setting, nothing bad will happen to her. Understanding each of these three emotions separately will help illustrate the associated therapeutic response that has been shown to be most effective in our center for easing symptoms. As we examine each of the emotional states depicted in Figure 7.1, we see that each has a corresponding therapeutic intervention.

Helplessness

Bryce Pitt (1968) provided one of the earliest descriptions of an "atypical postnatal depression" and provided the first glimpse into the heart of postpartum depression as a syndrome. As researchers and clinicians continue to observe and study women with postpartum depression, some have discovered that postpartum women present with comparable sets of symptoms. In our center, we have uncovered one such group of symptoms linked with postpartum depression that includes feelings of failure and inadequacy, leading to a

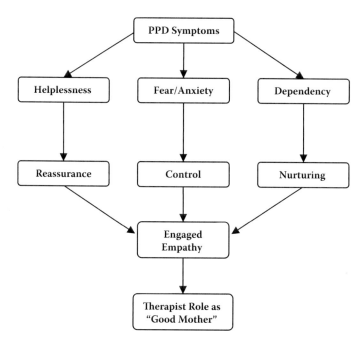

Figure 7.1 The Postpartum Stress Center voice of depression response model. (©The Postpartum Stress Center.)

generalized feeling of helplessness. Feelings of helplessness, whether perceived or real, can incapacitate a new mother.

What is the best response to a woman's expressed or unexpressed helplessness? A clinician's optimal response to helplessness is steady encouragement and *reassurance*. Initial reassurance can instill an early sense of hopefulness that, in turn, can motivate the client to seek additional support, either outside or inside the therapeutic environment. It can go only so far, though, and must be sustained with solid follow-through. Reassurance implies that we offer consoling words to soothe the wound, in addition to helping her advocate for her own healthcare and well-being. For example, a clinician might propose suggestions to help her manage time better or review her network of supporters to determine how she can enlist help.

The key to effective reassurance is empathy. If someone speaks words of reassurance devoid of the appropriate level of caring, the words will mean little, and feelings of helplessness will persist. Postpartum women are inundated with words of encouragement from all corners of their busy world. Unfortunately, much of it bounces right off their self-protective shield. By the time they come to see us, they have likely heard all kinds of reasons and theories about why they are feeling this way and what they need to do to feel better. They have probably been hearing how they are overreacting or worrying about nothing and that, perhaps, they will feel better if they just relax.

Remember the clinician's role here; we may be her only, or her best, guide. Our words of reassurance are more than just reassurance. If they are backed up with a central knowledge base and unmistakable empathy, they set the therapeutic relationship into motion. They may be the first hint of hope she has heard. They must be spoken calmly, with an air of competence and kindness.

Fear and Anxiety

We have already seen that postpartum depression presents as an extremely agitated depression. Anxiety thrives on the negative energy that generates it in the first place. The more that one worries, the bigger the worries become. The bigger the worries get, the scarier the scenario becomes. In women with pre-existing anxiety disorders, the first few months postpartum can exacerbate anxiety symptoms and increase the likelihood of panic and obsessive symptoms. In fact, the postpartum period is associated with an increased risk of women developing obsessive–compulsive disorder (Brandes, Soares, & Cohen, 2004). Regardless of where the symptoms fall along the continuum of anxiety severity, they can be one of the most disturbing aspects of postpartum depression for the woman and for her family, who feel helpless. Many women describe anxiety as the reason they feel so completely out of control; it can make women feel as if they are "losing it," as if they can no longer think.

Our response to her pervasive feelings of anxiety is to command the session with knowledge and expertise, creating a sense of *control*. This therapeutic intervention provides the client with an unwavering, consistent message that, for now, we have control of the situation that feels unmanageable to her, and we know what to do to help her feel better again. Her fear that she will always feel like this, that this is just what being a mother must feel like, and that she will never get better can send her anxiety soaring. Our response should be to model the control she desperately seeks. She can forfeit her desire for control for the time being and hand it over to the clinician, in the hopes of securing it herself later down the line. Our composure, acceptance of her disquieting symptoms, and management of the situation will go far to ease her crippling anxiety.

Dependency

For many women, feeling dependent is unfamiliar territory, as they find themselves in the uncomfortable position to need, ask for, and accept help. The discomfort from this dependent role can be so unsettling that postpartum women are actually less likely to get the help they need in an effort to reject the needy feeling it arouses. In fact, a study by MacLennan, Wilson, and Taylor (1996) concluded that only 49% of women who felt seriously depressed actually sought treatment. As expected, denial of the dependency can worsen symptoms, increasing a woman's feelings of anger, guilt, irritability, or despondency over her perceived helplessness. The best response to this weakened state of dependency is good, old-fashioned *nurturing*. It may be the last thing she thinks to ask for or even wants, but it is precisely what she needs.

What does it mean to nurture within the constraints of a therapeutic alliance? It means we support and encourage her, we educate and guide her, we help her cultivate tolerance for her symptoms, and we help foster healthy relationships and decisions during this time of transition. Though it may seem too obvious to mention, we must do it unconditionally, without judgment, without bias, and without criticism. Although nurturing is present in all therapeutic relationships, for postpartum women, the need for nurturing is highlighted by their recent childbirth experience. This notion gave rise to the current trend for postpartum doulas, who are trained to assist and support the mother and family, as an appealing option for many families.

Therapeutic nurturing also means clinicians need to monitor the self-help regimen. Is the client eating enough nutritional food—or anything at all? Is she eating junk food? Is she getting outside in the sunshine? Is she isolating herself from her friends? Is she able to take a walk? Is she able to rest when the baby is napping? Is she drinking enough fluids? Is she avoiding caffeine? Is she finding any time for herself? Nurturing a new mother can replenish her spirit, her physical recovery, and her strength of mind. The exchange of energy that takes place when she realizes she can no longer do this alone and relinquishes some of her power temporarily to us can be one of the most loving and most rewarding of the early therapy experience. This surrender, which may not always feel voluntary to her, can come from a place of trust or from utter despair.

ENGAGEMENT

In summary, we offer solid reassurance to a woman feeling helpless. We create a sense of control for the woman experiencing uncontrollable anxiety. We provide therapeutic nurturing to the woman who feels weakened by her uncomfortable reliance on others. When clinicians respond accordingly to these primary emotional states, they pave the way for empathy, a prerequisite for healing. Engaged empathy, although self-explanatory, remains essential for the advancement of the therapeutic partnership. There is tremendous emotional action and reaction in these moments. Without empathy, the energy gets lost in wayward tracks that can potentially lead the therapeutic alliance astray.

With this model of primary emotional states, we again see the paradox that characterizes a postpartum woman with depression. Often, she is hungry for the very attention (reassurance, control, nurturing) that she resents needing. Her awareness of this neediness is all encompassing, though she may desperately try to rebuff it. When we correctly acknowledge our clients' emotional states, appropriately respond, and accept them without reservation, we have entered a state of engaged empathy, a key to connecting on any meaningful level. When empathy is achieved, we assume the most precious and powerful role of all: we become the good mother.

CHAPTER 8

Therapeutic Models for Women at Risk

Postpartum women in therapy want to know why this is happening to them. They want to know what they need to do to get better. What will make a difference? What could they do to help prevent this in the future? What does all of this mean within the context of their lives right now? They want answers, and they want them fast so they can get better and go home to take care of their babies.

There are many theories regarding the nature of maternal depression, including anthropological, psychoanalytic, biologic, hormonal, genetic, environmental, relational, cognitive, psychosocial, and cultural models. Most experts agree that postpartum depression has many causes. Though we know that all women are at risk for some degree of emotional stress during this time, not all women get postpartum depression. Those that do will, at some point, surely ask, "Why did this happen?"

The hormonal changes of pregnancy and childbirth are known to contribute to a woman's risk for postpartum depression. But we know it's not all about hormones, because fathers get depressed during this time, as do adoptive mothers. In addition, caring for a newborn can be exhausting and overwhelming. Lack of sleep, unrealistic expectations, psychiatric history, family history, and social isolation can all play a role in the development of postpartum depression. This is why there is no single answer to the question of why this happened.

Here are some thoughts to keep in mind regarding risk factors:

- Some women may be more sensitive to hormonal changes, as is true with women who experience premenstrual syndrome (PMS) (Sugawara et al., 1997).
- Hormones, such as estrogen, progesterone, thyroid hormones, and cortisol, may become unbalanced in women who are especially vulnerable (Bloch et al., 2000; Pariser, 1993).
- Sleep deprivation or irregular, unpredictable sleep patterns will lower a woman's resistance to illness (Martin, Hiscock, Hardy, Davey, & Wake, 2007).
- If depression runs in her family, a woman is more at risk to experience it (Llewellyn, Stowe, & Nemcroff, 1997).
- Depression during pregnancy is a key risk factor for depression during the postpartum period (Dennis & Ross, 2006).
- There does seem to be an association between the tendency to be a perfectionist or a "control freak" and difficulty in the postpartum period (Mazzeo, 2006).
- Pre-existing anxieties, predispositions to worry or ruminate, or obsessive qualities, particularly during pregnancy, place a woman at risk. Depression and anxiety during pregnancy are strong indicators of postpartum depression (Beck, 2001; Liabsuetrakul, Vittayanont, & Pitanupong, 2007).
- Any premorbid psychiatric history (that which occurred prior to the current episode of postpartum depression), such as obsessive–compulsive disorder (Williams & Koran, 1997), a previous episode of postpartum depression (Llewellyn et al., 1997; O'Hara, 1986), and depression unrelated to childbirth (O'Hara, 1986) will be risk factors for certain women.
- An unsupportive spouse, marital difficulties (O'Hara, 1986), or a temperamental baby (Beck, 2001) can increase a woman's risk.
- History of early loss, trauma, abuse, or significant dysfunction in the family of origin will affect a woman's ability to cope after the birth of her baby (Buist & Janson, 2001).
- Obstetrical complications may put her at risk (Campbell & Cohn, 1991). Loss associated with this period such as miscarriage, stillbirth, and abortion is also associated with postpartum depression (Fergusson, Horwood, & Ridder, 2006; Hughes, Turton, & Evans, 1999; Neugebauer et al., 1997). An unplanned or undesired pregnancy is another risk (Beck, 2001).
- Other current outside stressors, such as major losses or changes related to job, move, illness, marital status, and socioeconomic pressures, will impact a woman's moods after childbirth (Beck, 2001; Kumar & Robson, 1984; O'Hara, 1986; Warner, Appleby, Whitton, & Faragher, 1996).

Postpartum depression is best understood within a contextual framework. It is never enough to see only the biological aspect, hoping that a pill will take care of everything. It is also insufficient to think that if we focus on a client's unstable marriage, she'll start eating and sleeping better. One of the pioneering models for understanding postpartum depression was developed by Milgrom, Martin, and Negri (1999). The authors developed a biopsychosocial model that addresses the multifactorial nature of postpartum depression. Specifically, the model is defined by biological factors (genetic influences, predisposition to hormonally related mood changes), psychological factors (family of origin experiences, coping techniques, defense mechanisms), and social factors (role of marital relationships and cultural expectations) (Milgrom et al., 1999). In this model, the authors show how a woman who is vulnerable (predisposing risk factors) responds to precipitating factors such as stress, which is impacted by sociocultural factors (unrealistic expectations), resulting in symptoms of depression, which is then intensified by negative thoughts or behavioral responses.

Thus, this model demonstrates the interactive and dynamic nature of all areas that impact the woman's life during this time. It covers the range of factors that are believed to impact the postpartum woman. Some women present with a stronger biologic influence, while others may manifest symptoms that may be more directly related to current life stressors. This is something clinicians should always consider when making an assessment.

PPSC MODEL OF PPD IMPACT AND ADAPTATION

In combination with the voice of depression response model and the belief that maternal depression can be understood as a trauma with devastating consequences, our center has developed the model of PPD impact and adaptation as outlined next. This model, adapted from the research of Peterson, Prout, & Schwarz (1991) and Epstein (1991) and their work with posttraumatic stress disorder, sets forth a theoretical framework within which we begin to understand the impact depression has on a new mother. Essentially, the trauma leads to distorted thinking, which in turn leads to impaired functioning, which leads to negative outcomes. This model underscores the importance of early detection and intervention for postpartum depression.

PPSC Model of PPD Impact and Adaptation*

I. Depressive symptoms leading to predominant beliefs
- I am a bad mother
- Everything is out of my control
- I am powerless over how I am feeling

---

* Adapted from the works of Peterson, Prout, & Schwarz (1991) and Epstein (1991). ©The Postpartum Stress Center.

- My loved ones will abandon me
- My environment is unsafe, unpredictable, or lacking in meaning
- I am weak and dependent on others
- I will always feel this way

II. Set of behaviors and emotions associated with acute distress reaction

- Panic
- Oversensitivity and/or hypervigilance
- Self-absorption
- Numbing or detachment
- Pervasive anxiety
- Isolation or withdrawal

III. Longer-term consequences of maladaptive responses

- Feelings of detachment
- Impaired attachment to baby
- Disruption in marital relationship
- Shame, guilt, self-blame
- Worsening of symptoms
- Illness that is harder to treat

Predominant Beliefs Based on Depressive Response   As discussed in chapter 4, when a woman has postpartum depression, she can barely distinguish her symptoms from her self: *If I'm thinking these things and feeling these things and doing these things, I must not be a good mother. Good mothers don't think and feel and do these things.* I might respond this way:

> Suppose you go to the doctor with a cold. You have a cough, fever, and fatigue. Your doctor checks your vital signs, listens to your breathing, and takes the appropriate steps toward treatment. Similarly, you come into my office and tell me, "I'm a bad mother. I shouldn't have had this baby. I don't think I can do it. I'm afraid my husband will leave me." It's as if I hear you telling me that you have a cough and fever. These are symptoms. They are treatable. When you feel better, you will no longer feel this way or think these things.

Admittedly, this is an oversimplification. Still, the bottom line is this: Postpartum women express feelings as *symptoms* but experience them as *self*. When a woman believes she is a bad mother, or weak and dependent, or that her loved ones will abandon her, she may think it's because she is not a good person or that she is flawed as a mother. Clinicians should respond by reframing these distorted beliefs. We do this by clarifying that when she tells us she is a bad mother or feels out of control, what we hear is that she has symptoms. The symptoms can be treated. This is not about who she is.

Set of Behaviors and Emotions Associated With Acute Distress Reaction Women experience acute distress with myriad response patterns. The set of behaviors and emotional responses to the agitated depression, as noted in the PPSC model, are not all inclusive; they are the ones we note to be most problematic for the women we see in our center. A clinician's awareness of the way clients typically respond to depressive and anxious symptoms will enhance the ability to intervene appropriately.

Longer-Term Consequences of Maladaptive Responses The third and final aspect of our model draws attention to the potentially serious outcomes of untreated postpartum depression. When the sets of behavioral responses listed in section II persist, they can develop into more serious problems in the larger picture.

THERAPY OPTIONS

While this model provides a foundation for deeper understanding and greater sensitivity to the issues, clinicians are apt to approach treatment options from many different perspectives. A postpartum woman comes into a clinician's office presenting with symptoms that reflect changes in her thoughts, feelings, and behaviors, as well as her biological functioning. Our job is to tease out which symptoms are most problematic, interfering with her ability to function, while we determine which intervention would be the most efficient and effective.

It is generally agreed that mild to moderate depression can be successfully treated with either psychotherapy or antidepressant medication, but severe depression requires both (Stowe & Nemeroff, 1995). It's interesting to note that in a study by Appleby, Warner, Whitton, and Faragher (1997) that compared individual psychotherapy with antidepressant therapy, both were found to be effective. Appleby et al. further note that since no therapeutic modality has been shown to be superior to any other, the choice of therapy for mild to moderate postpartum depression should be up to the client.

Nonpharmacologic treatment strategies are useful for women with mild to moderate depressive symptoms and may be especially attractive to women who are nursing or who wish to avoid taking medications for other reasons. Although a variety of psychotherapy modalities, such as supportive, cognitive–behavioral, psychoanalytic, family therapy, or group therapy, are effective (Holden, Sagovsky, & Cox, 1989), it is well established that interpersonal psychotherapy (O'Hara, Stuart, Gorman, & Wenzel, 2000) and cognitive–behavioral counseling have been shown to significantly reduce symptoms of postpartum depression (Appleby et al., 1997). Additionally, interpersonal group therapy intervention was shown to be successful in preventing postpartum depression in a group of financially disadvantaged women (Zlot-nick, Johnson, Miller, Pearlstein, & Howard, 2001).

Most therapists are eclectic and most subscribe to the notion that there are benefits derived from each of the leading therapeutic approaches. For years, we have utilized and seen the benefits of interpersonal, cognitive, and supportive psychotherapy at our center. Successful treatment for postpartum depression can include components from more than one of these theories. Here is a brief description of each:

- Interpersonal psychotherapy (IPT) is a time-limited, structured, short-term therapy based on the underlying principle that disruptions in relationships may contribute to the illness. The therapist and client primarily work with four specific problem areas: role transitions, interpersonal disputes, grief, and interpersonal deficits (Klerman, Weissman, Rounsaville, & Chevron, 1995). IPT helps the woman deal with changing roles and other stressors by teaching her how to communicate more effectively with others, offering emotional support, and providing help with problem-solving and goal-setting.
- Cognitive–behavioral therapy (CBT) targets negative thoughts and behaviors that tend to worsen depressed mood and helps by reframing old patterns of thinking (Beck, Rush, Shaw, & Emery, 1979). Cognitive therapy is based on the theory that the way we think and perceive the world affects our mood and daily functioning. This premise that negative perceptions can lower self-esteem, decrease energy and motivation, and increase stress levels is an important consideration when working with postpartum women.
- Supportive therapy, as the name suggests, often leads to improvement in adaptation and interpersonal functioning by fortifying the client's strengths and providing encouragement and direction. Brief supportive psychotherapy is a conversation-based therapy that uses a direct approach when offering support, such as praise, advice, clarification, confrontation, and interpretation (Rosenthal, Muran, Pinsker, Hellerstein, & Winston, 1999).

Using elements of interpersonal, cognitive, and supportive therapies in combination creates the ideal environment for the postpartum woman to flourish. One good example of the use of cognitive reframing can be found in *This Isn't What I Expected* (Kleiman & Raskin, 1994). Replacing distorted thoughts with more positive statements feels difficult for the woman immersed in negativity, but it's important, nonetheless. I will often tell a client that she doesn't have to believe these statements yet; she just has to say them to herself over and over. The first five from the list of twelve are:

1. I'm doing the best I can.
2. This is going to take a long time, whether or not I try to speed it up. I must take one day at a time.
3. I cannot expect too much from myself right now.
4. It is okay to make mistakes.
5. There will be good days and bad days.

Cognitive reframing can feel like a lot of work to the mother who is sleep deprived and anxious to get home to her baby. This is why I generally leave homework to a minimum and keep it simple during the early stages of our work together.

Ultimately, our goal in treating postpartum women in psychotherapy is to alleviate symptoms and improve psychosocial functioning. The particular modality used to achieve this goal has less influence over the final outcome than the style, authority, competence, and compassion with which therapy is executed and the sincerity with which it is received.

CHAPTER 9

Perfectly Postpartum

Pregnancy, childbirth, lactation, they all meant a temporary loss of control—of our bodies and of our careers. In response to this lack of control, we adopted a whole new range of controlling behaviors. We approached the enormous upheavals of pregnancy and childbirth as though they were normal life events we could in some way control. We sought to prove our mastery of them, our self-sufficiency, through natural childbirth, "birthing plans," and Olympic-level breastfeeding. We became mothering perfectionists.

Judith Warner
Perfect Madness, 2005

Ah, the pursuit of perfecting mothering: *How much is too much? What if it's not enough? What kind of damage will I impose on my children if I do it the wrong way?* Whatever the issue, whatever the question, whatever the proposed solution, mothers have for decades backed themselves into a no-win corner. It's never enough. Or it's not right. Not exactly. They've passed through phases of *The Donna Reed Show* and *Leave It to Beaver* mothers. They've tried working and staying at home. They have compared themselves to those mothers (*whom we all know*) who seem dangerously similar to the fictional character of the Stepford wife. They've tried holding on and letting go. Still, mothers today are left with one tenacious response: guilt.

Guilt is so pervasive that many mothers, particularly those who are depressed, presume it is a natural part of mothering, one that is inescapable in this day and age. Here's an example of how rampant this is: Question

number three on the Edinburgh Postnatal Depression Scale (Cox, Holden, &
Sagovsky, 1987) reads, "I have blamed myself unnecessarily when things went
wrong." (The Edinburgh scale will be discussed in detail in chapter 12.) This
question reads awkwardly, but the presumption is that women who are less
depressed blame themselves less. But many women, who are very depressed
and consumed by guilt, circle "No. Not at all." When questioned about this,
some say, "I blame myself, but not unnecessarily. I mean, if I do something
or am feeling something that's not right, I do blame myself, but I deserve the
blame, so it's not unnecessary." This guilt, as is the case with many destruc-
tive feelings associated with postpartum depression, can contribute to and
result from the illness. As she describes the plight of American women today,
Judith Warner (2005) writes:

> Too many [women] are becoming anxious and depressed because
> they are overwhelmed and disappointed. Too many are letting their
> lives be poisoned by guilt because their expectations can't be met,
> and because there is an enormous cognitive dissonance between
> what they know to be right for themselves and what they're told is
> right for their children.

Regardless of where this pressure to be the perfect mother comes from,
it has widespread persuasiveness and ends up as a force to be reckoned with
when we treat this population. If clinicians ignore it, we trivialize the context
within which many postpartum women struggle. If we do so, we can miss a
critical point of intervention.

Feminist researchers, such as Romito (1990), often link depressive symptoms to the inferior social status of women and to structural constraints,
such as labor pragmatics and division of household labor. Oakley (1980)
discusses four vulnerability factors related to these constraints, which might
offer insight into some women's emotional responses to childbirth: not being
employed, having a segregated marital role relation, housing problems, and
little or no previous contact with babies. Oakley believes that motherhood is
characterized by loss, particularly loss of identity, a notion that fits nicely into
the premise of this book.

Pressure comes from all sides and settles uncomfortably in the laps of
women trying to do everything the right way. Women say they are reluctant
to speak about their feelings:

> "I felt harassed. I didn't want to talk to anyone about how I was feeling.
> It's like I was a bad mother because I didn't want to breastfeed."
> "I didn't feel prepared to have a baby. I was afraid to tell anyone that I
> couldn't stand being alone with the baby. It made me feel incompe-
> tent and anxious. I was scared to death to be alone with him."

The conflicting messages espoused by countless parenting advocates are
enough to make anyone wonder if she is doing it right. *Babies should sleep on*

their stomachs. (Really? Mine would have protested.) *Babies should cry it out. Don't let babies cry for too long when they are too young. Baby-wearing is a great way to establish and maintain total need fulfillment* (whose?) *and maximize attachment. Does daycare promote socialization or will it increase separation anxiety?* (Whose?) *Do good mothers leave their children to go to work?* (Of course they do.)

I was one of the lucky ones who determined very early on, without much quilt, that I would be a much better mother to my children if I returned to work, part-time at first. The part-time option sounded good. I could be home early to spend more time with my baby, and it felt right, because I was too tired to work a full day, anyway. It was easy for me, I'm not particularly proud to say, to be selfish during those early postpartum months and put my needs right up there next to those of my baby. I have a slight rebellious streak that dates as far back as I can remember. I remember the exultation I felt walking into the high school gymnasium with my boyfriend, clad in jeans, to the formal prom. I remember the work boots I wore with colored socks accompanied by a mini skirt, long before it was a fashion statement, simply because I hoped I could get away with it.

Similarly, as I entered the world of motherhood, I recoiled from what was expected of me, whether that pressure came from my family or society as a whole, and found comfort in doing things that felt comfortable to me, even if it mean ruffling some feathers. That didn't mean I wasn't tempted to surrender, however, when I found myself sucked into the pressure cooker of "opportunities" for young mothers and their babies.

Longing for daytime companionship, I took my 4-month-old son to a local baby gym class. Hopefully, I won't offend any readers by saying I am almost positive he did not care whether he was in this brightly decorated room filled with expensive baby-friendly equipment or snug in our living room surrounded by unvacuumed dog hair and a Sesame Street video that had looped in repetition for the fifth time. I sat for a while in the circle of neurotic competitiveness, listening to mothers chatter on about whose baby was doing what and how many activities they had squeezed into their sleep-deprived schedules. *Why was I there, I asked myself. Who, exactly, expected this of me?* That was the first and last class to which I would drag myself.

It was then that I decided that if I were to maintain my sanity, I would pledge to:

Not go to baby classes programmed to make my baby smarter, faster,
   more agile, or speak foreign languages
Not compare myself to others
Not compare my baby to other babies
Do what I needed to do for *me* and bring my baby along in the process
Do the best I could
Not be hard on myself if I failed to live up to unrealistic expectations

Ask for help when I needed it

Trust my instincts

So what about the majority who don't rebel, who aren't even aware of the loftiness of society's established expectations? Do they even realize they have the option to reject them? It stands to reason that a particular woman's identification with her own customs and ethnic group would influence how she responds to pressure from the popular or mainstream culture. Therefore, clinicians must be open, not just to a mother's cultural traditions, but also to the significance these rituals hold for her. Each woman who comes to us brings a unique legacy: generations of mothering. We need her to teach us about her traditions and culturally specific practices. She needs us to understand how these practices have impacted her experience of mothering and depression. In this way we can help her draw upon those traditions that hold the most meaning for her and help her regain strength from her heritage.

If a clinician predominantly identifies with the mainstream American culture, the temptation may be to rely on familiar practices, which may or may not apply to the client. As Sue and Sue (2003) caution,

Counseling and psychotherapy have done great harm to culturally diverse groups by invalidating their life experiences, by defining their cultural values or differences as deviant and pathological, by denying them culturally appropriate care, and by imposing the values of a dominant culture upon them.

The role of culture and of gender has triggered much discussion within the context of postpartum depression. "As citizens of industrialized nations, we often act as if we have nothing to learn from the Third World. Yet many of these cultures are doing something extraordinarily right—especially in the way they care for new mothers," states Kathleen Kendall-Tackett (1994), a leading researcher in the postpartum community. She further cites the anthropological perspective of Stern and Kruckman (1983), who reported that the "baby blues" are essentially nonexistent in the cultures of the developing cultures that they reviewed. This contrasts with the high percentage of new mothers in more modernized nations who are reported to experience the blues.

Kendall-Tackett (1994) classifies and describes in great detail some of the characteristic rituals that are present in more supportive cultures, resulting in a lower incidence of postpartum illness: (1) *"a distinct postpartum period,"* a time when mothers are recuperating and, as Kendall-Tackett states so nicely, "when women were mentored by other women in the fine art of mothering"; (2) *"protective measures reflecting the new mother's vulnerability, including social seclusion and mandated rest"* (doesn't that sound good?); (3) *"functional assistance,"* described as a response to the need for rest—mothers are "relieved of their normal workload"; and (4) *"social recognition of her new role and status,"* which ranges from the symbolic gifts to crowning rituals complete with a beaded headdress.

It makes sense that strong social support and having extended family available to help will provide significant sustenance and subsequent relief from stress during this overwhelming period. It has been further suggested that in some cultures, family values and social organizations play an important role in protecting babies from the adverse effects of postpartum depression (Kumar, 1994).

THE PRESSURE TO BE PERFECT

In spite of all the ways women have advanced with liberated glory, sadly, there remains a pressure to be perfect. Nowhere do we see this with such fervor as in the American culture. So what's to be done? As we sit in our private offices far from the madding crowd, clinicians who work with postpartum women witness the crushing effects of this pressure. The pressure of cultural directives to be smarter, better dressed, and thinner than the rest looms over vulnerable new mothers and takes its toll.

We constantly note the insidious stress creasing the tired face that sits before us. How do we soothe her? It's a daunting task to try to offset such far-reaching demands put forth by the society in which we live. Yet, she comes to us, in part, for that.

Within her quest for comfort and meaning, we may represent the voice of reason amid the clash of cultural mandates. In today's world, there are way too much access to information, way too many opinions, and far too many choices. New mothers often spin with indecision, resulting in deadlock from both trivial (which never, ever feel trivial) and significant choices. A woman's mother-in-law might be telling her which decision to make and why, commercials are enticing her, social groups are encouraging her in a different direction altogether, and, then, just to top it all off, there's the shrill and constant tape in her own head looping over and over again.

By the time she reaches our offices, she needs someone to tell her that none of these things matters. That's a tall order and one that doesn't sit well with hypervigilant, control-freaky, symptomatic mothers who are desperately trying to take charge of their lives.

"None of this matters?" asked Jodi, mother of three, who obsessed about obsessing with the flair of an aficionado. I would inadvertently get so caught up in her obsessional loop that I would find myself spending way too much time trying to answer her unanswerable questions. Catching myself in this frenzy, I would pull back and point out what was happening.

"Jodi, you are so good at fixating on this, you've got me wrapped up right in there with you."

She loved that. "See?" She felt vindicated. "It's hard. How do I know the right thing to do?"

"How do any of us know?"
"What if I make a mistake?
"You will." (She didn't like that.) "Don't you think?"
"I suppose I will. But I'd rather not."
We live in a society that romanticizes motherhood and devalues it at the same time. How can any mother live up to the expectations that she and those around her set forth? In *The Myth of the Bad Mother,* author Jane Swigart (1991) brings the reader face to face with some stunning realities of child rearing and the intense experience it brings to both mothers and fathers. She writes:

> Whether we are male or female, parents or childless, the care of children reawakens our buried selves. For better or worse, childcare pulls us in two directions: outward toward the children we tend and inward toward our own earliest experiences of being cared for. Our first, most intense relationship with our mother often remains unconscious and inaccessible until we have children, at which point all the longings and ambivalence we felt toward her rise up in us again.

Women bring their childhood experiences and their history of relationships right into the office with them. Jodi had come to see me again when her third child was 8 months old; I had first met her after the birth of her second daughter. Jodi came from what she describes as a close-knit family who "helped me achieve near perfection in college. I did great. It almost killed me."

By the time she came to see me, she had spent several months recharging her uncompromising ways and trying to get things back in their proper order. She laughed when she told me how she could never live up to her mother's standards but, nonetheless, how hard she tried to "do things the way I know I should":

> There is no order to things with three children. I'm too tired. I am surrounded by things to do and screeching voices all over the place, and, still, I feel lonely and worthless. What am I doing? Did I really sign up for this? I keep going and going and getting nowhere. I feel like I'm walking backwards. I'm always running behind, trying to catch up with myself. Then, just when I think I've caught up, I still think I should be doing more. *My* mother certainly would have. Somehow she always managed to make everything look easy, but still, I never really caught a break. She was hard to keep up with, if you know what I mean.

"Why are you working so hard now, Jodi?" I asked, trying to help her look at her behavior from another perspective.
"I don't know. I wonder that, too. I have to, I think."
"Why do you have to?"

"I don't know. How else do you do it all? There's so much on my plate. If I don't run around doing it, it won't get done."

"And then what? What then, if it doesn't get done?"

She looked at me as if she had no comprehension of what I was asking.

"What if it doesn't get done?" I repeated.

"That's not an option."

"Maybe it is. Maybe it's one you can't see yet. Maybe doing it differently would feel better, in time."

"I don't know about that. It seems to me that figuring out a way to do less will only make me feel worse."

Women are making themselves sick with expectations of perfection. This can come from many sources. It can be the result of hard-driving, high-achieving parents, or it can be a personality type. It can stem from an underlying obsessive–compulsive disorder, or it can come from a biologic predisposition. It can be the result of abuse, trauma, or another major life disturbance, or it can just be because it is. Regardless of the origin, it needs to be identified and modified. In the end, women need to learn that they can indeed be alone with themselves and find peace there. It's a concept that is foreign to many.

Women may claim to be fed up with the myth of the perfect mother etched in their obsessive minds and reinforced by commercialism, but it remains pervasive, and we see the consequences of that pressure in our offices every single day. At the risk of oversimplifying a very complicated matter, one of our primary tasks is to present a healthy alternative to the pressure of perfect mothering. Mothers who are struggling with depression need to hear that it's okay for them to make mistakes.

Then, they need to hear it again, and once again.

PART 2

The Tools: Doing What Works

CHAPTER 10

The Phone Call

Initial Assessment

I wonder off and on whether I could hire a receptionist to return some of our calls, since much clinical time can be spent on the phone.

"Renee? This is Karen Kleiman, from The Postpartum Stress Center, returning your call."

"Hi." Her voice sounds brittle from the start. She says nothing else. This is when I worry most about someone who is not clinically trained taking the reins and returning these calls.

"You okay?"

"I don't think so," she says with her soft voice.

"Renee, is someone there with you?" At this point I have no idea who she is or why she called. I make early assumptions and rely heavily on my intuition.

"My husband is on his way home."

"Good. Talk to me and tell me what's going on. Tell me how I can help until he gets home."

This is when I realize, again and again, that these initial calls are best made by clinicians trained to listen for and respond to subtle cries for help. If we bypass this and head straight for the scheduling or logistical aspect of the call, not only do we lose the opportunity for an early connection, but we may also miss the urgency of the call.

For most women, regardless of how bad they are feeling, it's hard to make this first call. As noted in the earlier chapters of this book, many of them are calling with hesitation or in compliance with their doctor's or family's appeal.

But all the resistance or denial in the world cannot distract her from her earnest and immediate desire to feel better. And so, she waits for a return call.

Students of postpartum clinical practice are always surprised to hear how much time I spend on these first calls. Admittedly, this is one of the reasons I continue to toss around my fantasy of having someone else make these calls, simply because I seem to have run out of time to do it and do it well. We generally carve out a period of 20 minutes for a typical initial call—sometimes shorter, often longer. This time frame allows us enough time to assess for emergencies while obtaining additional relevant information.

The therapeutic objectives of this first call include:

- Establishing the first clinical interaction
- Establishing the role of a professional who is in a position to help
- Laying the groundwork for a potential relationship by clarifying this role as it relates to her expectations of recovery
- Gathering information regarding the client's perception of the problem and purpose of the phone call
- Rapid, early assessment of level of severity to determine whether emergency intervention is indicated

What's unique here is that, in traditional psychotherapy, the first contact is made in the office, in the form of the therapeutic interview; any initial phone contact is typically brief and rarely considered to be therapeutic intervention. With women in potential crisis, clinicians cannot afford to wait until that first meeting, which, due to scheduling limitations, may not be as timely as a clinician might like or the woman might need. Although clinicians need to be cautious not to diagnose or make presumptions over the phone prior to an evaluation in person, the phone contact remains a central vehicle for creating an alliance and assessing safety. How she speaks, what she says, how we react, and her perceived and misperceived interpretations of the current situation are all comments on how she is doing and what we need to do in response.

Here we recall Bruch's (1974) notion that the therapeutic exchange differs from the casual social contact in one important respect: the purpose. Because postpartum women are often thrust into unknown territory and not even sure themselves why they are calling, a clinician will find it useful to help them articulate why they are calling or what they think they need.

"Renee, you said you have a history of anxiety that's been treated in the past. Has it ever felt like this? Is this the same as it was for you the last time you experienced this?"

"Oh, my God, no. I've never felt this way. I've never in my life felt so out of control. I'm usually such an upbeat person, even when I felt anxious. I never felt so terrified and unable to do things. I just look around and everything is wrong. Everything is out of place. I can't sleep. I can't eat. All I do is think about how bad I feel."

"Okay, Renee, when anxiety gets this bad, it really is helpful for us to take a look and see what might be contributing to this so we can get you back on track and feeling good again."

Remember, we do not yet know, for certain, what she is struggling with or what the best intervention will be. All we know is that she is in distress. We can offer her a generalized statement of reassurance and hope she follows up with the evaluation, which enables us to take a closer look. It is also helpful to assess early coping strategies by getting a sense of what she has tried to do for symptom relief up to this point.

EARLY SCREENING

The first phone contact is a critical exchange. We have only a few minutes to evaluate and respond to her expressed pain and the nature of her suffering. Over the years, I've learned that it's not only *what* you are asking, but also *how* you ask it.

Are You Breastfeeding?

This was one of the biggest mistakes I've made. When I first started asking this question on the phone, I was inundated with stress-related responses such as:

"I tried, but I wasn't good at it."

"I wanted to so bad, but my baby couldn't latch on."

"Yes, but I think it might be part of the problem. He's not gaining enough weight, and I really don't want to supplement, but my doctor thinks I should and I don't know why he's not getting enough milk, and I have to go back to work in 3 weeks. I'm nervous that he won't take a bottle so I'm not sure what I should do, but I really don't want to stop breastfeeding. I've waited so long for this. No one seems to understand how much this means to me."

And the one reply that finally made me realize I was asking the question the wrong way was: "No. I'm not."

I realized in the silence that followed that my question stirred up a strong emotional response. *Did she feel I was passing judgment? Did she wish she could breastfeed? Was this a loss for her? Did she never want to breastfeed and was she just tired of the social pressure of people asking her? Whose business is it how she chooses to feed her baby? Did she feel like she had failed in some way? Was she feeling sad or guilty about this? Was I making all of this up and she just simply didn't want to breastfeed and was absolutely fine about her decision?*

The solution was simple, and the question was changed from that point forward to: Are you breastfeeding or bottle-feeding?

The question of feeding is quite relevant and does provide a platform for her to express any thoughts or feelings of anxiety that may be related to feeding issues. Feeding often represents her perceived capacity to nurture her infant, and her early response to this question can reveal her ease with this or signal trouble spots.

What's Your Husband's Name?*

I quickly learned that not all women with babies are married. Now I ask, "Are you married?" Although this still presumes that the majority are married, it is less likely to offend those who are not. I remember Dawn, who put me in my place when she answered,

> Yeah, I am. But my girlfriend doesn't think so 'cause we didn't have a ceremony. But I say, after all this hard work and deciding which one of us would carry the baby in our belly—I'd say it qualifies, don't you think?

Instead of asking a woman whether or not she is married, we can ask the name of the baby's father and whether he lives with them or not. Most women who reside in unconventional situations are most likely accustomed to presumptuous questions and will offer an early explanation of their living arrangements.

After getting the name of the woman's partner, my next question is typically: *Does (name) know how bad you are feeling?* Her answer may reveal a number of things:

- Is she telling her partner how bad she feels?
  - If so, what is the response?
  - If not, why not?
- Is her partner connected enough to her to know how bad she feels, whether she expressed it or not?
- Are her symptoms interfering with her ability to function in the relationship?
- Are there pre-existing or current marital concerns that are impacting the way she is feeling?
- What is her perception of the state of their relationship?
- Is her partner viewed as a source of support or as an additional stressor?

It is helpful from the outset to understand the role of her partner in this picture. At this point, I might ask if she'd be more comfortable with her husband accompanying her to the first session or if she would prefer to come alone. Although many women prefer to come with their husbands for support, just as many prefer to come alone; neither is a fair representation of the married state. And true to the nature of the psychotherapy setting, what you see

---

* It should be noted here that although any family unit with a baby is vulnerable to symptoms of depression, for our purposes in this book I will refer to partners and husbands interchangeably.

is not always what it is. Therefore, in our center, though we will want to meet with partners at some point, we opt to let the woman decide what is most comfortable for her at this first contact.

What's Your Baby's Name?

The mother's response to this question provides a glimpse into her relationship with her baby; one can gather much information regarding early attachment from this simple exchange:

> "Her name is Samantha."
> "What a sweet name. How's Samantha doing?" Asking about the baby is a
>   prompt for cues to how *mom* is doing in regards to their relationship.
> "She's fine."

At that point, I either make a note that mom isn't offering much information about Samantha, that she might be too tired to talk right now, or perhaps that a cigar is just a cigar and everything about the relationship is perfectly fine. My own emotional response—*that feels like an unimpressive thing to say about your 4-week-old baby*—may or may not be relevant. For what it's worth, I do find that most women, when asked how their baby is doing, by name, will answer this question with brutal honesty:

> "She's great. She's perfect. I just worry about how all of this is affecting her. My mother has been here helping me, so she's spending a lot of time with her. Is that okay?"
> "She's okay but she cries all the time and I have no idea what she wants. She's making me crazy."

Any response to our question about the baby will elicit an early peek into how she is feeling at that moment about her mothering.

Are You Having Any Thoughts That Are Scaring You?

This question is asked at the outset on the phone, at the first interview, and in subsequent sessions. It carries high anxiety, which is likely to inhibit her openness at one time or another. Our job requires us to check in repeatedly so we can (1) reinforce our readiness to respond if she is experiencing scary thoughts, (2) encourage her to divulge any discomfort in this area, and (3) determine to what extent this symptom is problematic.

Included in the appendix is a detailed outline of what should be addressed in the initial phone call. For now, heed these words of caution:

- Be careful not to make any generalizations about her concerns that you cannot account for without completing a thorough evaluation. For example, consider the questions "Do you think I'm crazy?" or "Could I really hurt my baby?" Chances are the answers to both of these questions will be "No." But until you evaluate the client and look her in the eyes, it is dangerous to speculate. To be safe, the response should be "Probably not, but I think it's important that we meet so we can take a look at everything and get you feeling better as quickly as possible."

- As always, take any thoughts of suicide, however passive they may be, very seriously and assess whether the client should be seen by a psychiatrist *before* she sees you.

Every time I revisit the concern that I am spending far too much time on the phone, I remember Patty and her sweet husband. Patty and David traveled far for our first session. She had been seeing a psychiatrist and was on medication, but her symptoms were worsening. Terrified that she would never feel better again, she said she didn't care how far she had to go to get the help she needed. She wanted to see me, and she believed I would help her feel better. After our first meeting, the three of us convened at my desk to make a follow-up appointment, and David shared his observation:

"You know, Karen, I just want to tell you something from a business standpoint. It's obvious that we are in the right place. Just look at Patty. I haven't seen a smile on her face for months. But I want you to know that she actually started feeling better after she hung up the phone with you the other day, when you called to set up the appointment."

"What a nice thing to say. Thanks for letting me know that. I'm glad it could make a difference."

"Honestly, Karen, talking to you on the phone was the first time she felt hopeful that she would get better. She believed in you. She believed she wouldn't always feel this way. It was the first light at the end of the tunnel. And I just wanted to thank you and let you know that it's an important part of what you do."

I knew that already. But it's always nice to hear.

CHAPTER 11

First Things First

Nobody would believe what an effort it is to do what little I am able.

Charlotte Perkins Gilman
"The Yellow Wallpaper," 1892

Postpartum women have lots of questions. Some questions are driven by anxiety symptoms, such as *How do I know if it's time to feed my baby again?* Others are complicated and have no easy answer. *Why did I get postpartum depression?* Some are related to things we swear we were taught not to answer. *What did you do when your baby wouldn't take the bottle?* Some we may want to research. *Do you think this is related to the birth control pills I started taking?* Still, there are some we *hope* we can answer but often cannot. *Do you think I'll feel this way again after my next pregnancy?*

If we proceed with the knowledge that women with postpartum depression are not likely to seek professional help (Cox, Connor, & Kendell, 1982; Whitten, Appleby, & Warner, 1996) and we recognize how difficult it must be for many of them to sit in our offices or even make the call in the first place, we are struck with the daunting task of making the best use of our first 50-minute hour. Comprehensive history-taking, rapid assessment, diagnostic screening, rapport building, determination of urgent intervention, reassurance, education, treatment planning, and our very best attempts to address a client's litany of questions are all taking place while we are observing, listening, and feeling what she may not be able to put into words. This forces us to cut to the chase.

Before we can make an assessment or determine which course of treatment would be most effective, there are some cautionary notes that merit special attention within this context: making assumptions, normalizing, making promises, and goal setting.

MAKING ASSUMPTIONS

In this line of work, as with all therapy, it is risky and never therapeutically wise to make assumptions. Most clinicians learn the hard way that once we presume something, subsequent sessions will invariably prove us wrong. So we must remain vigilant and open to any and all perceptions and possible interpretations. We cannot pretend to know what our client is feeling, and we should not project what we think she might be feeling. Nevertheless, when working with a postpartum woman, it is helpful to presume one thing and one thing only: that there has been considerable breakdown in functioning by the time she comes in for a first appointment. In doing so, we initiate passage into the holding environment. She doesn't think anyone can possibly know how bad she is feeling. With gentle authority, we convey to her that we know.

While supervising a new therapist at our center, I sat quietly (not an easy thing for me to do) in the background, observing as I scrutinized her interview skills.

"So, Lydia, what can we help you with?" The therapist put forth her question with the warmth and genuine caring I anticipated. "Why did you come to The Postpartum Stress Center today?"

My body stiffened and I'm certain the look on my face betrayed my effort to remain neutral. I surrendered momentarily and sat quietly.

"I need to feel better." She answered compliantly, with a look that seemed to say: *Why are you asking me that? Don't you know why I'm here? Isn't this what you do?*

I broke my silence, an occupational hazard of training with me: "Lydia, why don't you start by telling us how bad you feel and how this compares to how you usually feel. Since this is our first time meeting you, it's helpful for us to get a sense of how this compares to who you were before you felt this bad. Does that make sense?"

This sentence and request for elaboration provide several components that are crucial from the outset:

- It presumes a certain degree of sadness ("how bad do you feel"), which, in most cases, provides instant validation.
- It prompts for a self-reported description of the client's previous level of functioning, which can be a valuable measure for comparison and assessment.

- It establishes the outline of our initial goal for treatment, a line I will repeat in various ways throughout this book: *We do, indeed, know why you are here and we know what to do to help you feel better.*
- It tells her we believe her. Too often, a woman with postpartum depression has been (or felt) dismissed by family, friends, and healthcare providers, reinforcing her isolation. Listening to her is a good start, but *believing* her is imperative. She knows something isn't right. When those closest to her minimize her pain as "hormonal" or "normal," she either stops telling people how she is feeling or she begins to believe she must really be going crazy. Naomi Wolf (1991) describes in *The Beauty Myth*: "Pain is real when you get other people to believe in it. If no one believes in it but you, your pain is madness or hysteria."

NORMALIZING

Symptom relief is our initial, intermediate, and ultimate objective. This is why she is here and this is the goal for which we must strive. Focusing on the here and now is best, after a thorough history-taking. Long-term exploration of psychodynamic influences or family of origin difficulties is reserved for later. Therapists know there is nothing simple about the way any client presents herself in a first session; we know that everything is always related to everything else. But our first task is to reflect what we see back to her and present it as our assessment, as simply as we can, to a mother who is already overwhelmed. We review for her what she has told us and what her screening might show us, in terms of her symptoms. We confirm that we have interpreted this correctly before moving on to how we think we can intervene. Whether the task of obtaining symptom relief is straightforward and responds smoothly to treatment or is complicated and interwoven with long-standing premorbid factors, it should be stated up front, in words that make sense to the client:

"Let's go over how you are feeling, specifically, so we can help you feel better."

This is when it's important to talk about symptoms. All of them. Whether using an assessment tool, a list of symptoms taken from a book, or a wealth of postpartum depression knowledge, clinicians need to familiarize themselves with the cluster of possible symptoms the client might experience. Paradoxically, postpartum women are motivated to reveal their symptoms in an effort to seek support and, at the same time, well known to withhold how they are feeling in fear of judgment. Some of the literature points to the specific fear that disclosure of scary symptoms could result in a referral to a child protection agency (Heneghan, Mercer, & Deleone, 2004). This fear will keep a woman from talking about how bad she feels, even if letting someone know is her utmost wish.

When Annie sat nervously in my office for the first time, she didn't hesitate to spill her obsessive worry all over my words of comfort:

This is absolutely not who I am. I mean, if you knew me before, I am like always upbeat and in control. I don't know what is going on here, but it's not okay and I'm really afraid that this is just who I've become. My husband is telling me that I'm worrying too much, but he doesn't worry enough, and I know if I don't keep an eye on things, something may go wrong, especially at night when it's dark and she's sleeping. I'm afraid if I don't check on her, I might miss something. My mother said this is normal and I should just relax. I can't relax. Is this normal?

Research shows that most healthy mothers and fathers will experience unpleasant intrusive thoughts concerning their infants (Abramowitz, Schwartz, & Moore, 2003). Though obsessive thinking may be common in women with and without postpartum depression, clinicians need to pay attention to the specific nature of these thoughts. A woman without postpartum depression, for example, may obsess about feeding or nap schedules in order to establish a routine. A woman with postpartum depression may obsess about why her husband is 15 minutes late and wonder if something catastrophic has happened on his way home from work. The nature of the obsessive thoughts, therefore, can be an indication of symptoms that possibly require treatment. A woman's longing to hear that it is normal will not be helpful if she needs treatment. Efforts to appease her may not only postpone treatment but also can unintentionally lead her off track. Again, our words should be chosen carefully, taking into account that we may, in early stages of our work, have little information about what her previous or normal self looked like.

Keep this in mind: Because women with postpartum depression often will not recognize their symptoms as depression, most will not seek professional help. It is estimated that as many as 50% of women who experience clinical symptoms of depression during the postpartum period remain undetected (Ramsay, 1993). Despite what can be severe symptomatology, such as obsessional thinking about the baby's well-being or compulsive behaviors in response to persistently high anxiety, women and healthcare practitioners alike have difficulty differentiating between what is "normal" and that which requires professional attention. Symptoms of postpartum depression overlap with adjustments in the postpartum period that we anticipate women to experience, such as fatigue, early weepiness, and mood changes.

The dilemma is this: Women like Annie hope to hear from a professional that this is normal. That way, she thinks, there's nothing wrong with her: *I'm not sick. I'm not crazy. I'm just like everyone else. This is real; I'm not making it up.* That would seem to be a relief for her. But even if telling her "this is normal" provides a brief reprieve, if this *is* normal, she then thinks: *This is awful. How can I feel this way all the time? Maybe they don't understand how bad I really feel if they think this is normal. Maybe I'm not expressing it right or maybe they're missing something. Do I need to see someone else?*

Most therapists intuit that they need to be careful when using the term *normal* whenever responding to a client's need for clarification. After all, do we really know what normal means to the person asking us? If we don't take her frame of reference into consideration, we have no information (or right) to answer that question. But the painstaking quest for answers (such as, why did this happen to me?) deserves our attention. This is when we redefine normal.

Is it normal for women who give birth to feel depressed? Consider the research that indicates up to 85% of postpartum women experience fluctuations in their moods during the first few postpartum weeks (Hamilton, 1989). Baby blues are so common that experts are comfortable attaching the word *normal* to it. In this way, we can and should reassure the overwhelmed new mother that this is not a pathological state and that we expect her to feel weepy, irritable, and anxious in the first couple of postpartum weeks. This should be said only following an evaluation, so as not to overlook anything or reassure prematurely. As noted, when feelings of sadness, irritability, and anxiety linger beyond the 2- to 3-week time frame used as a mark of delineation, clinicians should suspect symptoms of depression.

In contrast to the blues, when a woman diagnosed with postpartum depression asks, "Is this normal?" our response can be any or all of the following:

- What you are feeling is very common for women with postpartum depression.
- When you are treated and your symptoms get better, you will no longer feel this way.
- Let's talk about how you are feeling and what we can do to help you start feeling better.
- What you are describing to me is typical for women who struggle with symptoms like the ones you are having.

In effect, what we are saying is: *No, it's not normal to feel this way after having a baby. Yes, it is normal for women with postpartum depression to feel this way.*

This is not, however, what she is asking.

PROMISES

Clinicians must always be careful about offering encouragement that may backfire, especially early on when we are less familiar with the particular dynamics that might be contributing to how our client is feeling. Reassurances such as *you'll be fine; no, you won't need hospitalization; you won't get worse;* or *your husband won't leave you* might feel good for her to hear, but we could be wrong and outcomes can attest to this. As we saw with the initial phone contact, instilling hope may be a primary intent, but we must be cautious not to assure her too hastily until we have more information.

Do you promise I'll feel better? Do you promise the medication will work? Do you promise I won't always feel this way?

Do not make any promises. Ever. We can and should be confident about our knowledge base, our therapeutic wisdom, and our plan of action. But the reality is that lives evolve and change is inevitable. Unpredictability goes with this territory. Presumptions can be a mistake at best and dangerous at worst. Clinicians must be careful to present only what they know to be true, along with a side comment that they will do the best they can to make sure that happens.

"Will I ever feel better than this?" a client might ask.

"We are doing exactly what we need to do to get you feeling better. You have seen the psychiatrist. You have started on the medication. Your husband is on board and knows how to reach me if he needs anything. Your mother will be staying here for 6 more days. Everything is in place."

"Are you sure I'll feel better?"

"I'm sure."

"Do you promise?"

Like a toddler anxious for the agreed-upon reward for his good behavior, fearful that his mom is going to forget, or worse, simply did not mean it in the first place, he squeals with persistence, "Do you promise? Do you promise, Mommy?" The teachings of child experts still lead the way as I revisit that treasured passage of time with each new client. *Don't make any promises on which you cannot follow through.* This may seem too obvious to mention, but when we are face to face with the desperate words of a woman who pleads for her very sanity and our promises in the same short breath, it can be hard to resist.

Do you promise I'll get better?

We know that this is likely the case—that she will, in fact, get better. It is the expected outcome to be sure. We could make that promise in another circumstance outside the therapeutic setting—for instance, to our child who is frightened by his first bad earache: *Yes, I promise you will get better.* But every single time I hear the cries of a woman begging for my promise of good health, I am haunted by thoughts of sweet Beth. I had seen Beth for years, off and on, after the birth of her daughter. After a long break in our work together, Beth started therapy with someone closer to her new home. "Besides," she said "I like you too much." It was true. We always felt like we were probably sisters in another life.

But Beth got very sick. Her symptoms of anxiety and depression soared and didn't seem to be responding to medication, therapy, or hospitalization. Beth called me for constant reassurance because her medicines and health-care providers continued to betray her diligent efforts. After months of little or no symptom relief and unrelenting, tortuous thoughts, Beth's desperate calls for help became constant and daily. *Karen, will I get better? Will I get better? Please tell me I will get better. Please tell me I won't always feel like this. Please! Do you promise? Promise me.* Her voice and my response echo in my head still. "Yes, Beth, you'll get better. I promise."

I promised her she would get better.

But she didn't.

She promised me she wouldn't kill herself.

But she did.

SETTING GOALS

From a practical standpoint, we have an obligation to identify those issues that are contributing to our client's depression or interfering with her recovery in some way. For instance, as the new mother reveals her story, we must listen to any background noise: *How is this related to her childhood abuse? Why isn't she talking about her baby at all? Is she drinking too much and minimizing that? When she says she checks a lot during the night, what does that mean? How many times? How does it feel to her if she doesn't check? Why isn't she looking at me while she's speaking?* And so on.

As clinicians, we are very tuned into our clients; after all, that's what we do. We are familiar with the feeling of asking a client a certain question that triggers a red flag in our minds. Those are the moments when we reach for our pen and paper, if they are not at hand, or we make a mental note: *That's probably relevant; I'll need to explore that further.* Upon hearing something that may be a contributing factor, clinicians must decide whether it should be probed at that moment or set aside for another time. Either way, its relevance should not be ignored.

Some issues that may be more conspicuous during the vulnerable postpartum period can leak into the early sessions, hidden within the client's words:

- *My husband travels a great deal.* This might suggest lack of adequate support.
- *My mother lives nearby, but we don't talk very often.* This might suggest impaired mother–daughter relationship.
- *My husband doesn't know how bad I'm feeling.* This might suggest marital discord or communication problems or both.
- *My baby's father is not part of the picture.* This might suggest lack of support resources.
- *I cannot get through the day without my caffeine.* This might suggest sleep issues, dependency issues, nutritional issues.
- *I knew I wouldn't be good at this.* This might suggest low self-esteem, negative thought patterns.
- *I'm so nervous all the time. I've always been like this, I guess.* This might suggest chronic or pervasive anxiety.

The issues that may have (probably) preceded the depression will now be incorporated into the treatment plan as goals. As the client speaks, she creates a portrait of who she was, who she is, and who she hopes to be again when she feels better. Actual intervention may be postponed, depending on the issue, but this is when we begin to understand the relevance and influence of each issue as an independent feature of the total landscape.

We presume that each therapist shares one universal goal, regardless of the client's unique needs—that is, to work toward the reduction of depressive and anxiety symptoms. Establishing specific goals at the outset can ease initial anxiety about the therapeutic process by offering a structure that helps dial down some of her symptoms, particularly those that are anxiety driven.

Goals should be:

1. Short term, easily achievable: *Here's the psychiatrist's number. I would like you to call me after you have made the appointment so I know when you'll be seeing her for the evaluation.*

2. Adaptive: *It sounds like you've been struggling with anxiety for some time now, long before your baby was born. It will be helpful for you if we spend some time looking at what works for you and what might not be working so you can have more consistent relief.*

3. Client driven: *When I feel bad like this, I just shut down. I'd really like to learn how to communicate better with my husband.*

4. Strategic: *First we are going to go over some of the things you can do to help reduce your distractions at night, which will help you rest. Then we'll discuss a longer-term plan to boost your current support system so you can get more sleep.*

At our center we use this shortcut for immediate goal setting in the first session (see appendix): We have a printed pad, about the size of a prescription pad, complete with logo and mother-friendly colors and images. On the pad we have printed a short list of top-priority tasks to help the client focus on what to do first, since we presume that this first session may overwhelm her with just another list of things to do. Therefore, we run down the list together, and each therapist checks off those tasks that are applicable to the individual client and adds text as needed. For instance, I'll check "call doctor for meds" and write the name and number of our psychiatrist or the name of her obstetrician if that's the course she is taking. I'll continue to check off my recommendations and spend a few minutes with each to make certain she understands what I am asking and what she needs to do. This way, she not only has a tangible script for action but also does not have to worry about whether she missed anything if her symptoms prevented her from concentrating on the details of what steps need to be taken. This is goal setting at its most base level, which, for many women, is exactly where they need to start.

Postpartum women are forever fraught with the pressure to do something—whether it's another load of laundry or getting their act together so they will appear in control when they go to the pediatrician. It never feels like enough.

"It does weigh on me so not to do my duty in any way!" Charlotte Perkins Gilman (1892) writes in "The Yellow Wallpaper," a short story inspired by her own postpartum illness in 1892. "I meant to be such a help to John, such a real rest and comfort, and here I am a comparative burden already! Nobody would believe what an effort it is to do what little I am able."

Nobody would believe it, indeed. Clinicians who work with the postpartum woman must believe it first and foremost. First we listen, then we believe, then we take action. We presume she feels bad; we make no other assumptions. We provide a frame of reference for her pain, we make no promises, and we help her prioritize her extensive inventory of things to do. One step at a time.

CHAPTER 12

Asking the Right Questions
Screening

As depression during pregnancy and the postpartum period continues to be a major threat to maternal health, identifying it and referring for appropriate treatment are becoming more important than ever. One study revealed that almost half of a sample of family nurse practitioners from Illinois and Wisconsin reported that they never screened for postpartum depression. If we generalize the presumption that screening for postpartum depression is not widespread, it is disheartening, but likely, that the statistics on the incidence of postpartum depression are on the low side (Goldsmith, 2007).

At our center, we have found that the most efficient and effective way to acquire accurate responses to those hard-to-ask, harder-to-answer questions is to have women write their responses down. It seems women are more likely to be candid about how they are feeling if they are reading the questions, as opposed to looking the clinician in the eye.

The screening tools for postpartum depression are satisfactory and certainly useful in the identification of some symptoms. The benefits of using these tools are clear. They provide statistically reliable and valid information that can help define and steer the course of treatment. Additionally, screening tools offer us the advantage of a concrete number—proof, so to speak, that the diagnosis is correct and treatment is appropriate. Women come in looking for that verification: "Isn't there a test I can take or a hormone you can give me to make this go away?" Screening tools are the closest thing to a blood test or x-ray that we have. Women are looking for something tangible, something that makes sense, something they can objectify, because everything they are feeling and thinking is so obscure. Women who are skeptical about their diagnosis of postpartum depression are more likely to understand that there is a real diagnosis when they can see a number that represents a score or severity of symptoms.

Joanne, being the perfectionist that she was, didn't like my determination that her depression was significant. "No," I told her, "it will not go away by itself if we just 'let it run its course,'" as she had hoped. Her symptoms were impressive, but still she resisted. After all, she protested, depression is a weakness and she was not about to surrender.

"Joanne, you are exhausted. You are working very hard, with very little energy left, I might add, to uphold your conviction that everything is fine. You have almost no appetite, you are crying much of the day, and you are having thoughts that are scaring you. You cannot sleep, you are blaming yourself for most of your symptoms and feelings that are getting in the way, and you tell me this is not at all who you usually are."

Her eyes tear up as I reflect back what she has reported.

"You feel disconnected from your 4-year-old and overprotective of your baby. You are worried that you will never again feel like yourself and wonder if your children would be happier, in the long run, with another mother."

She was sad, but not convinced.

"Here's the screening you took. Know what it tells us? A score of 10 or higher tells us that depressive symptoms are likely and a score of 12 or above indicates that depressive symptoms are probable."

She lifted her eyebrows waiting for my confirmation of what she already knew.

"Your score is 24."

"Out of a possible 30? Wow. Almost perfect," she mocked with sheepish acknowledgment.

"Well, it means you're not feeling good at all and we need to take care of that. You may not like to hear the word depression, but your symptoms are telling me that we need to treat this and we need to treat it right away. Okay?"

"Yes. I know. I want that."

Somehow, the score on the screening tool managed to cut through her resistance more easily than my words and years of expertise.

To date, there are three primary screening tools applicable for postpartum depression assessment: the Edinburgh Postnatal Depression Scale ([EPDS] see appendix; Cox, Holden, & Sagovsky, 1987), the Postpartum Depression Screening Scale (PDSS; Beck & Gable, 2002), and the Patient Health Questionnaire (PHQ-9; Kroenke, Spitzer, & Williams, 2001). All of the screening instruments are good; the EPDS is by far the most commonly used. For the most part, the tool selection may be less important than the subtle factors surrounding its use, such as: Have we created a space that feels safe and supportive that will enable our client to answer honestly? Are we presenting the tool in a nonjudgmental environment so she can explore and document how she is truly feeling and thereby accurately reflect the symptoms and clinical course of her illness?

Clinicians should pick a screening tool they are comfortable using and be certain they understand how it is to be used, scored, and interpreted. The next step is to talk with the client about what it means, why it is used, and what her answers reveal. For our purposes here, we review the EPDS, since it is widely used in the screening of postpartum mood disorders.

EPDS

Cox et al. (1987) developed this self-reporting questionnaire for the purpose of screening postpartum women during the first months after childbirth in the primary care setting. The EPDS has been utilized in 23 countries and carries a significant level of sensitivity (86%) and specificity (78%) in identifying those at risk of or potentially suffering from either prenatal or postpartum depression (Cox et al., 1987). Early screening is proving to be the single most effective and cost-efficient way to detect postpartum depression (Epperson, 1999), which is why so many states are following New Jersey's trailblazing efforts to enact legislation mandating screening for postpartum women.

The questionnaire is easy to complete and does not seem intrusive, even to women who are struggling with severe symptoms. In fact, in our practice, we include it as one of the forms we ask them to fill out in the waiting room. When asked how it feels to first complete the screening tool and then review it with their therapists, women consistently tell us it reinforces that they are in the right place.

Advantages of the EPDS include:

- It is a 10-item, self-rating questionnaire.
- It is user friendly.
- It is available at no cost.
- The test can usually be completed in less than 5 minutes.
- It is easy to administer and easy to score
- It can be implemented by a variety of healthcare practitioners in a variety of healthcare practices.
- It has been validated and is a reliable screening tool that accurately detects women with postpartum depression (O'Hara, 1994).
- It has been validated for use with postpartum partners (Matthey, Barnett, Kavanagh, & Howie, 2001).
- It can be used for screening depression during pregnancy (Evans, Heron, Francomb, Oke, & Golding, 2001).
- To determine its applicability across cultures, it has performed satisfactorily in most validation studies, in English and in translation (Berle, Aarre, Mykletun, Dahl, & Holsten, 2003; Small, Lumley, Yelland, & Brown, 2007).

Disadvantages of the EPDS include:

- It is a screening tool; elevated scores, in and of themselves, do not always indicate the presence of a clinical depression.
- It can miss some women who have a depressive disorder.
- It is not a substitute for a comprehensive psychological or psychiatric interview and should not take precedence over clinical judgment.
- It can leave healthcare practitioners with ambiguities or unanswered questions regarding appropriate referrals and optimal treatment options.
- If offered by untrained personnel, it may skew results.
- Some of the questions are confusing and lead to varying interpretations.
- It may or may not make a significant difference in the number of women who actually get help for postpartum depression. It has been reported that more than half of the mothers tested believed that their symptoms were not severe enough to warrant the label of depression (Whitten, Appleby, & Warner, 1996).
- The scale is limited in its measurement of the anxiety disorders and obsessive–compulsive symptoms that can be so prevalent in postpartum depression.

My experience is that women are receptive to this external measure of their symptoms and are somewhat relieved to know that there is a scale designed to help classify how they are feeling. Engaging in a dialogue to review the results is a critical part of the initial clinical interview.

Scoring the EPDS

Although somewhat variable, most experts in this field agree that scores of 10 or above indicate a woman may be at risk for postpartum depression. Scores of 12 or above indicate the presence of clinically significant symptoms and the woman should be further assessed and referred for treatment and follow-up. Some experts prefer that the cutoff score be lower to ensure that depressions are not overlooked. If the woman scores 1 or higher on question 10 ("the thought of harming myself has occurred to me"), which is referred to as a *positive* screen for item 10, immediate intervention is required.

Clinicians should consider the fact that even if a woman scores less than 9, if clinical judgment suggests that the client may be suffering from depressive symptoms or acute anxiety, an appropriate referral should be made. EPDS is a screening tool; it does not diagnose depression. Healthcare providers who are handing out the EPDS for a quick screen and sending women home may be flirting with disaster. Postpartum women need to be carefully screened, spoken with, and then referred for further assessment and treatment.

TWO-QUESTION SCREEN

In busy healthcare practices where there is concern that the screening will be time consuming, more attention is being placed on a two-question depression screen that is not specific to postpartum depression (Whooley, Avins, Miranda, & Browner, 1997) recommended by the U.S. Preventaive Services Task Force on Preventative Health Care (2002). This two-question screen has proven to be almost as effective as longer instruments (Whooley et al., 1997). It utilizes a dialogue instead of a written questionnaire and can be used in addition to the standardized tools. The screen is based on these two questions:

1. Over the past 2 weeks, have you felt down, depressed, or hopeless?
2. Over the past 2 weeks, have you felt little interest or pleasure in doing things?

For women who respond with "yes" to either of these questions, it's important to conduct a formal follow-up assessment.

Unrecognized maternal depression can be serious and debilitating. Studies indicate that depression screening leads to an increase in detection and treatment (Epperson, 1999), which is why experts now recommend that screening for postpartum depression take place in primary care settings, obstetrician offices, and pediatrician offices. Because pediatricians encounter mothers repeatedly during the postpartum year and may see the mother prior to her 6-week obstetric checkup, it is important that they recognize postpartum depression as well as educate and refer mothers for evaluation, if needed (McLearn, Minkovitz, Strobino, Marks, & Hou, 2006). Linda Chaudron (2003) points out that although pediatricians are treating the baby and not the mother, screening for maternal depression, which may affect the baby and the family, is appropriate and within the scope of their practice. However, in our center, we performed an informal survey and asked clients to whom they were most likely to disclose their symptoms of postpartum depression. The majority of women said they would not disclose to their pediatrician for fear of "being judged a bad mother." Most indicated they would reveal how they were feeling to their obstetrician and/or primary care physician, depending on to whom they felt most connected.

OTHER VARIABLES

In *This Isn't What I Expected* (Kleiman & Raskin, 1994), we included in the appendix an evaluation tool we designated as the "Raskin–Kleiman Postpartum Depression and Anxiety Assessment." Years ago, this clinical tool provided the earliest feedback to confirm the supposition that women were more inclined to reveal intimate information if they could write it down in a private moment, rather than speaking face to face with an interviewer. I can remember a few incidents when this discrepancy was glaring. Most notable was after I had had a couple of sessions with a new client, and she brought in the form after taking it home and completing it there. It was a long assessment, so we frequently asked women to complete it between their first and second sessions.

I had already run through my standard first-session interview questions:

- Family history of depression/anxiety? Personal history of depression/ anxiety?
- Any other mental illness in the family?
- Pertinent family history: parents, siblings, family organization, and relationships?
- Past medical history: illnesses, hospitalizations?
- Any history of drug or alcohol abuse?
- Any history of eating disorders?
- Any history of abuse? Sexual, physical, emotional? Other trauma?
- Currently taking any medications? Anything over the counter? Any supplements?
- Any recent physical exam to rule out thyroid problems? Anemia? Other medical conditions?
- Any alcohol in the diet? Any caffeine in the diet?
- Screening questions to help identify symptoms of depression, anxiety, obsessions, suicidality, or psychosis.

In addition to the standard questions noted previously, I took note of the client's appearance, mood, and affect: How is she speaking? Is she making eye contact? Are her facial expressions appropriate for what she is saying? How is she sitting? Are her thoughts clear? How does she sound? How does she make me feel while she's talking? What is her emotional state while she is speaking?

Assessment questions in an initial interview may seem straightforward enough but can still stir up a variety of responses. Typically, I would ask my questions, and the client would answer them. In this particular case, a week or so later, I reviewed the assessment she had brought to me after completing it at home. The answers did not match. "Any history of abuse?" I had asked her. Her answer was no in our first session. Yet on her assessment she had checked "I have been a victim of physical assault by someone I know" as well as "I have been a victim of childhood sexual abuse by a family member." When I explored further, she commented that she wasn't sure what I had meant when I asked the question.

Of course it may have been true that she misunderstood the question, but I suspect not.

Since that time, we have streamlined the screening questions at our center. By far, the most revealing instrument we use at our center is our symptom list (see appendix). It is a single sheet listing 94 symptoms, grouped according to categories of symptoms; for example, physical anxiety symptoms are one group. Women simply check off each and every symptom they are experiencing at the time they are filling out the form, providing valuable raw material for the initial evaluation. They tell us it is both distressing and reassuring to check off so many on the list. On the one hand, they think: *I must really be sick!* At the same time, they think: *I must not be the only one feeling this way if it's written on this standard form!* The latter is what we usually hear from women. By the time she is in the room discussing them in detail with the therapist, the woman has already overcome a major hurdle by acknowledging that those feelings are present.

Having these tools can expedite the interview process and provide a comfort level that enables the client to be candid in her responses. Filling out symptom lists or screening tools in the waiting room before meeting with the clinician provides the client with a journal of sorts. The room is quiet; no one is pressuring her to respond in a certain way. She is alone with her thoughts and her feelings. By seeing her feelings in print, she may be encouraged that they will be validated and understood. This can be a huge intervention in and of itself.

THREE KEY EARLY ASSESSMENT QUESTIONS

Suicide?

Every single woman with a postpartum depressive disorder who enters a clinician's office is potentially suicidal. She may not always admit it. She may not think that wishing she could sleep forever is a suicidal thought. She may think that keeping it to herself makes it less real. She may also think that if she tells us, we will take her baby away, call the authorities, lock her up, or think she's crazy. I suspect that more postpartum women than we even imagine have passive thoughts of suicide.

If clinicians do not ask a woman with postpartum depression whether she is feeling suicidal, we have no idea whether she is having thoughts of hurting herself or not. Thus, we ask each and every one:

- Are you having any thoughts of hurting yourself?
- Are you having any thoughts that are scaring you?
- Do you ever think it would be better if you weren't here?
- Do you ever think that life is just too hard or too painful to go on?
- Do you think your family would be better off without you?

The question of suicide is also addressed in the EPDS, item 10. Answered in the affirmative, it trumps any other score. Women who express any intention to harm themselves or their children should always receive urgent intervention. (Suicide will be explored in greater detail in chapter 27.)

Attachment to Baby?

Contrary to what media attention and sensational headlines might suggest, women with postpartum depression go to tremendous lengths to protect the well-being of their babies. They are far more at risk to hurt themselves than their babies. Still, it is prudent and good clinical practice to explore this relationship with probing questions:

Some questions, such as *how's your baby doing?* or *tell me about your baby,* can seem quite innocuous at first glance. But these questions lead the way for closer inspection of the relationship between mother and baby (a relationship that will be explored in greater detail in chapter 26):

- Does she address the baby by name?
- Does her affect match the words she uses to describe how the baby is doing?
- Do you have any gut response that something isn't right?
- Does she say anything that worries you?
- Is she concerned about the relationship?
- Does she seem to be worrying excessively about the baby?
- If given the opportunity to observe their interaction, clinicians should monitor mom's response patterns and contact with baby as well as check emotional, physical, and verbal responses.
- Look for evidence of "motherese" (baby-talk language).
- Is she comfortable touching her baby?
- Is she particularly anxious regarding feeding, crying, or fussiness?

Scary Thoughts?

Asking a new mom in therapy if she is having any thoughts that are scaring her may be open to interpretation, and she may respond in a number of ways:

1. "No. I'm not thinking of hurting my baby or anything!"
   This can be an instantaneous and defensive retort that may require further probing to ensure that she understood the question.
2. "No."
   She may be afraid of what we are asking and what she should say. She may shut down and resist sharing information until she feels safe to proceed.
3. "Yes. I'm afraid I'll never feel better again."
   This is an example of a thought that is indeed very scary for a new mother to have but is less of a concern to the clinician and is not, in fact, what we are asking.
4. "Yes, I am" or "Yes, I think so."
   This response requires immediate clarification and probing to determine the specific nature of these thoughts.

Therefore, the clinician's screening questions must be clear:

Are you having any thoughts that are scaring you?

Do you have any thoughts about yourself or your baby that you are afraid to tell anyone?

Are you worried that you might hurt yourself or your baby?

Do you have any thoughts that feel uncharacteristic or not at all like you?

Is there anything you think I should know that you might be afraid to tell me? (Scary thoughts will be explored in greater detail in chapter 19.)

We can conclude, from the research and from what women are telling us, that healthcare practitioners are not always asking the right questions. The implication for practice is that better clinical guidelines need to be established and better education curricula need to be developed to prepare graduates with the necessary information.

In our practices, clinicians must stay informed, keep up with the research, and, above all, ask the right questions. Then, we should continue to do our best to enable women to disclose how they really feel. Sometimes they do. Sometimes they need to wait until they feel safer. Either way, the questions need to be asked and, usually, asked repeatedly in subsequent sessions.

CHAPTER 13

Listening to Symptoms

Assessment

Years ago when I was the sole practitioner of my office, I asked a colleague to cover my practice or at least field the phone calls in my absence. His specialty was hypnotherapy, so I suspect he was accustomed to a fairly calm energy force, so to speak. Thus, his comment upon my return shouldn't have surprised me. "Wow, I don't know how you do it," he noted.

"Do what?"

"So much anxiety! The couple of women I spoke to were off the wall with anxiety. I mean, it was exhausting just talking to them for a couple of minutes. I didn't know what to do with them—send them to the ER or tell them to go take a pill!"

I was glad he was not treating women with postpartum depression. I thanked him for his help, reassured him that I would not be requiring his assistance in the future, and then thought about what he had experienced.

Essentially, the work we do needs to be understood within the context of a critical time frame. Generally speaking, the postpartum period refers to the first postpartum year. The continuum of postpartum mood disorders places baby blues at one end of the spectrum, emerging within the first 2–3 postpartum weeks. The onset of the blues usually occurs 3–5 days after delivery and subsides as hormone levels begin to stabilize. To complicate things, this same 2- to 3-week time characterized by dramatic hormonal fluctuation is also the time when significantly fewer women (1/10 of 1% of postpartum women or, on out of every 1000) experience symptoms of postpartum psychosis, placing this at the other end of the severity spectrum.

Because of this potential confusion of symptoms, it is crucial that health-care providers, particularly the physicians and nurses who are often triaging the initial calls, are not quick to dismiss early intense symptoms as "just the blues." To reiterate:

- Symptoms of the blues that last longer than 2–3 weeks should be referred for assessment and treatment.
- Symptoms of the blues that seem unusually severe should be referred for immediate assessment or medical intervention.
- If a woman complains of weepiness, moodiness, irritability, fatigue, etc. and she is *past the 3-week postdelivery time frame*, she should be referred for assessment and treatment.

Postpartum depression, whether mild, moderate, or severe, is generally a very agitated depression. The term *postpartum depression* itself can be misleading to both sufferers and health providers because it often presents with anxiety or obsessional thoughts rather than depressive symptoms. The acute anxiety may be unlike any the client has experienced and is easy to neither endure nor conceal. Anxiety, by definition, is never comfortable. Postpartum anxiety, however, is unique in that it often relates directly to the baby, ranging from overworrying to hypervigilant, obsessive worries to scary, intrusive thoughts about hurting the baby. When the baby is involved in the anxious thought process, it very quickly propels the anxiety to absolute panic. This state of intense agitation is difficult for the client to go through, difficult for loved ones to observe, and difficult for the clinician to interpret.

Is she at risk for hurting her baby?
Is she at risk for hurting herself?
Is this really anxiety or something else?
Could she indeed be "going crazy" like she fears?
Is she alone? Does she have an available support network?
What is your emotional reaction to it? Is it worrying you?

Your assessment of her anxiety will depend on a number of factors:

- *Is this a phone call or a face-to-face experience? (harder to assess on the phone)*
- *How early postpartum is she? (very early may be more problematic)*
- *Do you have an ongoing relationship with her, or is this your first contact? (first contact is harder to assess)*
- *Is this consistent with what you know of her personal/family history of depression/anxiety, or does it strike you as uncharacteristic? (your familiarity will be a key determinant of this assessment)*
- *Has she responded to your assessment questions with suitable answers, or are you more worried as a result of what she says?*

Clinicians should heed this warning: A client's fear or degree of reactivity to this anxiety—though not completely irrelevant—is not necessarily a sound indicator of how serious the symptom is. Separating her reaction to the symptom from the symptom itself is a fine distinction and a critical component of this early assessment.

FREQUENCY, INTENSITY, AND DURATION

Anxiety is only one of the symptoms of postpartum depression that can be a challenge to understand. The postpartum period is a time of heightened emotional experience and expression. Any sensation or feeling (whether it is a symptom or not) has the potential of intensifying during this time. Bodies are fatigued, systems are worn down, and nerves are frayed. Because of this, symptoms may not always be what they appear to be.

Sometimes the symptom speaks for itself; a mother with negative intrusive thoughts about her baby needs immediate attention and relief. Other times, a symptom may not be so clear, for instance, a mother who states she is crying all the time. As we've previously discussed, one of the primary reasons postpartum depression is often misdiagnosed is the ambiguity of symptoms. This is due to the intersection of symptoms with those generally considered to be within normal expectations for the postpartum adjustment period (Yonkers, 1995). Examples of those that overlap the most include fatigue, loss of libido, moodiness, weepiness, changes in weight, sleep disturbance, and low energy. Consequently, when carrying out an assessment, it is important to keep in mind that it is not the feeling (or symptom) per se, but rather the *frequency, intensity,* and *duration* of that feeling. Put another way, how much is that feeling interfering with the client's ability to get through the day?

For instance, all new mothers cry. All new mothers are tired. We know this to be true; it is absolute and undisputed. Thus, when a postpartum woman tells her doctor that she's exhausted and weepy, an untrained provider might assume this is the normal course of events. Furthermore, when this provider reassures mom that this is to be expected, she may be momentarily reassured. But if she is experiencing postpartum depression, her fatigue and weepiness are something else entirely. As her symptoms persist or get worse and do not resolve as her doctor insinuated, the assurance quickly dissolves into (1) *my doctor has no idea how I feel or what to do about it* or (2) *something is* really *wrong with me.*

If all new mothers cry, how do we tease out which crying is symptomatic? Essentially, we want to find out how much or how often she is crying (frequency); does the crying seem or feel excessive (intensity); and how long she is crying (duration).

A new mother reports she isn't sleeping at all. What does this mean?

- How much sleep is she actually getting?

- How much sleep did she require to function well before she had the baby?
- Is she able to sleep when her baby sleeps?
- Is her mind racing when she is trying to sleep?
- Does she awaken from sleep because her baby is crying or because she is having a panic attack?
- Is her interrupted sleep still totaling more than 5–6 hours?
- Is she getting less than 4 hours of sleep total for the night?

Our greatest concern here, other than the fact that she's exhausted, is sleep deprivation. Sleep deprivation can and will exacerbate all other symptoms and, if left unattended, can contribute to rapid decompensation. A woman's exhaustion may be normal when her baby is 2 weeks old and awake several times a night to nurse. We would be more concerned if her baby were 6 months old and sleeping straight through the night. Loss of energy can certainly result from lack of sleep, but if she is exhausted to the point of debilitation, this is not okay.

In these ways we can see how important it is to consider each symptom as a specific and complex expression that needs to be understood within the appropriate context. Screening tools are good, but they are not always enough.

A FINAL WORD ON THE SEVERITY OF SYMPTOMS

In reference to my colleague who felt bombarded by the degree of anxiety unleashed while covering my practice, I certainly understand how disturbing that can feel if one is unprepared for it or, dare I suggest, not in the mood. But within the context of a postpartum mood response, anxiety is predictable and severe anxiety is often unexceptional. Though I am accustomed to hearing and treating it, the panic-driven nature of postpartum symptoms should always inspire an immediate response.

Perhaps it's because I can hear what they are asking for, even when they don't ask. Perhaps it's because I know what kind of response I would want if I were feeling that way. Either way, anxiety is a symptom that calls attention to the sufferer. We hear it, we feel it, and we respond to it. It is a symptom that begs to be noticed. It is not, however, a symptom that worries me.

Symptoms that worry me are those that seek no audience—symptoms that, to an untrained eye or ear, remain inconspicuous: A voice that doesn't sound right. Behavior that doesn't feel right. Eyes that don't look right. Something out of character that sends a warning to our sensibilities that observers may not yet completely understand. Astute clinicians might hear it on the phone or might see or feel it in the first session. *Subtle symptoms that might otherwise go unnoticed can be urgent cries for help that require immediate intervention.*

The difficulty here is that this ambiguity of symptoms is most likely to impact us during our first contact with a woman about whom we know very little or virtually nothing. We have no frame of reference with which we can measure her presentation of symptoms. *Is this what she usually sounds like? Is this how she typically behaves? Can I trust my emotional response?*

The following are two examples that were notable to me at the time.

Sleep

When Erin didn't show up for her first appointment, I remember being worried. (Both things—missing appointments and me worrying about that—go with the territory, of course.) When a nonpostpartum client doesn't show up for a first appointment, I might think that he or she simply forgot or, more likely, changed his or her mind and didn't call to let me know—an occupational hazard, to be sure. But when a postpartum client doesn't show up for a first appointment, I always wonder if she's okay. Sometimes, she *is* fine—for example, she's distracted, she's exhausted, she doesn't have childcare coverage, she forgot, she's feeling better, she changed her mind, or she doesn't want to spend the money.

And, sometimes, something is terribly wrong.

I called Erin's home. Her husband answered. "Hi, this is Karen Kleiman from The Postpartum Stress Center. Is Erin available?"

"Oh, hi, Karen. This is Russ, Erin's husband. She told me she had an appointment with you. I didn't know it was today. She's upstairs sleeping. She's been sleeping a long time. She wasn't feeling well this morning, so I stayed home to let her rest. She's been sleeping since I got here. I'll go see if she can talk."

As much as it pains me to disturb a sleeping mother, I waited with uneasy interest to see why she hadn't come in, since I could easily recall our conversation from a couple of days prior, when she seemed motivated to make the appointment and get help. *She's been sleeping a long time.* His words resonated in my head. I didn't like the way it sounded, yet nothing in our brief conversation alerted me to any problems, so I continued to wait with the expectation that she would reschedule her appointment. When Russ came back to the phone, I could hear his desperation. "I can't wake her up."

"Russ, call 911, go back to Erin, try to wake her, and call me from the hospital."

Shit. Nobody trains us for this in graduate school. *What did we miss? How did this happen? Will she be okay? Who is she? What is her history? Why didn't I see this coming?* And so forth.

Erin would be okay after spending a couple of days in intensive care and having her stomach pumped to free her system of the Tylenol overdose that seemed, at the time, her only reprieve from the pain. I shudder to think what could have happened if the phone call had been an hour later or if her husband hadn't come home or checked on her when he did.

In our subsequent work together, Erin taught me a great deal about postpartum symptoms and how vigilant those of us who treat this must be.

Sometimes, women with postpartum depression will scream for help. Other times, they just sink into the background, hoping no one will notice.

Voice

Her name was Pauline. We never met. She called for information for a referral closer to her home, since she lived a couple of hours from our center. I remember she was sweet, but distant, on the phone. We exchanged information, she told me how she felt and I told her what her options were. Nothing seemed particularly out of the ordinary, other than a sense I was getting that something wasn't right.

"Pauline, are you okay? Right now? Are you all right?"

"Yes."

But she wasn't, and I could hear it. Her voice was hollow. It was flat and void of emotion. She was saying all the right things, but none of it felt right. Always careful to weigh what I'm hearing and feeling with what I do not yet know about a person (and what could be the presence of a personality disorder or Axis II diagnosis), I proceeded to check further.

"Pauline, how do you feel right now?"

"Okay," she replied like a compliant child who was hoping that this was my last question.

"I don't like the sound of your voice."

"I know." This surprised me.

"You don't sound good."

"I know." I could feel the heaviness in her words. I could feel her fear and disconnection. She could hardly speak, although her responses reflected a genuineness that spoke volumes. It was almost as if her awareness of her disconnection facilitated a connection.

"Pauline, are you alone?"

"Yes."

"Is your baby with you?"

"Yes."

"Is he okay?"

"Yes. He's sleeping. He ate an hour ago. He'll sleep for another hour or more." *Good, informative, alert response.*

"Are you having any thoughts that are scaring you?"

Silence. The only sounds were those of her deep breaths and anxious response to my intrusion.

"Not really." *That's never a sufficient answer.*

"Do you feel safe right now, Pauline?"

"Yes. But I don't feel good."

"I know. We're going to take care of that. First, you need to get someone home with you. And then, you need to see someone right away so you can take care of yourself and feel better. You know that, right? That's why you called here. You can either come here today and someone will see you or you need to call someone closer to your home. But you need to see someone so you can get some relief. Call your husband when we hang up the phone. Tell him to come home to be with you. Is there a neighbor you can call to come over while you wait? You'll feel better if someone is with you right now. I'll call you in a few minutes to follow up."

Pauline ended up going to a day treatment program where she could receive daily therapeutic and psychiatric support during the acute phase of her illness. As she continued to recover, she was followed by a therapist in her area and, from all accounts, is now doing well and enjoying her little one. But I will never forget her haunting voice, echoing with quiet despair. It was an early wake-up call for me that nothing can be overlooked or taken for granted in this work. Every single phone call we get brings us face to face with the potential for suicide and other very scary symptoms. Never make the mistake of presuming that all is well, unless you know for certain that it is. We must look into her eyes and ask all the right questions.

Even then, we might not know for certain.

CHAPTER 14

Collaboration

Many women with postpartum depression will be successfully treated with psychotherapy alone and will not need medication or a psychiatric referral. I do believe, however, that due to the unpredictable nature of this illness and potential for catastrophic complications, it is recommended that therapists do not work in isolation. This implies two things: (1) good supervision may be discretionary, but it is strongly advised, and (2) careful consideration of to whom one refers clients for medication or psychiatric backup must be made.

Ideally, women with postpartum depression should be treated by experts who are specially trained or, minimally, have a special interest in this field. But the reality is that there are a number of obstacles:

- Many communities do not have postpartum specialists.
- Many women are restricted by logistical concerns, transportation, finances, and childcare, making treatment compliance and follow-up difficult.
- Many women are startled by the recommendation that they see a psychiatrist (surely they can't be sick enough to see a shrink!) and are more comfortable initiating treatment with their primary care provider, who may or may not have expertise in this area. Careful explanation of this proposed referral to a psychiatrist should be made repeatedly until the woman understands why the recommendation is being made. Following up with her primary care provider may still be perfectly suitable, depending on the circumstances.

If we consider the fact that primary care providers such as pediatricians, family doctors, obstetricians, midwives, and nurse practitioners are often the ones who have the most consistent contact with postpartum women, it makes sense that women would feel most comfortable being treated by them. The problem is that, as studied by Logsdon, Wisner, Billings, and Shanahan (2006), practices are busier than ever, and screening for postpartum depression occurs infrequently in these primary care settings. This can delay treatment. Further complicating this picture is the fact that some providers who are in tune with the significance of this health problem may not have adequate training or skills to treat the disorder.

What's more, it is disturbing to discover the inadequate education primary care providers receive. Logsdon, Wisner, Billings, and Shanahan (2006) reviewed textbooks that are required reading in nurse practitioner and medical education programs and reported scant references and an overall lack of information on postpartum depression. One line or one paragraph here and there, which is literally what they found, hardly constitutes sufficient education.

The better news is that more and more effort and attention are being placed on raising awareness. Programs are being developed, educational tools and Web sites have been established, and the government is stepping in with policy recommendations and legislative measures. Hence, the larger picture is looking favorable, but when it comes down to the single clinician who is working with a woman in distress, decisions need to be made and treatment needs to be executed without delay. When treatment by a psychiatrist who has expertise and a special interest in postpartum depression is not possible, the alternative is to encourage the woman seeking treatment to contact the provider with whom she is most at ease. This is as important as the credentials of the treating physician because, as we've seen, if she's not comfortable, she's not going to disclose how she is feeling.

Increasingly, more obstetricians and family doctors are prescribing medications for women with postpartum depression. The upside to this is that women are getting access to treatment options earlier. The downside is that some of these women may not be sufficiently monitored throughout the course of their treatment process. As clinicians who are co-treating these women, we must be vigilant about monitoring this process. How is she doing on the medication? Is she having any side effects that are upsetting her? Do changes need to be made? Do explanations need to be given? Is there an ongoing dialogue with her prescribing physician? This collaborative and multidisciplinary approach involving the client, the therapist, and the physician is a crucial component of her treatment. It will enhance her feeling supported and maximize the continuity of care.

There is a problem that I confess I hesitated to put into writing. Some doctors simply don't have the right information. Too often, I am dismayed to hear that women are started on the wrong dose, given a medication that is not recommended as compatible with breastfeeding, or not informed of the side effects or how long they should be taking the drug. From time to time, a doctor will ask me for medication recommendations or dosing information.

Given that treatment for postpartum mood disorders involves special attention to issues unique to this population and that psychiatrists are comprehensively trained mental health professionals with a proficiency in psychopharmacologic issues, I strongly recommend that the medical collaboration be with a psychiatrist, whenever possible—primarily because the clinical course of postpartum depression is unpredictable and subject to deteriorate without warning. It may take time to find one well suited to a clinician's personality and professional requirements, but it will be worth the pursuit. Spend the time and energy to interview psychiatrists who may be interested in collaborating on cases, in order to feel confident about their style and professional service.

Recognizing that it may not always be feasible to obtain psychiatric backup, clinicians should work closely with treating physicians and be motivated to:

1. Support the incentives to increase awareness and education of all healthcare providers
2. Educate themselves with accurate, up-to-date information
3. Encourage clients to be their own best healthcare advocates by keeping an eye on changes in their responses to treatment, both positive and negative
4. Stay connected with the process and ask for a written report or a detailed voicemail so you can keep track of medication adjustments and progress
5. Ask questions when things are not clear and report areas of concern or progress; keep lines of communication open and remember that the physician needs information from the clinical perspective, too

The provision of medical backup to nonphysician therapists is an important issue in clinical practice. Having this backing enhances the clinician's efficiency, effectiveness, professional growth, and, perhaps most important in this setting with postpartum women, early access to a treatment option that is associated with a positive outcome.

Collaborative treatment implies that each practitioner works independently, and shared treatment approaches combine to augment the recovery process. There are, however, intrinsic issues that should be explored:

1. Clear role definition should be discussed regarding the specific expectations: Will this be, for example, a circumscribed prescribing role while the clinician delivers the psychotherapy? Is this person comfortable sharing the responsibility of care?
2. Do both the clinician and psychiatrist have complementary approaches? Is there a clear understanding of the psychiatrist's positions and practices regarding specific postpartum-related issues, such as medications during pregnancy and breastfeeding or

prophylactic treatment to prevent postpartum depression? It is important that beliefs coincide to reduce dissatisfaction as well as potential risk management issues.

3. Is the psychiatrist receptive and responsive to an ongoing need for communication and medical updates?

The advantages of collaborative treatment with physicians and all other healthcare providers cannot be overemphasized. There is really no downside to it, unless the parties involved find they cannot work well together. Care of the postpartum woman works best with this team approach, and it is often our job to make sure all players are on the same side with matching objectives.

Most clients appreciate the multidisciplinary treatment approach and feel supported by the team effort. After receiving permission for ongoing communication among care providers, clinicians may find themselves in the position of facilitating specific changes or running interference for the client. Personally, I'm never sure if this comes from my own social work background, my ubiquitous maternal instincts, my controlling nature, or is simply all about taking care of someone and having good common sense and clinical skills. Navigating the rough waters of postpartum distress requires a collective effort; still, clinicians may find themselves at the controls. Doctors are busy, families are in crisis, and clinicians may be in the best position to settle the vessel. In this way, once more, we manage, we care for, we hold. It is a tight framework that works well for the postpartum woman who feels she is unraveling. It is one of many ways in which we assume the role of good mother–expert therapist–coordinator of care.

CHAPTER 15

Sharing the Session

Life-cycle transitions such as the birth of a child often present as major stress points in family life, shaping postpartum depression into a family illness affecting all members. Including family members in the sessions can be enlightening as well as healing.

BABY

"Can I bring the baby to the session?" This may be asked because (1) mom has no babysitter at that particular time; (2) baby needs to be fed during that hour; (3) mom is uncomfortable leaving baby; (4) mom is complying with a rigid, self-imposed schedule with no flexibility to accommodate the appointment time; (5) mom wants me to see her baby; or (6) mom doesn't trust anyone to take care of her baby, to name just a few possibilities. Reasons for this question can range from a pure and simple inquiry to a deeper, potentially problematic symptom.

In our center, our response reflects our ambivalence surrounding this issue: "Of course you can bring _____ (baby's name is always preferred). It's our pleasure. You may find, however, that having him here is a distraction and it may be in your best interest to come without him, but he is welcome."

It can be argued that seeing the mother and baby together is ideal because it presents an opportunity to observe the mother–baby interactions. It can also allow us to act out specific interventions (for example, with attachment issues) and test some real-life suggestions with the baby in the session.

The downside of having the baby in the session is that the mother is less likely to concentrate on herself. The baby can be distracting and the presence of her baby may increase her guilt, thereby inhibiting her candor.

In our center we have found the best solution to our own ambivalence over this matter is to allow both possibilities, although the specific timing of these will vary. We remain open to the possibility that the mother may be more comfortable with the baby there or without the baby, and we will leave that up to her for a while. We will, however, ask her to bring her baby at some point during the early sessions.

Then what?

When we see a relationship that feels appropriate with no immediate concerns, we may want to comment on how well she is doing. This tribute to her mothering skills can provide much-needed sustenance for her hungry soul. If, on the other hand, we see something we are concerned about, we are obliged to bring it to her attention and use it in the session.

Marina was anxious about everything. She was anxious about being a mother and anxious about taking her baby out in the car. She was anxious about feeding schedules and anxious about what kind of mother she would be when he was a teenager. Marina was anxious about her husband getting up in the night, making him tired at work, and she was, to be sure, anxious about being anxious.

Moreover, she was anxious long before she ever had a baby.

I asked her to bring 2-month-old Oliver in with her after seeing her for a few weeks. He was a sweet and peaceful baby who rested comfortably in his car seat while mom answered my standard review questions: *What feels better at this point? What, if anything, feels worse? What feels exactly the same?* She reported much improvement in her symptoms and relief that she was closer to her "normal self," but she insisted that her confidence in her mothering was shaky at best. "I don't know, I try, I just never know if I'm doing the right thing or not. I mean he's doing great, but I'm never really sure if he's happy or if his needs are being met."

Marina's preoccupation with Oliver's well-being was impressive. She talked about him constantly. She looked over at him nervously while she spoke of his progress. "He's doing well, but I worry about him."

"You're good at that, aren't you?" I smiled.

"Good at what?"

"Good at worrying about Oliver."

"Oh, yeah. I'm a master at it." She turned in quick response to Oliver's whimper. "See? He just needs so much all the time."

I'm not even sure I would have noticed the whimper if she hadn't commented on it. I watched her for a few minutes while she bent down to rock his seat back and forth. "Oh, I don't know," she sighed with frustration. "He's so *fussy*."

He is?

Women with a predisposition to anxiety tend to have highly sensitive nervous systems. They might hear things before others do. They might smell things or see things before others do. Many times, their perceptions are accurate, a result of being keenly tuned in to their environment. Other times, they are responding to stimuli with hypersensitivity and overreaction. This paradox can make a postpartum woman, who is sensitive by nature, agitated and overstimulated.

Marina reached down to pick Oliver up and laughed fretfully. "I don't know what he wants." She scooped baby Oliver up and put his pacifier in his mouth, then removed it when he whined a bit. Then she frantically searched for his bottle. "He just ate an hour ago; I can't believe he's hungry again."

Maybe he's not.

She put the bottle to his lips. He protested. "See? I don't know what he wants." Her voice resonated with worry; her hands gestured defeat.

"Marina, are you worried that something is wrong with him, or are you worried that something is wrong with you?"

"I don't know what I'm worried about." Her anxiety mounted. "Don't you see how fussy he is?"

In some cases, depressed mothers interact excessively, which can result in overstimulating their babies.

"Marina, put down the pacifier. Put down the bottle. Let's try something, okay?" I paused for a few seconds. "Let's sit here. Hold Oliver and let's sit for a minute with him in your arms."

"And …?"

I quieted my voice and slowed down the pace of my words. "And nothing … just sit."

She looked at me and then at Oliver. Her arms gently circled him as he nuzzled into her lap. Together they sat quietly. Her breathing relaxed after a loud exhale. His whining subsided.

"Okay … now what do I do?" She raised her eyebrows as if awaiting my next instruction

"Nothing … you're already doing it."

"What does he want?" she continued to probe.

"You. It looks like that's what he wants. Just you."

"That's funny," she admitted after too long of a silence for her to bear. "He's calmer now and I'm not doing anything." She looked down at him, smiled, and looked back at me. "Maybe I'm trying too hard?"

"Maybe. But you're not 'not doing anything.' You are actively engaging with him. You might not be fixing or feeding or changing, but you are doing something. You are connecting with him and you are loving him. I'm thinking that's doing a lot."

"Maybe I'm too quick to respond; maybe I'm trying too hard to fix it, like I do everything else in my life; maybe I'm overthinking everything, hey, no surprise there! So, I have to get better at just being with him, right? And not reacting to every squeak he makes. I think he really is a happy baby. I just worry that I'm not doing enough or that I'm going to miss something. I'm afraid I'm not doing it right, not doing it well enough."

"I think he really is a happy baby, too. And I think you're doing a wonderful job. The only thing you're not doing well is believing that you're doing a good job."

She made a face befitting an annoyed teenage girl. "That's par for the course. That's been true my entire life."

"It can be different now. Maybe Oliver and I can help you believe that."

"That would be nice." She smiled contentedly as her eyes locked with his. "That would be nice for both of us, don't you think?"

"I do. I think that would be excellent."

DAD AND OTHERS

Having immediate family members join sessions can provide a wealth of clinical information that might otherwise be unavailable. When appropriate, extended family members such as grandparents should be invited, especially if the woman is single or if she is living with her parents, which may be the case with clients from culturally diverse backgrounds.

Partners should always be invited, encouraged, and persuaded to attend early in the work. The rationale for this is:

1. Postpartum depression dramatically affects the entire family.
2. Research has shown that the client's recovery will be smoother with the help of a supportive partnership (O'Hara, 1986).
3. He will have questions about her illness, her treatment, his role, his experience.
4. He should know who is in a position to make treatment decisions on behalf of his wife's illness.
5. He needs support and information about how difficult this is for him.
6. He may be depressed.
7. You need to make a quick assessment of the state of their marriage in order to determine how resourceful he will be as a support person.
8. Their relationship may make things easier or more complicated for her.
9. It is possible that he may sabotage her treatment due to lack of information or his inability to understand the nature of the illness. Even the most supportive partner can steer her off track without intending to and may need to be directed back on course.

Andrew was eager to accompany Victoria to one of her sessions. "She's doing great, isn't she?" he said. "She's so much better."

"I think some things are definitely better, I agree. Victoria is sleeping better, she's definitely panicking less, and her appetite is back, right Victoria?" She nodded in agreement, but appeared hesitant and anxious for me to clarify something.

"So some things are definitely better. This is just the direction we want things to go. What else, Victoria? How else are you feeling?" She waited to respond, smiling reassuringly at Andrew. The sweetness of their connection was distracting. It appeared that they were especially good at communicating—good eye contact, genuine concern, loving words. Still, something wasn't being said. Andrew broke the silence: "Aren't you feeling better, hon? It's been weeks now. It seems to me that everything is back to normal."

He seemed bewildered at her lack of response: "What? You're not okay? What's wrong?" His tone quickly sharpened.

Victoria looked at me for help.

"Victoria, it's important for Andrew to know how you are feeling. He thinks you're fine. Are you feeling fine?"

Victoria tried not to cry. "I'm much better. ... I—I—I just don't think I'm as good as you want me to be, or think I am."

"What do you mean, 'how I want you to be'? I just want you to feel better. You're very strong; I just know you're getting better and better every day. I can see it."

She took a deep breath, her eyes turning away from him. "I'm not feeling as good as you think I am. I'm trying. I'm trying to be strong. But sometimes, I just can't." Her words collapsed with her breathing. "I just can't."

"I don't know what you're talking about. You said you were better. You said you were back to yourself. Why did you say that if you aren't feeling good?"

"'Cause that's what I thought you wanted me to say. That's what I thought you wanted to hear. But when you told me I should stop coming to therapy, it scared me. That's why Karen told me to ask you to come here."

"I don't understand this. You look fine. You are doing a great job with the kids. You are taking care of everything. I don't understand what's wrong."

"I know you don't ...," Victoria wept.

Sometimes, clarity comes from great pain. Andrew had every reason to believe his perception of Victoria's recovery was an accurate reflection of how she felt. She was good at playing along. He now felt angry, a bit betrayed, and mostly frightened to hear that she had constant thoughts of running away and her obsessive thinking was making it impossible for her to sleep. Victoria revealed that her shame and deep desire to please Andrew made it hard for her to let him in. His equally strong desire for her to be well and return to her previous high level of functioning reinforced his false impression that everything was fine.

Very loving couples, with only the best intentions, can sometimes get in each other's way of complete recovery. It can be enlightening, if not inspirational, for a couple to come face to face with what they really need from each other. Andrew and Victoria's discovery of what they both expected from each other led the way for further discussions on the illness of depression in general. Navigating through the murky waters of depression will challenge a marriage in many ways. Only in fully experiencing this challenge, along with the ambivalence and discomfort, can the couple open themselves up to true intimacy and optimal recovery.

Expectations and illusions can provide hope or they can send a couple adrift. Bringing the couple into a session together can shed much-needed light on the status of recovery as well as the state of the marriage. At a time when both mother and father are confronted with parts of themselves they do not like and barely recognize, it is hard to rise above the shadow of depression to express what they are really thinking and really needing from each other. One step toward accomplishing this is for us to clarify the issues and help the two of them express what they need.

CHAPTER 16

Medication

Clinician's Perspective

I am not a doctor. For that reason, clinicians will not find information on specific medications in this book. The purpose of this chapter is to focus on the implications of using medication and how this impacts the postpartum woman in therapy rather than the specifics of which medication is used for what. It's an area of great interest and not without its problems for many nonmedical clinicians. It is best for clinicians to familiarize themselves with the medications commonly used for the treatment of postpartum depression in order to facilitate comfort and accuracy when addressing questions about side effects or what the client can expect during the course of treatment.

Though many clinicians reading this book do not have prescription privileges, clinicians are consistently confronted with and challenged by issues related to medication. The medication issue for many postpartum women is more than *Do I need medication, or not?* It becomes a therapeutic issue: *Why do I need it? What will it do to me? What will it do to my baby? I don't want to be crazy. Does this mean I'm crazy? I never take any medication, not even an aspirin.*

Starting out in private practice, still fresh with uncontaminated social work ideals, my intention with a client was simple: You talk, I'll listen. We will both work hard. Then, you'll get better.

That worked some of the time.

But the more contact I had with postpartum women, the more they enlightened me. Women described unbelievable waves of despair that took over their ability to think. Each story, though distinctive in detail, uncovered similar heartaches. Some faces showed the tired folds of unrelenting

125

sleeplessness. Others were tear streaked and lost in self-absorbing pain or seemingly, and remarkably, flawless. Still others were steady and breathless, as if the slightest movement would cause an avalanche of uncontrolled emotions.

I would meet with the women who came seeking relief. Together, we would come up with a plan, which largely included ongoing supportive psychotherapy. We talked and we talked. Many of the women did get better, but others continued to struggle with lingering symptoms longer than either of us would have liked. In due course, I discovered that the women who presented with more biological symptoms often needed more than I could give them with therapy alone. The symptoms that were biologic in nature, such as sleep impairment, loss of appetite, panic, and suicidal thinking, were, for obvious reasons, difficult to talk through and often responded better to a biologic intervention, such as an antidepressant. It's hard to move forward in therapy while obsessing, or panicking, or being stuck in a quagmire of symptoms. I discovered that, for the most part, women with serious postpartum depression responded well, and fairly quickly, to the use of antidepressants and anti-anxiety medications. Subsequently, as the symptoms improved, therapy became more effective.

Recently, with new research and challenging reports of short- and long-term use of medication for pregnant and postpartum women (Chambers et al., 2006; Grover, Avasthi, & Sharma, 2006; Levinson-Castiel, Merlob, Linder, Sirota, & Klinger, 2006; Misri & Kendrick, 2007; Urato, 2006), along with my ongoing recognition that more and more women are understandably concerned about taking antidepressants, I pause to rethink all options. At this point in the book, we will start by presenting some of the salient, evidence-based information on the use of antidepressants for postpartum depression.

Each woman is different, but generally speaking, experts agree that postpartum depression is best treated with medications, psychotherapy, or a combination of both (Stowe & Nemeroff, 1995). Medication is indicated for moderate to severe depressive symptoms or when a woman does not respond to nonpharmacologic treatment. Serotonin reuptake inhibitors (SSRIs) are the first-line treatment for postpartum depression. SSRIs are preferred because:

- They have a low side-effect profile, which makes them easy to tolerate
- They have a high safety profile and are not toxic when taken in overdose
- They work by enhancing the amount of serotonin available in the brain, which is associated with stabilizing and improving moods
- Although they are excreted in breast milk, there are no known short-term adverse effects to the breastfed baby (Lamberg, 1999)
- They are often effective for both depression and anxiety symptoms

Because postpartum depression is accompanied by severe anxiety, agitation, or both, anti-anxiety medications (anxiolytic agents) such as benzodiazepines are often used as an adjunct to antidepressants to treat the anxiety or sleep disturbance. Some practitioners who may be uninformed or unfamiliar with the unique symptomatology of postpartum depression may treat the agitation only with anxiety medications. This may provide initial relief in the short run, but these medications are not effective in alleviating the core symptoms of depression.

ANTIDEPRESSANT KEY POINTS

- Early intervention and initiation of treatment are associated with better recovery and prognosis (Kennedy, Beck, & Driscoll, 2002).
- Selective serotonin reuptake inhibitors (SSRIs) are effective in treating postpartum depression and anxiety (Wisner, 2007).
- Serotonin-norepinephrine reuptake inhibitors (SNRIs) are also effective for depression and anxiety (PDR, 2006).
- Less often, tricyclic antidepressants (TCAs; an older class of antidepressants) are prescribed. They may be especially helpful if sleep is a problem, since they tend to be very sedating. TCAs have not been associated with an increased risk of major malformations (Wisner, Gelenberg, Leonard, Zarin, & Frank, 1999), but poor neonatal adaptation has been reported (Eberhard-Gran, Eskild, & Opjordsmoen, 2005).
- Antidepressants usually take 2–4 weeks to improve depressive symptoms, though some women improve sooner. Full remission may take several months (Deglin & Vallerand, 2003).
- For the first episode of depression, experts recommend that women stay on the medication for 6–12 months after symptom resolution (Nonacs, 2006).
- The choice of antidepressant should be guided by the woman's history (and family history) of depression and any prior response to medication. It has been pointed out that this is best achieved while the woman is well, because depression can affect her cognitive functioning (Ward & Zamorski, 2002).
- Women with a history of bipolar illness in their family should always be evaluated by a psychiatrist because their symptoms could get worse if treated with an antidepressant alone (El-Mallakh & Karippot, 2002).
- Limited evidence suggests that estrogen therapy alone or combined with antidepressant medication may be effective in patients with postpartum major depression (Gregoire, Kumar, Everitt, Henderson, & Studd, 1996). It is doubtful that estrogen therapy will become a common treatment for postpartum depression. Research has shown that it increases the risk of blood clots and cancer in the uterine lining. Adding progestin eliminates the endometrial cancer risk but

is known to trigger depression when taken during the postpartum period (Flores & Hendrick, 2002). It is generally believed that more studies are necessary before this therapy should be recommended for general use.

- If effective treatment has been initiated during pregnancy, it should be continued during the postpartum period (Eberhard-Gran et al., 2005).
- If a woman and her doctor decide not to use antidepressant medication during her pregnancy, they can choose to initiate treatment immediately after delivery to reduce the risk of recurrent illness (Wisner et al., 2001).
- For women with recurrent major depression, long-term maintenance treatment with an antidepressant is recommended (Wisner, Parry, & Piontek, 2002).
- Efforts to ensure a woman's mood stability during her pregnancy through medical and psychosocial interventions may significantly improve her postpartum outcomes (Nonacs, Viguera, Cohen, Reminick, & Harlow, n.d.).

SIDE EFFECTS OF SSRIs

Ideally, women being treated for postpartum depression will be informed of the potential side effects by the prescribing physician, but often they will come to sessions with questions about their medication and how it is making them feel. These questions should be redirected to their physician, but it is helpful if you can reassure them in the interim. Most side effects occur within the first couple of weeks and will diminish over time, if a woman is able to tolerate them. Any side effect that feels difficult to tolerate should be brought to the doctor's attention right away. Each woman's tolerance of side effects is unique, and medications affect each woman differently. Therefore, it is prudent to assess an individual's response to make certain that the side effects are acceptable and not interfering with recovery.

When Cathy was overwhelmed by her anxiety, she was started on an antidepressant and came to see me 2 days after starting it.

"I'm worse," she declared. "I don't think the medication is helping."

"What's worse?" I asked for clarification.

"I'm so nervous all the time."

I explained to Cathy that sometimes the SSRI can cause early jitteriness; it might feel as if she's had too much caffeine.

"Yeah," she nodded with relief. "That's exactly how it feels. Oh, great, so now I'm taking a medication that makes me feel worse!"

I asked if it felt different from the anxiety she was feeling a few days ago, before she started the medication.

"Yes. This is like I'm jumpy and there's a buzz throughout my entire body."

We talked about this side effect and she told me she would be able to bear it, as long as it got better soon. I reminded her to stay off caffeine and that if she couldn't endure the feeling, she should call her doctor.

This brief exchange can be an important point of reassurance to the woman who is already overcome with bodily changes and symptoms. It is always good practice to refer all medication questions directly to her treating physician. Sadly, many doctors are busy, and the reality is they don't always have time to go over side effects one by one. Nevertheless, it is important to encourage and, if need be, facilitate this process by speaking directly with the client's prescribing physician.

Although one's brain will experience any of the SSRIs available in the same way, they have slightly different side effect profiles. The most common side effects of the SSRIs can include (PDR, 2006):

- Short term:
  - Anxiety, nervousness, or jitteriness (generally distinguishable from the anxiety associated with postpartum depression)
  - Nausea and/or diarrhea
  - Fatigue
  - Sleep disturbances
  - Headaches
- Long term:
  - Loss of interest in sex or diminished ability to achieve orgasm
  - Increase or decrease in weight

WHEN IS MEDICATION INDICATED?

The decision to take medication is always complex, from both the clinician's and the client's perspectives. In the next chapter we will explore this from the client's point of view. Here, we will focus on the clinician's assessment.

Ideally, the ultimate choice to take medication is best determined by considering the preference of the mother. Some women are relieved to hear that this is a real illness that responds well to medication and respond with flip urgency: *Yes, where's the pill? Can I start it now?* Others are alarmed to hear they are *sick,* and the prospect of using medication confirms their worst fear—they are afraid they are crazy.

General guidelines for the use of medication include consideration of all the following:

- Diagnosis
- Side effect profile
- History of previous depressive episodes, especially postpartum depression
- Previous successful treatment with antidepressants

- Family history of depression or other mental illness, particularly if it was successfully treated with medication
- Severity of symptoms
- Course of illness
- Suicide risk
- Degree of impairment that symptoms are causing
- Presence of depression during pregnancy
- How the client feels about taking medication
- Whether she is breastfeeding and her degree of commitment to continuing
- What her specific symptoms are; the following symptoms generally have a good response to medication:
  - Extreme agitation, panic attacks
  - Intrusive thoughts
  - Irritability, rage, feelings of loss of control
  - Depression worse in the morning or frequent waking in the middle of the night
  - Delusional thinking

BREASTFEEDING AND MEDICATION

Antidepressants carry some degree of risk when used during pregnancy and while nursing. Untreated maternal depression also poses risks for mothers and their infants. Therefore, the risks and benefits of treatment must always be carefully weighed for each individual woman seeking treatment and weighed against the risks of exposing the fetus or infant to the depression (Cohen & Rosenbaum, 1998). We must tell our clients that there is no perfect decision, and her wish for a risk-free decision is impossible. The best we can do is to inform them of both the risk of exposure and the risk of not treating the illness. Zachary Stowe, MD, director of the Pregnancy and Postpartum Mood Disorders Program at Emory University in Atlanta, has said, "I have spent the last 10 years of my career worrying about the impact of medications. I've been wrong. I should have been worrying more about the impact of illness" (cited in Doskoch, 2001).

An interesting factor that has been shown to influence a woman's risk perception is whether or not the decision to take medication is voluntary. For instance, the decision to take a medication during pregnancy may be perceived as carrying a higher risk than enduring the depression itself, which is not her choice. The decision to take action is perceived as incurring more potential risk. A second factor that appears to influence risk perception is a woman's comfort level with the option. Women who have been successfully treated with medication previously are more likely to opt for this treatment again (Wisner et al., 2000).

Depending on the circumstances, some physicians feel that a severely depressed mother poses a greater risk to a growing baby than low-level exposure to the medication. Women faced with this decision need to be educated and, whenever possible, husbands and significant others should be included in the decision to expose or not expose the infant to medication.

It is also recommended that the infant's pediatrician be involved in monitoring the infant when medication is used during breastfeeding (Burt et al., 2001). Monitoring an infant does not mean taking blood levels; it simply means asking if the baby has experienced any changes with feeding, sleeping, or irritability upon exposure to medication. Elizabeth Goldman, MD, notes that with SSRIs and low-dose anti-anxiety medications, it is extremely rare to see any evidence of a clinically notable change in the exposed baby (personal communication, November 16, 2007).

Facts related to breastfeeding and medications include:

- All medications are secreted into the breast milk, although concentrations vary (Misri & Kostaras, 2002).
- Untreated maternal depression has a negative impact on the infant (Lusskin, Pundiak, & Habib, 2007).
- Long-term impact of trace levels of medication is unknown (Pearlstein et al., 2006).
- Earlier initiation of treatment is associated with better prognosis (Lusskin et al., 2007).
- The decision to use antidepressants with a mother who is breastfeeding must always be a risk/benefit analysis (Kennedy et al., 2002).
- To date there are no data to support neonatal medication accumulation in tissue (Pearlstein et al., 2006).
- The lowest dose of medication that is effective should be used (Misri & Kostaras, 2002).
- In theory, the amount of medication to which the infant is exposed could be reduced by avoiding nursing during times of highest concentration (Spencer, Gonzalez, & Barnhart, 2001).
- The amount of drug to which the infant is exposed depends on a number of factors, including the dosage as well as the infant's age and feeding schedule (Eberhard-Gran, Eskild, & Opjordsmoen, 2006).
- Dr. Goldman explains that each SSRI is different, but in general, the concentration of medicine peaks in breast milk a few to several hours after taking the medication. This timing depends on when the medication is taken and the half-life of the medication. Half-life refers to the time it takes for a drug to decrease by half of its original dose (personal communication, November 16, 2007).
- At this time, no antidepressant has been associated with serious adverse events in a baby (Misri & Kostaras, 2002).

- To date, there is no evidence of significant problems in breastfed children exposed to medication. (Misri & Kostaras, 2002).

The bottom line is that breastfeeding is often a significant and emotionally laden subject for many new mothers. Although there may be times when a decision to take medication needs to be made swiftly, the decision to continue breastfeeding with medication, to discontinue breastfeeding, or to not take the medication at all is not one that can be made on the spot. This typifies how a medical decision becomes a therapeutic issue. A clinician's role is to educate, support, and provide as much access to accurate information as possible. Ultimately, women must decide for themselves which route to take.

WHO IS THE BEST HEALTHCARE PROVIDER FOR MEDICATION MANAGEMENT?

As discussed in chapter 14, many clinicians work closely with psychiatrists who have a special interest in this population. In my experience, this is the optimal arrangement for both you and your client. It is commonplace nowadays for general practitioners, internists, obstetricians, physician assistants, and nurse practitioners to medicate symptoms of postpartum depression. The benefit of this is that it typically provides clients easier and timelier access to assessment and treatment. I'm not certain who coined the phrase, but I do know that Kathy Wisner, MD, a leading advocate and researcher of postpartum depression, refers to the "magic appointment" as an interval between the identification of postpartum depression and when treatment actually begins. Dr. Wisner (2006) discusses how we, as clinicians, are best able to facilitate wellness during this time between the initial call for help and the scheduled appointment by encouraging self-care, mobilizing support, and offering expert reassurance.

In our center, we do our best to see someone within a day or so, always seeing an urgent case that same day, if needed. This may mean juggling our schedules or staying later than we had anticipated, but the clinicians who work with me know that this is an expectation of the practice. Many women who call our office have already called other clinicians who are unable to fit them into their schedules for weeks. This just isn't soon enough for most of them.

It's a difficult call to make. I don't think someone who is having scary thoughts about hurting her baby or who wonders if she should have had this baby in the first place should have to ruminate for days or weeks until a healthcare practitioner can fit her into his or her schedule. Postpartum depression is a crisis that is not always expressed in words, so women who are asked to wait for this magic appointment may respond with passive acceptance without revealing how truly bad they feel or how urgent it is to be seen. Worse yet, if they do express this, they may still be cast aside and inserted into an inflexible schedule.

The reality often is that when a woman calls her obstetrician or her primary care physician, she is likely to get a quicker response than if she wants to make an appointment with a psychiatrist. Although seeing a nonpsychiatrist physician may not be ideal for diagnosis and medication management, it can be an excellent intervention for a suffering woman when symptoms are acute. There are many nonpsychiatric healthcare practitioners who are exceedingly connected to their patients and who have proven to be outstanding resources for the treatment of postpartum depression.

CHAPTER 17

Medication

Client's Perspective

If I were diagnosed with diabetes I wouldn't think twice about taking medication prescribed to me. If I was told by my doctor that I had high cholesterol or high blood pressure, I'd take the medication prescribed to me. Sure, I'd need to change my lifestyle as well to address the underlying problems causing the high blood pressure or cholesterol—I'd exercise more, I'd eat better, I'd develop better coping mechanisms for stress—but I'd also take the medication to address the current crisis, until my other activities kicked in and my blood levels were safe enough that I could discontinue the meds.

Isn't it the SAME THING [original emphasis] with postpartum mood disorders? Aren't meds okay to help resolve the immediate crisis, while at the same time we can use exercise and/or talk therapy and support groups and whatever else works to resolve any contributing underlying factors and to recover and get back to our old selves? And when we do recover, we can reduce them until it's okay to stop taking them altogether.

It seems to me that psychiatric medication, where appropriate and prescribed by an experienced professional, is simply addressing a physical medical crisis. Our bodies don't differentiate between psychiatric illnesses and other physical illnesses. Only society does.

These words were written and posted by Katherine Stone, an advocate for women with postpartum depression who transformed her own experience with depression into the service of supporting and educating others in her trailblazing blog, *Postpartum Progress* (http://postpartumprogress.typepad. com). In her blog, Katherine speaks candidly and genuinely to countless women who seek her counsel and words of wisdom. In many ways, her words often carry more weight than those of healthcare providers because she has been there and is constantly monitoring things from all sides. Women with postpartum depression believe other women who have had postpartum depression. It is an affinity marked by their shared suffering and implicit bond. It's why support groups feel so good to many women in the postpartum period. Often, women say they feel better if others share their common experiences and feelings. "Things don't even have to be said aloud," someone once told me. "Everything's just understood."

Unless it is clear-cut from the outset (and it rarely is), I typically introduce the topic of medication in the first meeting, either by inquiring through history-taking or asking how a woman generally feels about it. I do this to get an early sense of how open or resistant she may be to the possibility.

The following are some of the more common responses and some suggested navigation strategies.

"I WOULD PREFER NOT TO TAKE MEDICATION, BUT IF I NEED IT, I WILL"

Depending on how long she has been feeling bad and how severe her symptoms are, I do my best to honor a woman's request not to take medication when she expresses it. I will, however, clearly state my reservations, if I have any. If I am concerned about particular symptoms or if her history tells a story of previous success with medication, I may indicate that medication would be helpful. I clarify that we can start by increasing supportive measures and see how the therapy progresses. Then I point out that we will continue to reassess how she feels. If her symptoms get better, we'll know we are on track. If she continues to struggle, we will reconsider the use of medication. This is usually a fair and mutually agreeable path to take.

When Marilyn called to make a follow-up appointment, she said she had things to talk about and didn't like the way she was feeling. Months before that, she had decided to stop coming to weekly sessions. At that time, she said she was feeling better, but not great. She said she wanted to take a break and that maybe the way she felt was just as good as she was going to feel. She was obsessing less and attaching well to her baby. She left this final session saying she would call "in a while" to set something up, but she would see how she felt first.

Seven months later, she called and left a message on my voicemail, "Hi, Karen, it's Marilyn. I know it's been a while, but I'd like to come and see you. I'm not feeling as well as I had hoped."

When Marilyn came in to see me, she described how she was feeling. "It's hard," she said, holding back her tears:

I really thought I'd feel better by now. I really tried to think positively and focus on everything that is so good in my life. But my brain kept defaulting to how I usually think. It's like no matter how hard I tried, I would still end up obsessing, worrying, thinking something was wrong with Sean. I would look at him and think he was having a seizure. He wasn't, and I'd think, "What is wrong with me?" You know how wonderful my husband is? Well, he's had just about enough of this. My anxiety is turning into anger and my anger is being dumped on him! It's crappy, actually.

I sat back as she continued to review that past few months: "I can't turn my brain off. I've had lots of good days, days where I thought I had found my old self again. Days where I could laugh and be in the moment with the kids. Mostly, though, I spend every day trying to make myself feel better."

The tears turned to sobbing. "I hate bawling like this. What is wrong with me?"

"Marilyn, this is a long time for you to be feeling this way."

"Yep, it is."

We sat and I waited for her to pick up my cue.

"I know what you're going to say, Karen."

I smiled, "Go ahead then."

"I have a prescription for the antidepressant. My OB gave it to me when you and I talked about it the last time I was here. When I told her how I was feeling and that I was seeing you, she wrote me the prescription and said, 'Absolutely. Take this; it will help you feel better.'"

"What did you do with the prescription? That was months ago."

"I still have it. It's in the kitchen."

I couldn't help but mock her determined procrastination. "Is it helping yet?"

"I know. I know. That's why I'm here. I should have decided this long ago. I'll fill the prescription and start taking it."

"I think that's a good plan."

"THERE IS NO WAY I'M GOING TO TAKE MEDICATION"

Many women do express a stern objection to medication. This could be for a hundred reasons, including a previous bad experience with medications, a family member's bad experience with medications, or a preconceived misinterpretation about psychiatric medications. It may be shame induced, stigma related, or fear based. Whatever fuels the protest, women who don't want to take medication do not want to take medication. So first, I listen. I listen to what they say, how they say it, why they say it, and why they feel so strongly about it. Then, I add my song and dance about needing to inform them of all options, particularly if I feel their symptoms would respond well to medication.

"I knew this would happen. This is why I didn't even want to come. I knew we'd be talking about medication." Jill came in repelling the suggestion even before it was made. And she was unwavering. "See? Like a pill is going to fix all of this. I knew I shouldn't have come."

Ah, she protests too much.

At the risk of overgeneralizing, it does seem that the majority of women who come out of the gate objecting to medication, without adequate preparation and discussion, usually do so because they are scared and misinformed. Some of them do go on to recover without medication. Others learn along the way that their opposition may have been premature and decide that symptom relief, in any form, would be welcomed. So, this subset of women might ultimately change their minds and decide to start medication. Soon after, these same women might marvel at their resistance: "Why did I wait so long?" Then, they often follow with a flip commentary, "I don't ever have to get off the meds, right?"

"I AM CONSIDERING ANTIDEPRESSANTS FOR ANXIETY AND DEPRESSION, BUT I AM SCARED OF SIDE EFFECTS, ESPECIALLY WEIGHT GAIN"

Weight gain to a woman who is trying desperately to lose 30 extra baby pounds can be an unwelcome prospect—so much so that it can cloud her already distorted thinking and become the single reason she refuses to take medication. The mere possibility or potential, along with the very real possibility that it may not even cause any weight gain, is still not even enough to enable some women to consider this option. Just the mention of the remote likelihood of weight gain sends these women darting off in the opposite direction.

The association between antidepressant use and weight gain is unclear. Regardless of what the research may show, it is my experience that weight gain from antidepressant medication is usually negligible. Some women do gain some weight. Some women lose weight. Many notice no significant difference at all.

Consider also that depression can cause appetite suppression and weight loss. When women take the medication and start feeling better, they may eat more and therefore gain weight. Weight gain, like sleep, can become an object of a woman's obsession, taking on more power than it might otherwise if she were thinking more clearly. We certainly want to respect and support her concern over not wanting to add extra pounds, but we need to be assertive with the information we have, to help her understand that feeling better is worth the trade-off.

"MY HUSBAND IS OPPOSED TO MY TAKING MEDICATION"

Partners need to be educated along with the women in treatment. Both need information and evidenced-based literature to support decisions they will be making. It may be helpful to have copies of current research on hand to share with them to avoid an anxiety-provoking search on the Internet. In the end, most partners are open to options that are likely to yield a positive outcome.

"IF YOU THINK I NEED MEDICATION, IT MUST MEAN I'M REALLY SICK"

As we've noted, women who have recently given birth and end up in a therapist's office often express great disappointment in themselves. *If I were a good mother, I wouldn't be feeling this way.* Early on, our role is to define postpartum depression and help clarify what it may mean to each individual woman. Symptoms that warrant the use of medication are frequently scary symptoms, such as panic, intrusive or suicidal thoughts, and confusion. When the topic of medication is introduced, some women associate this with the severity of their illness.

One explanation that sheds light on this distinction is that there are certain sets of symptoms that respond better to medication than others. Particularly in the psychiatric world, there are some very serious illnesses that do not respond well to medication, while a mild illness can have a good response to the use of medication. A good analogy to which women can relate, referred to in *This Isn't What I Expected* (Kleiman & Raskin, 1994), is when one goes to the doctor with a sore throat. Her glands are swollen, and it's difficult to swallow. She's tired and might have a fever. If the sore throat is bacterial, such as strep, the doctor will prescribe antibiotics to ease the course of recovery. If it is negative for strep, it is deemed a viral infection and treated with rest and lots of warm tea and honey.

In this way, it can be reassuring for a woman to hear that medication is being discussed because it will help her feel better, not because she is so very sick.

"WILL I HAVE TO TAKE IT FOR THE REST OF MY LIFE?"

The answer to this is "probably not," but we are not in a position to determine the long-term course of her medication treatment. To repeat, the SSRI antidepressants, which are the most widely used for postpartum depression, usually take 2–4 weeks to for initial symptom relief and usually a few weeks or months beyond that to achieve symptom resolution (Deglin & Vallerand, 2003). The goal in treatment is, ultimately, resolution. It is recommended that women remain on the medication for at least 6–12 months after they start feeling better (Nonacs, 2006). With medical supervision, most women can successfully discontinue the medication when the time is right, as determined by their history and clinical course. A common reason for women's discontinuing prematurely is that they begin to get some relief. This translates into *I don't need the medication; I feel good.* But the truth is that she feels good because the medication has helped reduce her symptoms. Discontinuing the medication impulsively or too soon can result in a relapse with symptoms that are more difficult to treat. The decision to remain on the medication long term is based on her history, her family history, the severity of her depressive episode, the degree of impairment, and a thoughtful dialogue between her and her treating physician.

"THAT'S FINE. WHATEVER YOU THINK IS BEST. I JUST WANT TO FEEL BETTER"

One of the things we can do best for a postpartum woman in crisis is to present all of her options in a space and place that helps her feel protected and heard. Chances are she has already been advised by a number of well-meaning friends and professionals and is swirling with options and opinions. All she says she wants is to go home to her baby or go back to a time before the baby was in the picture. Making a decision about the course of her treatment can feel like more than she wants or is able to do. Clinicians should make the options known, discuss the pros and cons, listen to the set of values that guides her thinking, interpret what she is saying, and help her make a decision that feels best to her at that time.

Then, remain open to the possibility that all of that may change the next time you meet together.

CHAPTER 18

Alternative Therapies

Psychotherapy for postpartum depression is a well-established treatment (Epperson, 1999), but many women may find it difficult to attend a weekly session or are unable to afford it. Some women are hesitant to take medications while nursing, or at all, because of the side effects or a host of personal reasons. When considering complementary treatments, clinicians should remember that the evidence continues to support the efficacy of psychotherapy and/or antidepressant drug therapy for the treatment of postpartum depression. The use of alternative treatments, however, is becoming increasingly prevalent due to the fact that most are readily accessible and generally well tolerated.

Over the course of my clinical practice, I remained entrenched in the medical model, believing that much of what I was dealing with could be understood and best treated within that framework of diagnosis, symptoms, and medicine. For years, I remained steadfast, if not stubborn, about the effectiveness of research-based trials and treatments. It's different now. New experiences have fostered new beliefs. My eyes are open to the promise of untapped options. Though I remain unwavering about what I know is proven to be effective, I now listen to, support, and believe in a broader range of possibilities.

As my years mount to mark the wisdom of middle age, I must confess I have become quite the spiritual thinker. I believe this surfaced when I tiptoed to the other side of 50 and began seeing things a bit differently. I found myself redefining what I wanted in my own life and being more creative in my efforts to get there, sometimes stumbling from one point to the next with my eyes wide open. Paralleling my own personal discovery with that of my work, I now find I am much more enthusiastic and open-minded about alternative interventions than ever before. Maybe it's because I'm getting older. Maybe it's because women are asking for more choices. Maybe it's because these alternatives work.

When Rose came to see me, she was weary from life. Her 2-year-old was in a body cast to correct a congenital problem, and her 7-month-old was waking two or three times a night for a feeding that probably could have waited until morning. Her husband had recently lost his job, and his search for another was stymied by his own symptoms of depression. She was used to being "the one who does it all." What started out as a behavioral response to early sexual abuse was continuing well into her adult years. She tried to keep it all together so that everything would look good and no one would know the depth of the pain that shadowed her every step.

And she did look good. Belying the chronic fatigue and red eyes swollen from lack of sleep, she had a contagious smile that made me smile back instinctively. She smiled big and often, despite her exhaustion, or perhaps because of it, trying hard to shine through the darkness.

It was clear from the beginning that she didn't want to "dwell on the past," and her fleeting references to significant past events left me hungry for details. She shared glimpses of childhood molestation, early parentification, her mother's premature death, unprecedented financial strain, family history of mental illness and criminal behaviors, and impaired interpersonal relationships. Then, there was her singing.

"When I was 2, I told my mother I wanted a piano so I could play Mozart. Turns out it was Piano Concerto No. 17 in G Major. I got better as I got older." She smiled with all teeth aglow.

I listened to her describe a connection with music that was unfamiliar to me. My own piano lessons enabled me to do little more than annihilate Beethoven's "Für Elise," which I periodically pull out of my bag of tricks when I want to impress someone with my pathetic musical aptitude. It's always good for a few laughs.

Rose's appreciation for music was something I had never known or ever seen in my work. When she talked about the music, she was transported to a place she wanted and needed to be but refused to go.

"I have always equated singing with joy. When I feel bad, I don't sing. I can't sing. I need to sing, perhaps, but I can't. Or I don't want to. I haven't sung in years."

Rose was a gifted opera singer. She was instructed by a beloved singing coach who unexpectedly died in her arms after a heart attack. At that moment, Rose revoked all association with this exceptional piece of herself. Her heart crushed by one more unbearable loss, she shut down all avenues of expression. Once again, she found herself on automatic pilot, doing what was expected of her, doing it well enough, while she silenced every creative cell in her tired body. She told me that singing at Marietta's funeral 10 years prior was the most difficult thing she had ever done in her life.

It was the last time that she had sung.

FIND THE JOY

On this particular day in our work together, I told Rose the story about the day I got news of this book contract. More precisely, I told her how I opened myself up to the universe and told the powers that be I was tired of getting my work rejected and that it was time to publish the book on which I had been working diligently. She smiled kindly, cheering on my ridiculous storytelling.

Trying to conceal my own skepticism, I asked:

Are you familiar with the laws of attraction? It goes something like this: You focus your thoughts on something that you want. Picture it in your mind. Feel as if it is actually happening and you are (here's the important part) open to receiving it. … Well (this is shady part), the idea proposed in this theory is that you will get what you want. The most vital component of this universal law is the energy of our emotions. When a person focuses on a thought or desire and combines it with strong emotion, this union pulsates from self to the universe and ultimately attracts the very thing that one desires. Hmmmmm …

I realize I'm opening myself up to criticism at best and accusations of narcissism at worst, but here's the truth of what happened to me and what I shared with Rose. I remember sitting in the waiting room of a doctor's office trying to pass the time and decided to take a stab at this. I closed my eyes and took a deep breath. I tried to shut out the noises in the room around me and focus in on my thoughts; that, alone, is almost impossible for me to do. The act of visualizing in one's mind means one has to simultaneously clear the slate of all extraneous distracting thoughts, such as: *What am I making for dinner? How will I get another chapter written? Will I have time to exercise? Will I get out of here before rush hour? Did I remember to send out that group e-mail for our research? Did my husband remember to take the dog to the vet?*

I sat breathing in and out, clearing my mind. *Okay,* I thought to myself, *I can do this.* I focused on not thinking; I worked hard to do so little; I concentrated on nothing—all of which pertain to states of being that are not natural for me and the way I am wired. But I persevered, in my head, until I was able to picture the book. This book. I had been writing a book and sending it out to a number of publishers and was impatiently awaiting a verdict from those who had expressed interest in it; this became the object of my meditation. Much to my surprise, I was indeed able to visualize a vague outline of the book in my head. This was not a crystal-clear image by anyone's standards, but it was there, in my mind's eye, sketchy and hard for me to imagine. Still, it was there. *This is good; I can do this,* I repeated to myself.

I pictured what the cover would look like at the end of this process: *Therapy and the Postpartum Woman*. It looked good, just the way it would look if I had designed it myself; after all, this was *my* fantasy. I could see the book resting on the publisher's desk while some dark male figure nodded approvingly. He liked it. This was good. Then I saw myself holding the book out and fixing my eyes on it, staring at the cover, feeling proud and accomplished. Then, I think I called my mother.

That was fun. The whole thing lasted about 9 seconds, which was all I could muster. At that moment, the nurse came into the room and called my name, snapping me out of my self-induced trance. The point of the story is this: When I got home from my appointment a couple of hours later, I sat at my computer to continue with my work. I checked my e-mails and saw the one from Routledge: "We have reviewed your work and will be sending you a contract," or something like that. I'm sure I didn't really read it. I just felt it. When I was done celebrating my success with great relief and great joy, I remembered my contact with the universe. A life lesson? Perhaps. A coincidence? Almost certainly. A good story to help empower women to believe in themselves and the power they hold within? Most definitely.

Rose loved the story, too, because it appealed to her imaginative senses and hidden, but burning, desire to believe in something again. I said,

> Rose, do you think you can do this? Just for fun? Why don't you try, when you leave here, to find a quiet space for yourself and have a moment with the universe? Try it. Maybe you can picture yourself singing. You may not feel ready to sing again, but maybe you're ready to imagine it. What would it look like, feel like, sound like? When you do it, close your eyes and picture it in your mind. Where would you be? What are you singing? Who else is there? Do you know what I mean?

She smiled her precious smile. "I know what you mean. I'll try," she replied with perfect obedience. "I'm just so tired. It sounds good, but I feel like I'm too tired to do anything right now. I'm not sure my mind can conjure that up at this point."

Finding the joy is hard when you're tired. If singing was the key to Rose's joy and she was too tired to sing and too tired to care, we needed to find another way. There was reciprocal power to her singing, and this is true for many of us, whether the source is music, children, art, work, relationships, travel, or whatever brings us the joy. It's the proverbial chicken and the egg factor. When we feel better, we are better able to find and experience the joy. If we can find the joy, bring it back into our lives, and experience it, we will feel better. Regardless of its point of entry, the way in which it comes to be matters less than the ultimate experience of joy. One of our jobs, as clinicians, is to facilitate this process.

In Rose's case, we had been meeting for weeks, and she wasn't feeling better. I could feel that the sessions were meaningful to her and the support was appreciated, but the depression persisted. She was sad, despondent, and exhausted. There were days she felt as if she couldn't do it for one more day. She had made it clear, at various intervals, that discussions about the sexual abuse she had endured, or Marietta's death, or the loss of her mother would spiral her deeper into despair, so those topics were off the table for a while. "I have to function," she would claim. "If I talk about those things that bring me so much sadness, I will never get out of bed again." I knew that wasn't true, but I also knew what she was saying. We agreed to wait until she was feeling better to talk about the pain she had buried for years.

The antidepressants weren't helping, and the therapy was palliative but ineffective. Her overwhelming fatigue cried out to me. How could I help her rest when her baby's sleeplessness merged with a lifetime of agonizing losses and she was being tugged from all sides? From what pool do we draw when treating women with postpartum depression when we have already implemented the two most common interventions—psychotherapy and medication?

I talked to Rose about seeing our hypnotherapist, who was certain to transport her into a peaceful spot where she could indulge in the fantasy of being free from external strife. As a bonus, she might even fall asleep and really get her money's worth. She left our session with two homework assignments: to open herself up to the universe and to sit for 45 minutes, as daunting as it might seem, with a therapist who had his own brand of magic to help soothe her exhaustion.

Upon her return, Rose reported to me that she had tried to envision herself singing as I had prompted her, but her weakened state wouldn't permit it. She claimed she "just couldn't do it." For what it was worth, she explained, she did find the time and the space to sit alone with her thoughts. "Besides," she reported back to me, "I did *try*." She was hoping that maybe the universe had heard her modest effort.

In the meantime, she had scheduled her appointment with our hypnotherapist. She reported that she liked the experience and it went well—though something weird had happened.

"What do you mean by 'weird'? What happened?"

"Well, he was putting me into this trance thing, or altered state of being, or whatever he called it—a relaxed state of awareness, I think. I closed my eyes and thought, 'Hmmmm ... This would be a good time to imagine myself singing' like you had asked me to. But, instead, I found myself ... *singing*, actually singing in my head." Her eyes perked open; her eyebrows stretched upward into the crease of her forehead.

"When I'm happy, I sing Italian. When I'm angry, I sing German. When I'm sad, I sing French. While I was in his office, he was doing his thing in the background and I found myself singing in my head. I was singing, *"Je dis que rien ne m'epouvante."* Her voice lilted and danced into the air as it left her lips. "I wasn't really singing, not out loud, anyway, but I found myself singing the aria. I was aware that I could hear him talking, my hands loose in my lap. I felt like I was singing—the breath, the power that comes through when I've just completed an aria and nailed it. When I focused back onto myself, I actually felt like I had just performed; I was energized, tired, excited, proud, all at once. There's no feeling like it in the world."

"When was the last time you did that, Rose?"

"Never." She laughed. "I mean, I always, always hear music; sometimes it's so loud I wonder if other people can hear it inside my head. But I never sang an aria word by word in my head like that."

"How'd that feel?"

"It felt … unbelievable. It felt like … I was singing. I felt totally and completely embraced by the fever of the aria and the passion of the words. It's hard to explain. It's where I live."

As she spoke, I could feel an aura emerging from her tired body that lifted her up and out of herself. She sat up tall, stretching out her left arm to match the symphony in her head, as she explained. "The words are not words; it is a language that is only known to those who sing it. It's *je dis que rien ne m'epouvante*. It's Micaela's aria from Carmen. The music. It speaks to me in a way I can't describe. Singing is a high—some use actual drugs or alcohol; I have always used music and singing, specifically, to 'escape.'"

Her words resonated with the gift of her voice. "You know what I mean?" Her body swayed in rhythm with her voice. *"Je dis que rien ne m'epouvante,"* she sang.

I sat mesmerized, soaking up her essence. I, too, felt captivated by the melody. I spoke slowly, so as not to distract the spell she was lost in. "Are you aware that this is the third time you sang in here today?"

"No." She smiled, "I did?"

"You did."

She inhaled deeply. "Well, then. How nice. It's the *je dis que rien ne m'epouvante*. It must be."

I raised my hand and designated four fingers, keeping count on behalf of her brilliant, yet restrained, concert. There would be three more times throughout the rest of that session—seven occurrences—where she chimed in tune with her classical training, almost as if she could no longer restrain it.

When she left that day, there was newness to her smile, something pure and fresh. This must be what hope looks like. These are times when I feel I am witnessing a miracle. It was joy coming back into her life. It was beautiful to behold.

ADJUNCTIVE THERAPIES

Was it the hypnotherapy? Was it our supportive union? Was it the antidepressants? Was it the universe? Was it perfect timing? Was it some absolute or random combination?

Sometimes, clinicians need to be creative. Sometimes, transformation takes place as a result of proactive intervention and dead-on intuition. But we always need to keep in mind that women with postpartum depression may benefit from a number of interventions other than medications and traditional psychotherapy. Although more research is necessary to determine the effectiveness of alternative interventions with respect to postpartum depression, many are attractive options to women struggling during this time of their lives. By and large, they are not terribly expensive and may appeal to women who would prefer not to take medication. However, I would caution clinicians not to rely on an alternative therapy as the sole course of treatment for anything other than a mild depression. Alternative approaches may be best used as adjuncts to methods such as therapy and/or medications in which efficacy has been well documented.

Some of the current options, in no particular order, include:

1. *Omega-3* polyunsaturated fatty acids have been shown to offer health benefits to pregnant and nursing mothers. Low levels of omega-3 fatty acids are associated with postpartum depression (Hendrick, 2003), and a 1- to 2-gram daily dosage has been used to augment treatment with antidepressants (Nemets, Stahl, & Belmaker, 2002; Peet, Murphy, Shay, & Horrobin, 1998). Further substantiation of the preliminary data reflecting the positive effects of omega-3 fatty acids on mood will likely lead to this alternative's being considered a safe treatment option for depression, both during and after pregnancy. When their symptoms are mild, women seem eager to try these supplements as an initial option prior to starting antidepressants.

2. *Light therapy,* often used for seasonal affective disorder, is another intervention that may be preferred by women who are interested in nonpharmacologic treatments. It's a small investment (usually about $200 for a portable light box) and can be used in the comfort of their homes. In a small study of pregnant women with major depression, the bright light therapy produced antidepressant effects (Oren et al., 2002). Similar results were reported in a study of two women with postpartum depression. The first woman had been depressed for more than 4 months and chose not to take antidepressant medication; the second had been depressed for an undetermined period of time but had not responded to a trial of psychotherapy. In both women, the Hamilton Rating Scale for Depression (Hedlund & Vieweg, 1979)

scores dropped significantly after 4 weeks of daily 30-minute pho-
totherapy sessions (Corral, Kuan, & Kostaras, 2000). Though more
research is needed with respect to postpartum depression, experts
agree that this is a favorable option because it is easy, well tolerated,
and safe for the nursing infant.

3. *Herbal supplements* do worry me a bit. Many women presume they
   are safer because they are "natural," but they are not regulated by the
   U.S. Food and Drug Administration. This leads to my concern over
   what exactly a woman is ingesting. St. John's wort is the most widely
   used supplement for depression (National Institutes of Health,
   2008), but it should not be taken in combination with antidepressants. Research is too limited to recommend it for use by pregnant or
   nursing women (Dugoua, Mills, Perri, & Koren, 2006).

4. *Estrogen* may appeal to some women because, again, it sounds natural, and diminished levels contribute to the hormonal flux associated
   with postpartum depression. Estrogen levels drop dramatically after
   delivery, leading some women to believe (and hope) that this hormonal deficiency is the root cause of postpartum depression. However, according to Victoria Hendrick (2003), postpartum depression
   has not been conclusively linked to low levels of estrogen or any
   other hormone. Additionally, she points out that the use of estrogen
   is associated with a decrease in breast milk production and the risk
   of other, more significant problems, including endometrial hyper-
   plasia, stroke, and deep vein thrombosis. As mentioned previously,
   one study did report that *transdermal estrogen* (the estrogen patch)
   may be useful in the treatment of postpartum depression (Gregoire,
   Kumar, Everitt, Henderson, & Studd, 1996). Although these studies
   do suggest a possible role for estrogen as a treatment or augmenta-
   tion option, it remains experimental. In our center, women who have
   come to us already on the patch (some obstetricians are prescribing
   this), do well for a while and then, typically, start antidepressants for
   more consistent relief. This is purely an anecdotal observation.

5. *Massage therapy, acupuncture,* and *relaxation techniques* are wonderful ways to improve mood as well as to promote a positive mother–
   infant interaction when enjoyed as a pair. A promising study at the
   University of Arizona in Tucson suggests that acupuncture may be
   as effective as psychotherapy or drug therapy in the treatment of
   depression (Allen et al., 2006).

6. *Exercise* has been shown to reduce mild to moderate depression and
   anxiety. The recommendation is 30 minutes of physical activity at
   moderate intensity, 3–5 days per week. Furthermore, a program of
   vigorous exercise was determined to be as effective as other treatments for depression (Dunn, Trivedi, Kampert, Clark, & Chambliss,
   2005). The greatest challenge for postpartum women, of course, is

time and tiredness. Although it is not easy to do when the temptation is to remain inert, small steps make a difference, and encouraging women to get out in the sunshine and walk will help. Postpartum women involved in a regular exercise program and informal support sessions improved their depressive levels and general feelings of well-being (Armstrong & Edwards, 2003). It can be argued that both exercise and support will contribute to a postpartum woman's sense of well-being.

7. *Hypnotherapy*, a longtime useful tool for childbirth preparation, can be an effective intervention for postpartum depression (Yexley, 2007). In our center, we use it adjunctively, particularly for women with insomnia, extreme anxiety, and obsessive thinking. Although there is limited information on its use specifically with postpartum depression, it's a no-risk option that, at the very least, is certain to help women feel more relaxed. And, at best, magic can take place.

8. *EMDR* (eye movement desensitization and reprocessing) is a treatment method that was originally intended to diminish the distress associated with traumatic memories (Shapiro, 2004). More recently, its use has generalized to be effective with depression and anxiety either with or without trauma. EMDR is a therapeutic process that helps the client work through negative cognitions and trauma-induced responses by reprocessing the traumatic memories in a more adaptive manner. At this time there has been no research on its effectiveness specific to postpartum depression.

9. *Electroconvulsive therapy* (ECT) can be very helpful when severe depression is associated with suicidal or homicidal thoughts, psychosis, or resistance to drug therapy. Two separate studies have indicated that both severe depression and psychosis respond well to ECT (Berle, Aarre, Mykletun, Dahl, & Holsten, 2003; Reed, Sermin, Appleby, & Faragher, 1999). ECT is an important effective option for depressions that are not responsive to other interventions.

10. *Support groups* can decrease the isolation and stigma that depressed mothers often feel encumbered by and can provide an invaluable outlet for expression and unconditional support. Postpartum Support International (PSI) is a nonprofit organization that has spearheaded the support network in our country and across international borders. PSI has long recognized that, in conjunction with accurate information, screening, and treatment, women supporting other women during a postpartum crisis can be another key to a smoother recovery. Although group therapy for postpartum depression has shown inconsistent results (Fleming, Klein, & Corter, 1992; Meager & Milgrom, 1996), support groups, whether facilitated by mental health professionals or led by peers, continue to be a preferred option by many women with postpartum depression.

The advantages of the support group experience are:

- Safe place to disclose feelings and fears
- Reduces shame
- Feels like more acceptable form of treatment and therefore may increase compliance
- Assists with working through feelings of grief and loss by reducing isolation
- Can help promote more realistic view of motherhood
- Can expand social support network
- Groups generally free of charge or low cost
- Can distribute accurate information about PPD, treatments, resources, and coping skills

There are some logistical constraints worth noting that can make postpartum support groups particularly challenging, such as:

- Attendance may be poor due to childcare, transportation, money, denial, anxiety, or motivation issues.
- Practicability may be limited in rural settings.
- It is important not to mix groups of depressed and well mothers within the same group.
- Some women identify themselves as not being a "group" person and prefer individual support.
- There is a risk of exacerbation of symptoms. Sometimes women can over-identify with the symptoms of other women in the group, or hearing other stories can intensify their anxiety.

Whether we view postpartum depression as a biological crisis, a neurological glitch, an existential aspect of the human condition, or an illness of the soul, it becomes evident that scientific research is not the only frame we can put around the human experience of new motherhood. In practice, clinicians must operate from a number of perspectives—sometimes simultaneously with and sometimes independently of each other, but always in the best interest of the client.

In many ways, my experience with Rose heightened my own awareness of the joy we all harbor deep inside. Joy comes in many forms. It can manifest as that glorious feeling of laughing so hard it hurts—that pure, raw expression of laughter that consumes our being, rendering us breathless and unable to speak or think. In its simplicity, joy is what can connect us to ourselves and to others. It is what makes the unendurable endurable. Finding the joy is not always easy. Sometimes, as clinicians, we need to help that process along. Finding joy might be possible as a result of neural reprocessing, an unconscious trance, or healing through the channels of our bodily energies. Joy might be possible with the right medication, a supplement, information reprocessing, or a meaningful connection. Maybe bright light, fitness training, or a roomful of like-minded comrades will make it possible. Any or all of these tools and pathways can help bring the postpartum woman closer to herself again. Help her find the joy.

PART 3

The Work: Clinical Challenges

CHAPTER 19

Scary Thoughts

"Are you having any thoughts that are scaring you?"

This has become a standard question when assessing for depression after childbirth. Sometimes it is asked at the doctor's office. Sometimes it's written on a screening form. Sometimes it's posed by a clinician who is experienced with working with postpartum women.

Sometimes, unfortunately, it is not asked at all.

Years ago, before I had the advantage of a clinical pool of women who continually teach me what I need to know to help them, I set out to learn more about the relationship between childbirth and depression. I had an office, but no clients. I had passion, but no direction. I needed information. Simply put, I needed women to tell me how they were feeling and what they needed.

The ad in the local newspaper was straightforward: *Therapist researching postpartum depression. If you've had a baby and are concerned about the way you are feeling, please call for an interview.* This was before postpartum depression had captured mainstream attention. But long before celebrities battled over who had it and who didn't and before books were written on the subject, women were indeed suffering. The word wasn't out yet, so women weren't speaking.

Only three women responded to the ad. That didn't surprise me. What surprised me was that two of the women were more than 65 years old. I couldn't imagine why they were contacting me. With much curiosity, I met with each individually and asked them my prepared script of questions. Each independently told me that this was the first time she had spoken about the private pain she had endured almost 50 years ago. Each described different but similar stories of isolation, feelings of deep loss, sadness, fear, and despair.

The inappropriate feelings. The socially unacceptable thoughts. The symptoms that kept her shut in from the outside world for endless periods of time. The shame of it all. No one knew how she felt. Not her doctor. Not her mother. Not her husband. No one.

The shame attached to feelings and thoughts associated with postpartum depression is unimaginable. Today, women remain steadfast in their determined fight not to let anyone know how they are feeling. Why do they do that? Why *must* they do that? Fear of recrimination? Fear of judgment by others? Fear that they are essentially unequipped to be mothers?

The prevailing notion that mothering is instinctual is everywhere we look. Evidence abounds culturally, anthropologically, and biologically. Thus, when symptoms get in the way and thwart a process that's believed by most to be natural, it's hard not to take that personally. As a result, women may mistakenly believe that they are flawed in some significant way. *Everyone else is able to do this mother thing right, why can't I?* Cultural ideals aside, women tend to be extremely good at pressuring themselves to compete with their own expectations of how this launch into motherhood should look. Perceived failure in this area can lead to an exhausting internal struggle.

Sherri taught me a great deal about this struggle. She was 30 years old. This was her first marriage, first pregnancy, first baby. She sat down and looked straight at me with a look I'm very familiar with: a look of hesitation. It's a look that reflects both uncertainty and hope. It's an anxious gaze that seems to say *I don't know if I'm in the right place or not but I certainly hope that I am because I'd really like to tell you what I'm thinking, but I don't want to tell you what I'm thinking, so maybe I'll just sit here until I know for sure that I'm in the right place and can safely say what I need to say.*

Sherri proceeded by telling me she was overwhelmed with thoughts of her son. She said all she could do was think about her baby, all day long. It's not uncommon for new moms to become hypervigilant about their babies' safety. It's natural for all new mothers to worry about the well-being of their babies. In fact, it is believed that some degree of anxiety can help foster a protective instinct or alarm, such as the "fight or flight" response, that helps women take action when there is a threat or perceived danger (Lark, 1993). But when these instincts kick into high gear and take the form of constant, unremitting, unwanted thoughts that bombard a mother's sacred space, they have exceeded the ranks of natural and protective responses.

Sherri continued:

> I can't sleep. I'm up all night checking on him. Is he breathing? Is he okay? It's like, if I could watch him all night, maybe I could prevent something bad happening. I need to sleep. I keep getting up and checking on him. It's insane. I'm seriously up every hour, maybe two. I get up. I go to his room and I look to make sure he's breathing. Then I go back to sleep for an hour and wake up and do it again. When I

try my best not to get up, I can feel the pressure in my head; the chatter in my head gets worse. This sounds crazy, doesn't it?

It didn't sound crazy. But I could tell from her demeanor and her quick check on my interpretation of this behavior that it felt extremely crazy to her.

"Are you having any thoughts that are scaring you, Sherri?"

Cut to the chase. Don't waste time waiting for disclosure that may take minutes, hours, days, or weeks. If we don't ask this question, we cannot assume that women will tell us if something is scaring them. Sherri looked straight at me but paused before speaking, as if she were both surprised and relieved to hear my question. Her baby was 5 months old. Her obstetrician referred Sherri to me after hearing the revelation that she hadn't felt like herself since the baby had been born and continued to feel worse instead of better. Sherri's history of anxiety was unremarkable, but it did bring her to therapy late in high school and intermittently through college, where she learned and practiced cognitive–behavioral techniques of anxiety reduction. She reported that both of her parents were "nervous people"; her father had recently been diagnosed with obsessive–compulsive disorder and was doing well on medication. Furthermore, she claimed to be rather at home with her anxiety, which, for the most part, hadn't caused a huge problem in life. But these feelings were different, she said. The anxiety she had experienced since the birth of her son felt more invasive and disruptive.

"What do you mean, 'thoughts that are scaring me'?" She knew what I meant but needed to test me to pave the way.

Reassurance of our expertise is essential at this point. A woman's trust in our ability to understand, cope with, and ultimately provide relief for her symptoms will determine how early on in the process she can reveal what she is really thinking. What stands in her way of trusting this relationship from the outset? Usually, it's her very real fear that someone will misunderstand what she is saying and criticize or reject her or—her greatest fear of all—take her baby away.

Sherri had told her mother she wasn't feeling good. Her mother had told her that this was normal and she shouldn't expect to feel good at this point. She further told her daughter that having children was hard and he should stop indulging in so much thought about herself at a time when she should be thinking about her family.

Sherri told her girlfriend (who was recently married and didn't have children) she wasn't feeling good. Her friend told her everything would be fine. Her mother-in-law told her she was overreacting and should stop complaining. Her husband told her she was strong and she was doing great. The stranger at the park told her she should tell her doctor so she didn't end up like that crazy woman who killed her baby.

So she stopped telling people how she felt.

"Sherri, if you're having thoughts in your head that worry you or thoughts that you're afraid to tell anyone, it might help you to know that this is common. We are not surprised at all when we hear women tell us some of the scary thoughts they are having."

She waited. She was not quite ready yet.

"So it's common to have scary thoughts? How common?"

"Very common. Close to 30% of women with postpartum depression experience obsessional thoughts, and some of them are very scary." We sit together, her eyes locked into mine. "I know it's hard. But there's a good chance that you'll feel a bit better if you talk to me about the thoughts you are having."

She didn't believe me.

"Sherri, you don't have to tell me anything that makes you uncomfortable."

For a moment, Sherri seemed ready to leap. "I don't think you've heard what I'm thinking before." Whenever I'm struck by obvious body language, I revisit Psychology 101: classic demonstration of closed body language, which indicates defensiveness or protectiveness: crossed arms against chest, crossed legs, head tucked down, avoiding eye contact. At this moment, Sherri typified this portrayal. I could feel her tension mounting. Again, she found herself vacillating between telling me and withholding, between disclosing and denying, between trusting me and following her desire to protect herself. I said,

Listen, Sherri, here's what happens. When these thoughts come and go and it feels like you must be going crazy, the natural response is to try to shut them off in an attempt to block them from coming back. But, actually, that can make it worse. You see, trying to make them go away gives the thoughts more power. It's like you push and push and push and use all this energy to keep pushing and still they persist. It's not until you release that pressure and let them be that they can settle down a bit, at least long enough for you to tolerate. Telling me will not make these thoughts real. It will not make them happen. These thoughts are symptoms. They are not about who you are or what is going to happen. They are symptoms.

Sherri sat up with rigid determination, as if her posture could somehow prevent the thoughts from intruding. She pushed back her short blonde bangs and squeezed her hair between her fingers:

I can't get these thoughts out of my head. I cannot get them out of my head. Why would I be thinking these things? I keep thinking I'm going to hurt him. Something terrible is going to happen. Like picking up a knife or holding his head under water. I can see the whole thing happening. I can see blood and body parts and awful, awful—unbelievably awful—stuff in my head. Why would I want to hurt him? What is wrong with me?

Sherri covered her mouth in disgrace, choking with each inhale. "It's so awful, I can't believe I'm thinking it. I can't believe I'm saying this out loud. I'm disgusting. I'm repulsive." She closed her eyes, gasped quickly to inhale several shallow breaths, and wiped the tears across her buried face.

Nothing in our training adequately prepares us for this. Books that reference postpartum depression and the pain of negative intrusive thinking don't tell you what it feels like to absorb that much suffering. When pain permeates the air with such force, I can almost feel my own breathing become shallow in sync with hers. The shared rhythm can create a bond of unmatched proportion. It feels unexpectedly raw.

Rarely do we talk about mothers who have thoughts of hurting their babies. It conjures up all kind of images of monster mothers: How can a loving, nurturing woman admit to having such evil thoughts about her own flesh and blood, especially while she simultaneously declares great love for him? The incongruity of this notion is what fosters our society's denial. It's too hard to understand or to believe that a mother could think or feel such deep displeasure; thus, many pretend it isn't there. Worse yet, when people only partially understand, they risk perpetuating misinformation and widespread misperceptions.

The women I see in my office have never had their names splashed across headlines, although many have feared that's where they would inevitably end up. Each woman who has trusted me enough to disclose her private anguish has confided that this is her greatest fear—that she will spin out of control, be sucked into the vortex of madness, and end up lost forever.

Any number of things can make a woman feel like she's a bad mother: ignoring a child's plea for attention, resenting a baby's midnight wail, or feeling too tired for just one more diaper change. The range of reasons for self-blame and guilt that can annihilate a woman's self-esteem is endless. It's hard to be a mother. It's hard to reconcile the conflicting feelings. It's especially hard to try to do everything right. The exhausting quest to be the perfect mother can render a woman defenseless against the onslaught of societal pressures and impossible expectations.

That's on a good day.

When we add to this the distorted thought process that can accompany a postpartum illness, the impact is nothing less than torture. Negative intrusive thoughts are so widespread with postpartum depression and so misunderstood. For postpartum women, these thoughts typically focus on the baby, although themes will vary. In a study of 100 depressed mothers and 46 nondepressed mothers, 41% of the depressed mothers reported the occurrence of negative thoughts of harming their infant, while only 6.5% of the nondepressed mothers reported having these thoughts. According to the study, the prevalence of these thoughts has been widely underestimated (Jennings, Ross, Popper, & Elmore, 1999).

The nature of the thoughts can range from annoying and worrisome to graphically violent thoughts and images that quickly extinguish any fantasy of idyllic maternal bliss. They are unwelcome at best and, at their worst, they are agents of unrelenting torment. Research does support the notion that efforts to dismiss or block these intrusive obsessions are counterproductive (Larsen et al., 2006). Strategies to distract oneself—for example, distracting or reassuring oneself—actually compounded the problem and reinforced the threatening nature of the unwanted thoughts. The research further suggested that the temptation to suppress the thoughts did not, in fact, help to control them. Rather, it led to an increase in the preoccupation. The authors conclude that management of these thoughts involves encouraging the client to speak freely about them and helping her understand that this is a common manifestation of postpartum depression with obsessive thinking.

I continued to reassure Sherri that these thoughts, no matter how horrific or gruesome they may be, are symptoms of acute anxiety. Thoughts are thoughts, I reminded her. They do not lead to or encourage action. They are thoughts. Repeating this concept can be valuable, although admittedly all the reassurance in the world can be insufficient when one is locked into the full swing of an obsessional loop. Sherri would affirm this with her anxious ruminations: "Tell me again that I'm not a terrible person." And I would. Then, in a few minutes, I would tell her once more.

Sherri agreed that she was very aware of how irrational these thoughts were. This is always a good sign. The discrepancy between what she thinks she should be feeling and what she is feeling causes high anxiety; this is further evidence that these thoughts are anxiety driven.

Her distress over these intrusive thoughts tells us that the thoughts are ego-dystonic, or not characteristic of who she is. Ego-dystonic obsessional thoughts are essentially inconsistent with what she wants or believes. Although the obsessional quality is disturbing, these thoughts are rarely acted upon ,except when psychosis is present (Miller, 2002). Ironically, a high level of distress regarding these thoughts is reassuring to the clinician. This is because it helps to rule out a far more serious condition. Women with psychotic symptoms are not troubled by their delusional thoughts, because these thoughts seem consistent with their distorted reality. In women with postpartum psychosis, thoughts are ego-syntonic, and no distress is associated with them (Brandes, Soares, & Cohen, 2004).

This distinction was comforting to Sherri, who, like so many others, was very good at obsessing about her obsessing.

How could I put her mind at ease when it was spinning so feverishly? Could my words even slightly appease her distress if she believed that she was damaged goods?

"Sherri, you should know that this is not worrisome to me. I don't like the fact that you're feeling so bad, but I am not worried about what you are telling me."

"You're not?"

"No. I'm not. You feel terrible, that's for sure. But these thoughts that you're having are not what you think they are. You are not going crazy. You are not going to hurt your baby. You are not psychotic. You have a history of anxiety that, since the birth of your baby, has resurfaced and manifested itself in the form of obsessive thinking. Add the excessive checking of your baby at night and the pre-existing compulsive behaviors that you have shared with me, and we've got a diagnosis of postpartum obsessive–compulsive disorder. You told me your father has OCD, and we know there is a genetic link."

She laughed with relief. "Oh, my God, is that why I'm going nuts making sure everything is put away so nothing will fall on him or hurt him? And why I am constantly rearranging things even though it makes no sense at all? You're right." She nodded her head in affirmation. "I think you're right."

I smiled back.

"How are you feeling right now?" I asked.

"Better."

"What do you mean, 'better'? In what way do you feel better?"

"I'm not sure. I think I feel better because you know what I'm talking about. There's a name, and it's a real thing. Because you've heard of this before, and I'm not making it up or going crazy. That part feels good."

That part *is* good.

Sherri left my office with a plan. She would bring her husband in to our next session so he could become better informed about her symptoms and how they were getting in her way. She would call our psychiatrist and make an appointment for a medication evaluation. Because her father was doing so well on the antidepressants, she was hopeful that she would respond similarly. She would continue with supportive psychotherapy for the short term, and she would stop asking everyone she knew for advice, since this only seemed to overwhelm her. Together, she and I would explore the cognitive–behavioral skills she had learned in previous therapy and apply them within this new context. The plan was good. But the key to her initial relief came from something else.

The critical reassurance came from my assertion that I understood her suffering, that it had a name, and that together we could make a plan toward feeling better. This declaration of confidence and expertise by a clinician is what separates the women in treatment who hope they will get better from the women who know they will. It's an important message that can be insinuated by how we act and project ourselves or can be explicitly stated. Either way, it is a message that will damp fears and augment recovery.

CHAPTER 20

Help-Resistant Complainer

It never ceases to amaze me how much someone can reveal by her initial phone call. One afternoon, I received a page on the beeper. A page generally indicates one of two things. Either someone is seeking immediate assistance for a crisis or, more commonly, someone is having difficulty tolerating her symptoms. This perception or *misperception* can be experienced by either the woman herself, her partner, or another loved one who is genuinely worried about her. We know that without adequate knowledge of what is happening and what it means, symptoms can escalate into panic mode. When this happens, we see a phenomenon where a woman may *feel* as though she is in crisis, though, in fact, there may not be one. Admittedly, this is a difficult distinction to make if one is not trained to do so and, of course, it is always best to be safe.

After receiving the page, I checked the office voicemail, as callers are instructed to leave a message in addition to their page. I listened to the plea for help:

> Hi. My name is Nicole. I had a baby a few months ago, and my doctor told me to call. I'd like to make an appointment as soon as possible. I'm having a hard time breathing, and it's probably anxiety or panic or something. I don't know what it is, but if someone could please call me back, I would appreciate it so I can make an appointment. Hopefully, I can get in sometime today.

At our center, we try to be as accommodating as possible. Each one of us will do our best to shift our personal schedules around, stay late, or skip lunch to make sure someone in immediate need gets an appointment as soon as possible.

Sometimes that makes us heroes. Other times, it means we go out of our way for someone who could have waited until tomorrow.

I called Nicole back and, after assessing that there was no emergency, told her I could see her Thursday morning at 11:00, but someone else could see her this afternoon or tomorrow if she felt she couldn't wait the 2 days.

"I'd really like to see *you*, if I could," she sighed, with a shallow, panic-inspired breath.

Her anxious and urgent request for my expertise tugged at that vulnerable spot I work so hard to conceal. Could she wait until Thursday? Probably. Was she connecting with me sufficiently to influence a shift in my availability? I suspect so. Was she manipulating me? Definitely. Did my awareness of that dynamic keep me in control of the situation? Absolutely.

"Nicole, someone else in the office can see you this afternoon or tomorrow; everyone here is wonderful and can help you. Why don't you talk to your husband and call me back if you'd like to be seen either today or tomorrow, and we can arrange that. If you prefer to wait until Thursday, you can let me know that, too."

"Okay, that sounds good. I'll call you back this afternoon and let you know."

Tuesday afternoon came and went, as did Wednesday morning. By Wednesday afternoon, it occurred to me that I hadn't heard from Nicole, so I pondered the possibilities. Either she felt better and didn't feel the need to come in or she felt worse and perhaps she was in trouble and needed our immediate intervention. I called and left a message indicating that someone could still see her that afternoon.

On Thursday, I received a message from Nicole at 10:00 a.m. "Hi, this is Nicole. I know it's last minute, but I was hoping you could still see me at the 11:00 appointment today. Please call me if that's possible."

It wasn't possible. But it did start me thinking about what was taking place and how often we see this incongruent exchange, this "help me, but …" or "come here but not too close" syndrome, as it were.

I like to think that if I'm aware of being manipulated, then I'm not being manipulated. This isn't exactly true, of course. Still, what I'm doing is giving permission for someone's anxious symptoms to burst forth aimlessly while I do my best to keep a check on them and provide structure to contain them. In the end, however, we frame it; we understand that being influenced by women with intense anxiety symptoms that are all too vicious to endure is part of the job.

We scheduled an appointment for the following Monday. Nicole presented as an attractive 34-year-old mother of a 3-month-old baby and a 2-year-old. Her primary complaint was acute anxiety. She was a bright girl who worked hard and loved her job promoting pharmaceuticals to local doctors. Her black, button-down shirt was tucked neatly into her flowing skirt, finished off immaculately with (I couldn't help but notice) a pair of grown-up, highest-heeled shoes. She expressed her relief that her demanding job was flexible enough for her to "run out in the middle of the day for an appointment."

I listened carefully as she described the nature of her anxiety. She described the crushing pain in her chest: "I know I'm not having a heart attack but it feels like a heart attack. I mean this must be what a heart attack feels like"; the rapid heartbeat: "like my heart is beating right out of my chest. It feels like I can almost see it pounding when I look at my chest"; ruminating thoughts: "My head never stops. I worry all the time. I overanalyze everything. If I'm not worrying about something, I worry about not worrying. I've always been a worrier, but it's much worse now"; and sleep difficulties: "I have never slept well, even before the baby, but now, it's much more complicated. I'm just so tired all the time and I need to function at work and at home. I can't catch a break."

Still, in spite of her depiction of distress, as well as her score of 14 on the Edinburgh screen, something didn't sit right with me. I wasn't sure what it was. She just didn't seem to be as upset as she was saying she was. This contradiction between what a client tells us and what we see for ourselves is not so unusual. As we've seen, a client will try to present as "well put together" to disguise or distract from or maintain control of her suffering. This tendency to uphold the illusion of perfection is conduct a postpartum specialist should be quite familiar with, although, honestly, it never fails to intrigue and challenge me. But in Nicole's case, I was seeing something a bit different: a woman who, from all outward appearances, presented well, reported symptoms that were interfering with her ability to function, and complained about how bad she was feeling. Her demeanor did, indeed, contradict her reported symptoms, but in this instance, something other than a severe illness seemed to be at the crux. I wasn't sure, early on, what this was, exactly; was it a personality issue? Was it an Axis-II diagnosis? Was it attention-seeking behavior?

Even after prolonged probing, I wasn't convinced that she was as sick as she felt and needed to dig deeper in order to determine how I could best help her. It's not always what it looks like. Because postpartum women can present in ways that are incompatible with what they are saying, clinicians must rely on precise diagnostic skills. Clinicians with less experience in this area would benefit from close supervision in order to sharpen the diagnostic picture. The bottom line is that clinicians must remain plugged in to both what the client is saying and how she presents. Any incongruity might be a diagnostic clue. If this pretense catches a clinician off guard, the clinician is at risk for missing the essence of what the client needs, and both will be wasting their time.

I continued to take note of Nicole's history: Mother and father both have a history of pronounced anxiety; neither was on medication, as far as she knew. Her sister had been treated for panic attacks, but she wasn't sure if she had ever taken meds, either. Both her paternal and maternal grandfathers had a history of alcoholism, as well as her father's brother and her mother's two sisters. Her brother had been diagnosed with bipolar disorder 10 years prior and, instead of taking his medication, had been in and out of rehab for his ongoing struggle with drugs and alcohol abuse. She didn't say much about her brother at that juncture, but I sensed her uneasiness.

When asked if she had a history of any alcohol or drug use, she said, "No." Aware of her significant family history of substance abuse, I pursued this further: "Did you ever do any drugs, in high school or college?"

"Not really. I mean, I smoked pot a few times, but I hated the way it made me feel, all paranoid and everything."

"Any alcohol?"

"Not really. I mean, I used to drink beer in college, you know, at parties."

"Do you drink any alcohol now?"

"No, not really."

"Not really?" I mirrored.

"Well, I have a glass or two of wine."

"How often? Once a week? Twice a week? Every night?"

"It helps take the edge off. It's the only time I get to relax. Between work and the baby and my husband being gone so much and all the things I have to do."

"The wine helps you feel relaxed," I reiterated.

"Yes. I really love the way the wine makes me feel." She smiled like a child caught with stolen candy in her mouth.

"How often? Every night?"

"Every night."

She reported no significant history of previous medical or mental health issues and boasted, "This is the first time I've ever seen a therapist." Her appetite was good, her relationships were strong and supportive, her thyroid screen was normal, and she reported no suicidal thoughts. She stated her fatigue was overwhelming and heightened by the fact that her husband often traveled on business. Her family doctor had suggested she start an antidepressant and also gave her a prescription to help alleviate her anxiety. Nicole told me she took the antidepressant for a few days but couldn't stand the way she felt, so she went off it.

"I know it can take a while to work, but I couldn't wait a while. It was awful. I felt spacey and depressed and not at all like myself. I'd rather feel anxious than how I felt on the medication!"

"Did you take the anxiety medication, too?" I asked. I believed that the anti-anxiety properties would indeed give her relief, but I was concerned about the interaction with her alcohol consumption.

"No. It scares me. I don't like the way medication makes me feel. There's no way I'm going to take that."

"Are you taking any over-the-counter medication? Any supplements? Any herbal remedies?"

"Nope."

"Any caffeine in your diet?"

"Oh, yeah," she chuckled. "Are you kidding? Oh, my God, that's my favorite part of the day."

"How much caffeine?"

"A lot. I need it. I mean, how would I get through the day? I'm so exhausted. I drink a lot." She used her hands to approximate the height of the cup. "I guess the equivalent of five to six cups. I'm sure I'm addicted. I need it. I'm totally addicted."

As someone who buzzes from decaffeinated coffee, I thought she was right; this *was* a lot of coffee. If her recollection of her coffee intake was anything like her recollection of her wine intake, it might even be higher.

"That's a lot of coffee for someone who's having anxiety attacks. Did you know that caffeine can exacerbate anxiety or even trigger an attack?"

"No, I didn't know that. That's not good news."

"Well, it's not terrible news, but do you know what that means?"

"I'm *not* giving up my coffee. I can't give up my coffee."

So then we talked.

We talked about how insidious anxiety can be and how a family history of anxiety can predispose a woman to experience it after childbirth.

We talked about how much stress she was under with her job, her husband's traveling, and taking care of a new baby and a toddler.

We talked about how many of her symptoms are not new for her but are in a state of sharp exaggeration as a result of her childbirth experience. We discussed how the combination of hormonal changes, sleep deprivation, family history, and current stressors from work and home created the opportunity for her anxiety to spiral out of control and make her feel so sick.

We talked about the pros and cons of medication and how her family history of addiction did pose a special risk that we needed to take into account.

We talked about the fact that she did not present with pronounced depressive symptoms. Though she reported intense symptoms, our discussions did not seem to substantiate the severity she said she was feeling. Some of the depressed feelings ("I notice I'm crying more than usual") could possibly be secondary to her anxiety ("I'm depressed about feeling so much anxiety all the time"). I knew I needed to be careful about making presumptions that might not be true, never forgetting that she could, indeed, be more symptomatic than she appeared or reported.

We talked about what she could do to get some relief. That's where we got stuck.

"So what should I do? I can't stand the way I feel and I'm not going to take medication."

Being one who doesn't have patience for the more traditional psychotherapeutic dance of waiting for the client to come up with her own solution—not to mention that many times symptoms prohibit clients from being able to do so—I prefer to answer a question with precisely what the client wants (or needs) to hear. So I offered Nicole my list of suggestions:

> *You need to cut out your nightly wine.*
>   "I can't. I need to relax."
> *You need to avoid caffeine.*
>   "Not possible. How will I get through the day?"
> *You need to consider nonpharmacologic interventions to facilitate sleep.*
>   "I know I should exercise and eat better and stuff. I just don't have
>   the time. And I'm not interested in that hypnotherapy you were
>   talking about. I just don't think it will make a difference."
> *You might want to consider adding the anti-anxiety medication on an as-*
>   *needed basis to break the cycle of anxiety. It works wonderfully on a short-*
>   *term basis, and if you take it as needed you won't have any long-term*
>   *problems with it. Your doctor and I will be monitoring this with you closely.*
>   *I'm not going to let anything get out of control.*
>   "I'd really rather not take medication," she responded with clear
>   determination.

I found her opposition to every suggestion quite interesting.

"What would you like me to say, Nicole?"

"I don't know. Just *tell me what I can do to feel better.*"

"I am."

She sat quietly for a moment, seemingly stifled by the paradox she presented.

"Is this what you do sometimes, Nicole? Do you find that sometimes you set things up and make it hard for others to help you? And hard for you to help yourself?"

She listened, as I continued.

"Remember when you first called a couple of days ago? And how anxious you were to get in for an appointment? And how I offered you a number of options but you resisted? And then sabotaged things for yourself by trying too late to get in, when you had missed the opportunity?" She nodded. "Do you see how you are doing this again? Let me explain how you get in your own way":

> You have a strong family history of addictive behaviors, but you self-
>   medicate with alcohol because it feels good.
> You are exhausted, haven't had a good night's sleep since you can
>   remember, but you (1) drink alcohol, which is a depressant and
>   interferes with sleep; (2) aren't interested in any medication that
>   may help you sleep; (3) aren't willing to give up the large amounts of
>   caffeine you consume during the day, which further obstructs your
>   body's ability to rest; and (4) resist any suggestion for safe, alterna-
>   tive interventions that may set a successful sleep plan in motion.

You say you don't like the way medication makes you feel funny and "alters your mind," yet you love the way wine "takes the edge off" and you look forward to it nightly.

So, medication is out of the question. Hypnosis is out of the question. Exercise does not fit into your schedule now. You will continue to drink one to two classes of wine at night and five to six cups of coffee per day. I'm thinking this course of action isn't working well for you, and I suspect talk therapy won't help much. What do you think?

Because she was bright and insightful and despite her self-proclaimed stubbornness, I shared with her the label that my clinical director identifies as a common interference in the work we do. She was a *help-resistant complainer*, which characterizes a hostile–dependent relationship between the client and therapist, setting up a push–pull, "yes, but" relationship between the two.

"I think you might be right," she agreed with a smile, yielding to my way of thinking, if only temporarily. This was partly because she suspected I might know what I was talking about, partly because she was feeling so bad that she knew she needed to do something different, and partly because she was tired and unable to fight. It was then that I saw something in her eyes I had not seen earlier, and it needed to be addressed.

"Are you afraid, Nicole? Right now, is something scaring you?"

She inhaled deeply, "I'm not sure."

I waited.

"Maybe I'm afraid to take medication because it will mean I'm really sick or totally insane or something."

"'Or something'? Something like your brother?"

"Yeah, I guess, like that. He's so sick and so out of control. I'm the perfect one. I'm the one that doesn't get sick. I don't want to be crazy. I have to stay healthy. I'm the one that has everything together. Everything will fall apart if I get sick."

"No, Nicole, everything is much more likely to fall apart if you do not take care of yourself. If you learn how to take better care of your symptoms, you are much *more* likely to keep things under control, not *less* likely. I know it's scary because you've seen the darker side of mental illness in your family. I don't know what you've seen that has scared you so much; we can talk more about that later. But I do know that you are not 'crazy'. You are not out of control. You are having terrible symptoms of anxiety that are interfering with your ability to function well, and you need to treat it. This doesn't necessarily mean with medication, but you do need to treat it."

"I know," Nicole spoke softly as she reached for a tissue. "I know."

Together, we sat in that space that felt so right, when the two energies merge into a place of shared oneness. It's when the client feels the most cared for and most safe. It's when she knows she's in the right spot. This is when she is most likely to move forward in the direction of healing.

"All right, all right," she acquiesced. "I got it. I hear you."

"What do you hear?"

"I'm not taking care of myself now. I'm just avoiding it by doing things the way I've always done them. It's not working."

"No, I don't think it is."

"Okay, I'll try. No, I'll do my best. It's a deal. No caffeine. No wine. *And no medication,* as long as I stick to the deal."

"Okay, Nicole. It's a deal."

CHAPTER 21

A Good Girl

We all hope our baby is perfect. Ten fingers, ten toes, ten Apgar score: normal pulse, regular breathing rate, good reflexive responsiveness, active muscle tone, and perfect baby pink skin. When all goes well and all the stars are in alignment, some of us are lucky enough to hold that perfect baby in our arms after 9 months of restless anticipation.

For some women, it is more complicated.

What happens when something goes wrong? What happens when everything a mother fears might happen, happens? How does one make sense out of something that makes no sense?

Take, for instance, the mother who claims she's done everything right. She dutifully followed up with all prenatal visits and adhered to doctors' orders. She abstained from any remotely impure substances that she may have previously swallowed without a second thought before becoming pregnant. She obsessed about every little thing that went in or on her body, lest her delicate system be contaminated with any foreign matter that would be incompatible with her growing belly. She avoided things that were bad for her and tried her best to surround herself with loving forces, aiming for a balance that exists better in theory than in practice, for sure.

Still, something unforeseen happens. Dreams are blown apart. Lives are changed forever. No one is prepared when blindsided by an unexpected turn of events.

Melissa sat rocking herself back and forth on my couch, arms crossed against her chest and her head down, so sweet and young looking for her 35 years, like a wounded child who could hardly bear the suffering. Her eyes were bright and soulful, despite, or perhaps because of, her endless crying. "I cannot do this," she wept. "I do not want to do this. I cannot be a mother right now. I cannot do this. I will not do this. Not now. Not this way. Not this baby."

Poor, sweet Melissa, I thought. What could I possibly say or do to help her? What words? What tools? What magic did I have that could even begin to make a difference? I had none at that moment, so I sat with her and her pain.

"I don't want this baby. He's not normal. All I wanted was a normal baby. Is that too much to ask? I feel terrible saying that, but it's true. I mean, a good mother wouldn't say that. Someone else should raise him."

When a mother declares her ambivalence about being a mother, it is often frowned upon as a failing. There is a universal expectation that mothers want to be mothers. It is expected that the maternal instinct will surface on cue and everything will fall into place.

Or so it seems.

"I'm better now than I was." She smiled slightly at the reference to her previous state of collapse that landed her in the inpatient unit of a psychiatric hospital. "Killing myself doesn't appeal to me quite as much, but neither does waking up in the morning."

Melissa spent 8 days on the inpatient unit of a facility that presumably did its best but fell short of meeting the unique needs of a woman who had just given birth to a baby. Melissa denied any previous history of depression and stated that her relationship with her 6-year-old son was, quite frankly, the sole reason she didn't kill herself. Before she was discharged, the social worker on the unit called to make the referral:

> Melissa is a lovely young woman who was admitted on the recommendation of her treating psychiatrist after she stated she was not able to take care of her baby. She has a 6-year-old son and her baby is 2 months old. He has Down syndrome. She's not handling it very well; she seems to be in shock. Her family is in the area, mother, father, and brother. Oh, and her brother is impaired in some way, not sure to what extent, but I think it's pretty severe. Her husband seems to be very supportive and says there are a number of helpful friends and family members who can help take care of the baby until Melissa feels better and can deal with this.

"Deal with this"? I wondered what she meant by that.

The social worker went on to say that she thought Melissa felt a bit "entitled" and perhaps she was spoiled in some way that compromised her ability to adapt to the situation. She presumed, because Melissa had done well after the birth of her first child, that she was simply overreacting to the shock and disappointment brought on by the birth of Brandon and his diagnosis of Down syndrome.

I thanked her for her referral and privately took note of her simplistic and dreadfully insensitive analysis.

In fact, I would discover that Melissa had a history of dealing quite well with life. Raised by parents who were loving and supportive, she learned early on how to take responsibility for herself and the importance of being a good girl. And good she was. Always top in her class, she worked hard to achieve and maintain her own high standards. Clearly, she had been successful in her life and, aside from some intermittent and clinically relevant distractions, her striving for excellence and her desire for control in her life had brought her great satisfaction. "I didn't have an eating disorder or anything, but I do obsess about what I eat and I exercise all the time. I mean, all the time. Like, if I skip a day, I'm a mess, in my head, I mean."

During our subsequent sessions, she admitted that things at home were stressful while she was growing up. It went without saying that her brother's severely low functioning created incredible demands on the entire family; he was unable to care for himself in any way. Melissa said she had to work hard to keep things running smoothly.

"What do you mean, 'running smoothly'?" I asked, curious at this early point in our work about the link between her mentally impaired brother and her newborn baby, whom she also perceived as vastly impaired.

"Chris is great. He's 2 years younger than me. It's been him and me, my whole life. He's severely disabled, like a child. He can't do anything on his own. I love him. I always have." She smiled the loving smile of an older sister who had decidedly taken very good care of him and protected him from the dangers of living in a world that does not tolerate individual differences very well—not to mention total incapacitation.

"How difficult that must have been for you." I could not imagine what life must have felt like for a younger Melissa, as I traversed the range of possible emotions in my head.

"I knew something was wrong right away. I remember my mother telling me, when I was very young, that Chris was different and that he was very special, and we would have to take special care of him. So we did."

Sounded simple enough and, at first glance, seemed to have worked well.

"Where is Chris now?" I asked, wondering about the profound and lingering impact on both Melissa and her parents.

"He's home with my parents. It's been 31 years. They are wonderful with him. My mother never, ever complains. Never says a word about it. Never."

Wow. Impressed with the dedication from all sides and inspired by her mother's enduring sacrifices, I couldn't help but wonder how this affected Melissa when she was so very young. *How does a child learn to put all her own needs aside for the needs of a sibling who requires faithful attention and constant care? How does a child pretend that everything is okay when she is not sure what any of it means? Where does a child go for help when she is taught and modeled that the family does not ask for help? What does a child do with all of this? How does it feel to have a brother who is so drastically impaired?*

"It was fine. It's just the way it was."

Fine? It was "fine"? I asked myself.

Ah, her mother had taught her well, indeed.

Every once in a while, a therapist is caught in a struggle among what she is hearing, what she is feeling, and what she thinks her response should be. When details of the session tap into the sacred ground of countertransference and we are forced to assess our own emotional response, exquisite things can begin to unfold in therapy. Of course, we must be careful not to misinterpret the feelings or project them haphazardly onto the client.

I took a close look inside and thought to myself: *Oh my God, how did this child* (the same embodiment of a child I now see gently rocking back and forth in my office) *learn to integrate so much negative information? How awful.* I remember how hard it was for me when my own sister was sick and I felt the need to make excuses to my friends when we were forced to come home early from our vacation to take her to the hospital. Everything we had planned came to a halt. In a flash, the mood shifted from fun to fear. Everything screeched to a stop and shifted course. There is no choice in situations such as these. No one likes it, to be sure. But while the adults kick into high gear and take action, children can remain caught in the crossfire. It may be the only way, but it's not always fair. And it's very, very scary.

I continued with Melissa, presuming too much, perhaps, but giving her permission to dive into that scary place. "Melissa, it must have been hard for you, when you were young, to know what to do with all of your feelings. Even though Mom wanted you to be strong and positive, I imagine some of your feelings didn't feel so good."

She lowered her head and hesitated. "No. Sometimes it didn't." She spoke quietly to make sure her words remained safe within the room.

"What did you do with some of the bad thoughts or feelings you had? Who could you talk to?"

She raised her eyebrows and looked at me as if she didn't understand what I was asking. "No one."

My question seemed to have stunned her into a silent, unfamiliar place. The silence, a hallmark of psychotherapy, can create enormous anxiety for unseasoned therapists. It can feel too awkward, deafening in a way, creating an urge to fill the space with words and premature interpretations.

I am quite at home in this quiet space.

If I am welcomed to stay (if the silence persists) and the silence is long enough (some inexplicable time frame), therapy can shift to an entirely new level. The silence, then, provides an entry to the soul. It's as if a veil lifts. For Melissa, the stillness seemed to be saying, *Will you come inside with me and let me show you what it felt like for me, when I was so young and scared? Will you listen to me? Do you promise not to judge me? Or scold me? If I tell you how I'm really feeling, will you be able to keep me safe from bad things happening?*

Melissa filled the empty space with tentative words, testing me, testing herself: "Gosh, I remember being embarrassed. I mean, no one really talked about bad things. It's even embarrassing talking about it now. Mom kept saying that nothing was wrong—that this is just what is. It's the way our life is.

But I never had friends over, and I couldn't go play after school 'cause I had to help her, and I didn't know what to say when kids asked what was wrong with my brother or why they couldn't come over to play."

She squirmed to find a comfortable spot; her smile vanished.

"Why couldn't your friends come over?

"Oh, my God, 'cause it was too strange. I mean, no one would understand. I was so embarrassed!"

"What age does this take you back to, Melissa? How old do you feel now, when you are thinking about these feelings?"

"I guess about 8." Her leg started shaking up and down. "This is so weird," she laughed nervously. "I mean, it's weird to feel these feelings. I didn't even think I had them. I really didn't. You know if you feel one way long enough, you just figure that's all there is to it. You know, everything was always tucked away, I guess."

She giggled nervously.

"What feelings, Melissa? What feelings were tucked away?"

"Geez, I don't know. All kinds of things, I think."

Her hesitation spoke volumes. How could she put these feelings into words when she had worked so hard to keep them from being exposed? What a formidable task. Shrouded by years of embarrassment (her word) and shame (my word) and denial (her mother's mandate), her voice was soft and her words were slow to emerge.

"It's weird to think about all of it. I love Chris. I really do. But it was so hard."

I noticed her breathing became more rapid and her voice cracked with sadness.

"God, everywhere I went and every single thing I did was for him, or about him. And you know what?" She inhaled deeply and brought her hand to her chest as if it hurt to breathe. "It was terrible. I can't believe I'm saying this, but he was so … so … hard to look at. He was so … ."

Her head shook, as if to dismiss the thoughts racing inside. Maybe she could just wish them away like she tried to do when she was younger.

"He was so *what*, Melissa? My tone of voice shifted as if to address her 8-year-old self, as I repositioned my body closer to her to catch sight of her closing eyes. I repeated her words softly. "He was so … what, Melissa?"

"He was so *ugly*." Her tears were old tears, held back by years of suppression, imposed restraint, and great self-discipline. God, how does one hold that in for so long? *If I cry,* little Melissa used to think, *I will not be strong. I will disappoint my mother. I won't be able to do what I need to do to take care of my brother. I'll betray my mother's trust in me. I'll be a bad girl.*

"Ugly." Not a pretty word, for sure. But it is not a word that conjures up any particular disgrace, for me. Yet for Melissa, for little 8-year-old Melissa, she was teetering on the edge of discrediting her family when she, just once, said aloud that her brother was ugly. In a home where structure was required in order to maintain control, as well as manage the overload, there was no room for insubordination. Everyone knew the rules. They made no excuses and asked for no sympathy. It's just the way it was.

Melissa had never uttered that word again. Until now.

Melissa brought Brandon into every session with her. Despite her constant worry that she would not attach appropriately with Brandon, she was, not surprisingly to me, a wonderful mother. Her ability to take the work we were doing and connect it to how she was feeling about her baby Brandon was the key to her progress.

"I brought in my journal today," she said, "the one I kept while I was in the hospital. I know I kept saying I would bring it to you, but I just kept putting it off. It's like I want you to see it, but I don't want you to see it. It's been on my mind to bring it, but I couldn't seem to do it. I guess I'm embarrassed."

Same word. Same feeling. Chris and Brandon. The more our sessions delved into her past relationship with her brother and her parents, the more I understood what she had meant when she had said at our earliest session, "I just can't do this. I'm too tired."

She held the journal out to me, not quite far enough for me to reach it from where I was sitting. *Did she want me to come get it? Did she not want to let go of it?* Her ambivalence was striking, straight out of a scene from a bad Freudian movie bursting with symbolism. "Would you like me to read it, Melissa?"

"I'm not sure."

"If you're not ready, then hold on to it. I can look at it another time. Or, I don't ever have to see it. Whatever makes you more comfortable."

"I want you to see it." She smiled her familiar, gentle smile, opening her heart with her typical hesitation. "I really do. It's just that I'm so embarrassed."

We learn that when clients use a descriptive word repeatedly, it is likely to have particular meaning for them. The meaning to them is not always what we think it means.

"What does that mean, you're 'embarrassed'?"

"I don't know. It means I'm afraid to show you what I was really thinking. I'm afraid you'll think I'm a terrible person. I'm afraid you won't like me, I guess, if you know who I really am. Or, was. Or something like that."

Melissa struggled to sort her past from her present and wanted so badly to rid herself of a lifetime of shameful thoughts and feelings. But releasing oneself from the grip of familiar feelings, regardless of how negative they may be, creates a vulnerability that can feel intolerable. *If I let these feelings out, what will happen? Will I be rejected? Will I have anything left inside me? Is there a core self that can sustain itself despite potential disapproval? How will I think and feel after this? And, ultimately, will I be abandoned and left with nothing?*

I also knew that the heart of her uncertainty rested with the relationship between her and her mother—a mother who, by all rights, was exhausted, overwhelmed, and most likely overcome with her own grief on a daily basis. Melissa's mother saw the challenge of a special-needs child as a gift from God and insisted that her daughter not surrender to the temptation of distracting thoughts. I would not begin to speculate whether her mother was struggling with her own depression or whether her way of coping with such a life-altering event was the best way to do it. What I do know is that when it came to understanding and dealing with any of her unwanted and shameful feelings, Melissa was left to fend for herself. She learned very quickly that these thoughts were unacceptable.

"Melissa, there is nothing you can say, nothing you can write, nothing you can think or feel, that will shock me, alarm me, or change the way I feel about you. I know you had awful, indescribably awful thoughts after Brandon was born. I can only imagine that giving birth to a baby with any disability was one of your deepest, darkest, unspoken fears. I also understand that you have had no place to talk about this. You have worked so hard to keep those thoughts private and intact."

She sat quietly, listening to everything I said, hungry for words to soothe her soul. "I feel so guilty. Some of the things I wrote are sickening."

"Only to you, sweetheart, only to you."

More silence. More reflection. Both of us trying to find our places: Melissa wanting to trust me, yet fearful to take the leap, and me grateful for the opportunity to slide into the role of the good mother. For myself, I know that most of my professional instincts are a direct outcome of my own experience as a mother—most often, from my not-so-perfect moments. I've had my share of perfect mother moments, but they are few and very far between, as life inevitably gets in the way. But sitting in my office, it is something altogether different. Suddenly, all my best intentions as a mother, all my high standards of ideal-mommy responses, all the things I realized I should have said and done with my own children but didn't, are actualized right there and then.

For all her mother's trials and trouble, from all accounts, Melissa's mother had done a wonderful job raising her. Our discussions were not intended to condemn those efforts in any way. Melissa had grown into a lovely, thoughtful, compassionate, and quite adorable young lady. But right now, at that moment, she needed a good mother, one who was not distracted with one challenge after another.

Melissa glanced down at her journal. "If I give it to you, will you read it later, not in front of me?"

"If you would like, I could do it that way. Or, we could talk about how it might feel if we looked at it together."

"Really? I don't know," she said, shaking her head and curling back up into her comfortable corner of the couch. "I'm *so embarrassed!*"

Trusting our relationship, I pushed further: "Let's try. If it feels too bad, you'll tell me, and we'll stop. How does that sound?"

"Okay."

Melissa reached toward me to hand me her journal. I took it into my hands and felt as though I were carrying a bit of her inner, younger self, vulnerable and defenseless. I held it closed shut again my chest: "Melissa, let's be clear about this. There is nothing written in here that will surprise or upset me. You can be very sure of that. Nothing bad is going to happen. You are the boss here. If, at any time, you change your mind and want me to stop, you just say so. Any bad feelings you may have about this right now are from you and your past experiences; they are not about me and how I may feel reading your words. Does that make sense?"

She nodded in agreement.

"Can I open it now and read some of it?"

She nodded her head for me to continue.

"Would you rather I read it to myself or out loud?"

"To yourself."

I opened the journal and read the words of which she felt so ashamed and protective:

What is wrong with my baby? I swear there is no way I can take care of this baby. He's not normal. He's not right. He's so ugly. No one will come see my baby. No one will love my baby. There's been a mistake. A terrible fucking mistake. He's SO UGLY. So ugly. He's so U-G-L-Y!!!!!!!!!!!!! God, what will I do? Please someone take him away from me. I wish I could do this over. I wish I had another life. I'm so embarrassed. I'm so tired. There's something really wrong with me. No one will help me. I need help. Take him away.

Brandon was sitting beside her in his infant carrier. She turned to him while I read, reaching her hand out to touch his. He smiled. He always smiled his precious smile.

I continued to read her words of panic and despair that colored those early, dark weeks after his birth. After reading a few pages, I lowered her journal and watched her with Brandon. Sweet Brandon.

"He's a good boy," she said, guilt ridden and always the good girl. "You know, it's funny, Karen. I looked over some of what I had written this morning, before I came here, wondering if I should show it to you. And you know what? It was strange, but while I was reading, it was like confusing, almost as if I didn't know who I was writing about—was it Chris or Brandon? Know what I mean?"

I knew what she meant. How do we make room for more hard work ahead of us if our head is already so crowded with layers and layers of unresolved grief? Quite simply, she needed permission to grieve the loss of her perfect brother before she could fathom the notion of moving forward with her son.

The work that followed in therapy centered on Chris, not Brandon. This not only made sense to Melissa, but it also came as a welcome relief. She often interrupted the seriousness of the work with her playful distractions: "I had no idea I felt so bad while I was busy being so perfect!" As her attachment to

Brandon evolved into one of splendor and comfort, she never stopped trying to understand what it all meant.

"Maybe I'm supposed to do this again."

"What do you mean, Melissa? Do what again?"

Maybe I'm supposed to learn how to love again. Only this time, I can do it differently. I can do it better. Maybe I was blessed with Brandon so that I could do this again. So I could learn that it's okay to have negative feelings. That *I'm okay* if I have negative feelings. That the world won't crash down around me if I admit that I don't feel good about something. Maybe Brandon was given to me because I am, in fact, the best person to be his mother. Because I know how to do this now. Because Chris taught me. I don't have to do it the way my mother did it. Maybe it worked for her, but that's not the way I want to do it. I'm not weak if I admit this is hard for me sometimes. Good mothers can have bad days. And as long as I leave room for those days that don't feel so good and let myself feel that way without feeling guilty or beating myself up, maybe, just maybe, I can do this really well.

She leaned in toward Brandon and tickled him with gentle stroking. "What a lucky little boy you are to have me as your mommy!" They giggled simultaneously. I absolutely loved watching her with him. She had come so far and worked so hard to get there. I admired her ongoing interest in finding meaning to her life and her ability to express it so eloquently.

Melissa possessed many of the characteristics associated with resilience: humor, insight, ability to transform traumatic events into something positive, and, perhaps most appealing to me personally and professionally, her ability to trust the therapeutic relationship. When healing takes place in the therapeutic setting, it takes place for both of us.

I looked at Melissa and then at Brandon. I watched him wiggle with joy, his eyes fixated on his loving mother. She smiled at him, then at me. "He's perfect, isn't he?"

"Yes, Melissa. I believe he is."

CHAPTER 22

Breastfeeding to Death

Several years into my clinical practice, I was compelled to write an editorial on breastfeeding to help empower others to make informed decisions that might potentially alter the course of their recovery. It was never meant to be contentious, but, as it turns out, the piece stirred up much more controversy than I anticipated. Emotions run high regarding this topic, and the article evoked opinionated responses from avid breastfeeding supporters as well as those seeking permission to bottle-feed as an alternative to breastfeeding. I was surprised to discover it also angered a subset of women who never wanted to breastfeed and felt I was prejudging their decision to bottle-feed. It seemed that whatever my motivation, the article touched many of the already frayed nerves of women with very strong opinions on the subject. "Is Breast Always Best?" was my effort to reconcile my strong belief that breastfeeding was, indeed, one of my greatest pleasures in life, and yet, for *some* women, under *some* circumstances, it can mean a totally different thing.

We are all familiar with the pressure. *Breast is best.* The American Academy of Pediatrics has been sending this message to women for years. The first line of their breastfeeding initiative on their Web site is: "From its inception, the American Academy of Pediatrics has been a staunch advocate of breastfeeding as the optimal form of nutrition for infants" (2008). I have no doubt that this is true. Nor do I doubt that breastfeeding is associated with strengthening the immune system, nutritional and economic gains, and protection from diseases and allergies, while benefiting mom at the same time. The American Academy of Pediatrics recommends that women breastfeed for the baby's first year. At best, this message promotes the rewarding relationship between the two and facilitates a healthy start for the new baby. At worst, it can impose unbearable guilt on a mother who is already struggling to breathe.

I first met Lindsay at a talk I was giving to new mothers. It was at a monthly meeting sponsored by a local breastfeeding support group. She was one of a number of women who blended into the background of enthusiastic new mothers, eager for information and support during this time of transition. Over 1 year later, Lindsay called my office:

"You probably don't remember me. I came to hear you speak at a breast-feeding support group last year. I'm calling because I'm 3 months pregnant again and would love to come in for a consultation because I had postpartum depression after my first child."

Lindsay had a therapist and a psychiatrist who had treated her previously, and she intended to contact them when she was further along in her pregnancy. For now, she hoped to schedule one meeting with me, to strategize and help her feel better prepared for the upcoming postpartum period. Then, she would follow up with her previous therapist.

When we met, she reported that her pregnancy had been uneventful, and she felt good both physically and emotionally. She continued to work on her advertising career as well as spend as much time as possible at home with her sweet son. Her previous postpartum depression had been treated successfully with medication, so we discussed the option of starting the same medication when she delivered. She said she was planning to breastfeed, so she needed information on that.

There's no easy answer for this dilemma of medicating while breastfeeding. Many women do it. Many women choose not to. The best thing we can do as clinicians is to stay on top of the ever-changing research, read as much as we can on the subject, and make certain our clients have current, impartial information on which they can base their decisions. Our clients need to be informed, and they need to make their own decisions.

But that's where the problem lies.

Women who are depressed are not always in the best position to make a decision. After all, difficulty in concentrating is one of the hallmark symptoms of postpartum depression. How, then, can we expect a woman to come to a clear decision if she is not thinking clearly?

As Lindsay continued to speak, I could hear how important breastfeeding was to her. As with many women, it was more than a way to feed her baby. It provided a mutually gratifying liaison that felt, quite honestly, necessary to her. It was way up on top of her list of things to do after she had this baby. She said she was comfortable taking the antidepressant while nursing and that this was what she had done the last time. *Good.* We both felt comfortable with this plan. She said she loved her therapist and she felt comfortable with her psychiatrist. She reported that her marriage was strong; work was fulfilling. Lindsay was a passionate, creative, and energetic woman who was looking forward to a fairly smooth postpartum period. She felt confident that she had taken the steps toward making a plan, and everything felt in position to proceed with cautious optimism. When she left my office, she told me she'd call and let me know when her baby was born.

I can still bring to mind her next phone call to me. I remember how difficult it was for me to tell who it was on the phone. Her voice was not familiar. She was panicking and frantic and wanted me to call. She didn't leave her number; she just said, "Karen, call me; it's Lindsay. I feel terrible. I need your help." *Lindsay?* I wondered for a minute and struggled to recollect the voice. I went through my appointment book, back through months of names, until I found Lindsay's number. It had been months since our only meeting. I wondered why she was calling me, rather than her therapist. I called her back.

"Karen, it's awful. I've never felt like this. It's much worse. I don't know what to do."

Are you seeing your therapist? Did you call your psychiatrist? Are you on medication? Is someone home with you now? The questions poured out, as Lindsay desperately told me that, yes, she had been taking a low dose of the antidepressant for some time now, but things were getting worse. I remained calm for the most part, as I sought to guide her to safety. However, every once in a while, the panic pierced the boundary between her and me, and it suffocated me. We're not always sure why certain people or certain feelings affect us the way they do. We are taught there may be a number of countertransference interpretations. I think that sometimes it's just a simple exchange of energy when two people occupy the same space in time. It's another universe thing that defies any explanation that I develop. It doesn't happen very often. When it does, something profound and indescribable takes place.

I told her she needed to call her psychiatrist now.

"I can't," she gasped.

"Why not?" I snapped back.

"Because. Because, he'll want me to increase my medication."

"Sweetheart, you must call him. You can't just continue to feel this way. If you need to increase your meds, then you need to increase your meds. You'll feel better. Trust your doctor. Call him."

"I can't. I'm breastfeeding. I don't want my baby to get all of that medication. I have to breastfeed. I have to breastfeed," she sobbed.

"Lindsay, your baby will be okay. You can breastfeed. Call your doctor. Call your husband. If you can't, then give me the number so I can call your husband and let him know you need him."

Lindsay agreed to call me back after she heard from her doctor. She also promised me she would call her husband and ask her neighbor to come sit with her. Since I wasn't treating her, I felt helplessly out of the loop and secretly hoped that everything would be okay. She did leave me a message later that day, telling me that her doctor did want her to increase the antidepressant, and he was able to see her the following day for an appointment. *Good. That's a relief.* So I went back to the business at hand and presumed everything was all right.

Two weeks later I received another phone call. It was from a police officer who called to inform me that Lindsay had been missing for a couple of days and had been found the day before in her car, 2 miles from her home, with a fatal gunshot wound to her head. They found a note to her loving husband and her sweet children, telling them that she couldn't live like this and that they would be able to live a good life without her. The officer had found my business card in her wallet, so they wanted me to know.

I was stunned and sickened. There was too much sadness at that moment to sort out what I was feeling, but I knew, in my heart, that Lindsay made a choice between breastfeeding and taking more of the medication that would have likely saved her life. She was undermedicated. Her symptoms broke through and did not respond to the low dose she was taking. In her depressive mindset, she could simply not reconcile increasing the medication while she was breastfeeding. What made sense to her when she was healthy was incomprehensible in her depressed state. That was the decisive moment when I knew that this conflicting issue needed to be addressed and women needed a new message.

Because of Lindsay's untimely death, one thing has changed for me. I have no ambivalence and zero tolerance for this issue. If a woman with postpartum depression is breastfeeding and experiences severe symptoms, such as suicidal thoughts, that necessitate immediate treatment with medication, she has two choices.

She can take the medication and breastfeed, or she can take the medication and not breastfeed. Not taking the medication is not an option.

And so I repeat the message I expounded on in my editorial:

What should the message to women be? *It's okay not to breastfeed.*
 It's that simple.

 It doesn't matter who we are in relation to this woman. We might be her friend or her counselor. We might be her sister or her doctor. If this woman is suffering with postpartum depression and breastfeeding, we might have to help her through this process by explaining her options, by telling her there are medications that are compatible with breastfeeding, or by giving her permission to stop. That option doesn't feel good to a depressed mother. It feels like someone is yanking the anchor from the very last thing that is keeping her afloat. It feels terrifying and incapacitating. It feels absolutely impossible and nothing short of catastrophic.

 This is because breastfeeding, to the depressed mother, is more than breastfeeding. It is a lifeline. It's as if it provides the single opportunity for her to feel that her presence is making a difference. This is why we need to help her navigate the rough waters and make the right decision, particularly if she needs medication. It may be to continue breastfeeding. It may be to stop. Either way, she may not be able to make this decision without the clarity of an outside perspective.

This process is complicated and raises important questions:

Does she need medication?

How does she feel about taking medication while breastfeeding?

Is it possible that breastfeeding may somehow contribute to her feelings of despair?

Is breastfeeding depleting her of her strength and energy, thereby worsening her illness?

Is her insistence on breastfeeding interfering with her treatment?

Does she have proper guidance to wean sufficiently so as not to aggravate the delicate hormonal balance?

Does she have enough information and support to discontinue the breastfeeding relationship, should it come to that?

These are considerations that I daresay have been largely ignored by breastfeeding organizations and the medical community. Frankly, I'm afraid for the women who continue to work so hard, with painstaking determination against such formidable odds, to stay on track, to prove something to someone, to breastfeed at all costs. I'm not sure what they are trying to prove, exactly. Perhaps they strive to meet their own self-driven, impassioned expectations. To follow the rules they've always believed in. To do it right. To be the best mother they can be.

It's time we let them off the hook. So they can rest easy. So they can learn that good mothers, indeed, have lots of choices. So they can get the treatment they need.

So they can get better.

CHAPTER 23

Countertransference

When Is Yours Mine?

Meeting Monica and Bobby was hard from the start. I knew from her phone message that they had lost their dear son after 9 months' gestation, during delivery. No matter how much experience we gather and how many years we refine our craft, it never gets any easier, hearing one very sad story after another.

"He was perfect." She sat close to her husband in my office and shook her head in disbelief. "Perfect. He was 8½ pounds of solid boy." Monica tried to stop herself from crying while she reached for her husband's hand.

The three of us sat together waiting for the details of the story to unfold. Planned, uneventful pregnancy other than a late delivery, 2 weeks post-term. No history of miscarriages or difficulties related to reproduction. Married for 3 years, both eager to start a family and anticipated no problems. Monica was referred to me by her obstetrician who was worried about Monica's "prolonged grief," suggesting that she should be "over it by now; after all, it's been 5 months." Monica did have a history of depression, so she agreed that it could be helpful to find a safe place to talk about her huge loss.

"It's hard to talk about this to anyone. My family is also suffering, so, honestly, I don't want them to feel bad about how bad I'm feeling. My friends have their own problems and don't need to hear about mine. Besides, many of them have a new baby, which isn't a place I want to be right now.

"I don't know what happened," she continued. "No one has given us an explanation that makes any sense. All I know is … that … I don't know … it's not supposed to happen like this. One minute I was pregnant with a big healthy boy and the next minute they tell me he's dead. When they put him in my arms, he didn't look dead. He looked perfect."

She cradled her arms and gazed into the emptiness. In a flash, I could see her baby there, in her mind and in mine, plump and perfect as she had described him. Unexpectedly, I was overcome with a feeling that brought me way too close to home, and, for an instant, I was transported back to the birth of my son, 16 years earlier.

My pregnancy was also uneventful. I loved being pregnant, and the bigger I got, the better I felt. When my due date came and went, no one was particularly concerned other than eager relatives who called for hourly updates. After 3 weeks past the due date (hard to believe this was so long ago that it was before doctors were doing routine ultrasounds) and a failing placenta, a C-section was the only way my baby was going to come out. We packed, we prepped, and we let the doctors do their thing, given that nature's course had stalled.

Though memories of the moments after delivery are vague as my aging brain rummages through the past 24 years, I remember the hurried response and the flurry of scrub-clad, nameless figures around me. My baby was whisked away to an undisclosed, *oh-my-god-what's-wrong-with-my-baby* location as my belly was meticulously stitched closed. After what seemed like forever due to either my altered, medicated state or my panic—I'm not sure which—my baby boy was brought to me, swaddled neatly and capped with the sweet striped infant hat that today is packed away in a box of things with which I simply cannot part. He embodied perfection to me, apart from his misshapen head that resulted from being overcooked and pelvis-squeezed for too long. I would later learn that the critical moments just before he was perfect were, in fact, life threatening. When they wiggled his big head out of my tiny incision they saw he wasn't breathing. His Apgar score was 2 at 1 minute. Scores below 3 are generally regarded as critically low and above 7 as generally normal. To this day I don't know which specific criteria he fell short on, but I do know that when the test was repeated at 5 minutes, his score was 8. All was well.

But for an instant, he wasn't breathing. He had aspirated on meconium, a risk to postmature babies and, thanks to split-second intervention, had an endotracheal tube down his little throat to suction his mouth and airway. Before I knew what was happening, he had been intubated, observed closely, cleaned off, and, literally within minutes, returned to my swollen chest, which was yearning for the warmth of my newborn baby. He was, as Monica had just described her baby boy, perfect.

In addition to aspiration, another risk of postmaturity is intrauterine fetal demise or stillbirth.

The ache I felt in my chest as Monica recounted the events of that heart-rending evening at the hospital was too deep and too personal to ignore. I took in a full slow breath as Monica pulled out a picture of her son and said, "Can I show you a picture of Mathew?"

"Of course," I said, digging deep for the most soothing and tender voice possible.

The moment of silence while she glanced at for her one enduring keepsake of his precious self seemed eternal. The room felt still and empty. Then, the emptiness started to throb, as if in sync with my rushing heartbeat. What would I see? How would he look? Could I separate this from my own experience? Would I be able to stop thinking of my son? Would I be able to hide what I was feeling? Could I remain neutral in my response?

Bobby bent forward to grab a peek at the photo before she handed it to me. I leaned toward her, accepting the picture as a delicate gift she was sharing, as if she were handing me a sacred piece of herself. I looked at Mathew. He was just as she had described him, big and gorgeous. His eyes were closed. He looked peaceful and, as we so often hear, as if he were sleeping. I remember being bothered by my quiet thought that she was right, he didn't look dead. The dull pain in my heart grew sharper as images of my own son's birth flooded into my vision. I could almost feel my objectivity vanishing.

"I'm so sorry." I looked at Bobby and Monica. "It's so awful, sweet Mathew, he's so beautiful." Another moment, in therapy as in life, when the right words are nowhere to be found.

Her eyes filled with tears as she said, "I miss him so much." Her sobs became heavy with unimaginable grief.

My instincts led me to sit quietly after saying, "I know you do."

One of my students asked me whether, when the pain is that excruciating, it is ever okay to go over and sit with her or hug her. From time to time it is okay, but, generally, it's better not to. I say this because without knowing the particular client, her degree of healthiness, the severity of her symptoms, the strength of her personal boundaries, what she needs, and what the therapeutic relationship means to her at that moment in time, it's hard to know what impact that level of intimacy might have on her. Clinicians should trust their instincts but then still wait. Sit with it. Think about it. Then decide what to do.

When the pain is that great, and that palpable, two things are certain: (1) She needs to express it, and (2) she needs to know we can tolerate it. The space we create between the client and ourselves during such time of incredible emotion is as important as our desire and ability to comfort her. Bear in mind that a loved one who responds to her weeping might hold her and console her in the hopes of helping her control the pain to some extent and perhaps cry less. Loved ones unite against the unbearable pain, hoping to lessen it, even if only slightly. *If you stop crying you won't be in so much pain,* they might think.

Our job, on the other hand, is to let her know that no matter how bad she feels, how hard she cries, and how much it hurts, it's okay. The message is that she has permission to express the inexpressible and that it will not unnerve us and we will not try to inhibit the process. To the contrary, although we, too, want to be consoling in our response, the difference is that we want her to stay in that painful space for a bit longer than she might like so she can say the things she needs to say and feel the things she needs to feel in order to get some relief and make room for healing.

I am not saying a hug is always inappropriate. I am saying that sometimes, with some women, a hug can be misinterpreted as *I'm here for you, but I'd feel better if you'd stop crying,* and that's the last message we want her to get. Moreover, it can violate an important boundary, one of personal space. Clinicians need to be mindful of their own emotional response and perhaps reassess whether giving her a hug would be the best thing to do at that moment. Timing is crucial. At another moment, such as when she's leaving the session, I do believe a hug not only is an appropriate gesture of comfort but can also provide closure on a difficult session that tells her all is okay; she is safe here.

I confess that the feeling I struggled with while listening to Monica and Bobby explore their sadness was one of tremendous guilt. I thought about our similar tales of pregnancy and post-term deliveries and, still, any way I looked at it, my baby lived and their baby died. Any time a strong emotional response invades the therapeutic setting, we have the ingredients of countertransference material that can be (1) useful to the session, (2) harmful to the session, or (3) incompatible with the work we are doing. In this case, it had honestly never occurred to me that my son had been so close to death until I sat alongside their anguish.

Freud introduced the concepts of transference and countertransference within the therapeutic relationship as labels for the irrational, stereotypical, and patterned responses that are inappropriately transferred between the client and the therapist (Alexander & Ross, 1952). Just as we expect some clients to project some of their emotional responses into our relationship, we must also be prepared for the possibility that this intimate work with new mothers will provoke strong emotional responses of our own.

Using a broader definition than originally conceived, countertransference has evolved over the years to apply to any emotional reactivity on the part of the therapist, not just the inappropriate ones. The construct applies to both positive and negative experiences, which are more often than not currently seen as tools for deepening our understanding of the therapeutic experience. When countertransference problems arise, though not surprising to us, they should be attended to and dealt with as they emerge. Honest introspection and ongoing supervision can safeguard against potential intrusions into the therapy (Alexander & Ross, 1952). This may seem obvious to many, but the slope is slippery, and the scrutiny of emotional truthfulness cannot be emphasized enough.

When we are moved beyond words and overflowing with emotional resonance, it can be one of the most authentic moments of our work. If mindful, the degree to which we allow ourselves to experience these emotions, understand them, and use them in our work enables us to move through the process with finesse and proficiency. It can inspire therapeutic action that makes sessions richer and more meaningful for both the clinician and the client.

Monica and Bobby observed my sadness on a number of occasions during our work together. They later told me it was a part of what made it so meaningful for them. I was constantly moved by how poignantly Monica expressed her grief and the shattering of every one of her fantasies. She would describe hearing her baby cry or phantom movements in her belly. She often dreamt that Mathew was alive and recalled vivid tales of things they did together in the middle of her deep sleep. Early in our work these dreams were hard for her to talk about; later they became a source of comfort to her.

The death of a child must be the most difficult to mourn.

My own sadness needed to be understood within this context and saved for future sessions without their ever hearing a word about my son's birth. We must remember that we are there for our clients and for our clients only. They are entitled to every fragment of our attention. When it wanders off course, we are obliged to regroup, focus, and cast aside our temporary diversion for later inspection. We do that on our own time with our own supervisor or therapist.

That moment in time, locked within their nightmarish sorrow and the awareness of my own blessing, stays with me today as a reminder of how to get in and get out of the vortex of pain. We can step inside only so far. Then we stay, we empathize, and we leave. It was a single bittersweet moment that unveiled life's cruelest sorrow and its utmost gratitude.

CHAPTER 24

Sleeplessness

I met a woman in line at the grocery store who was frantically trying to juggle her few-month-old in one arm and her way too many items for the express lane in the other.

"Can I help you there?"

"Oh thanks," she grimaced as she shifted her baby from one hip to the other. "Everything's so hard right now, you know."

"I know," I said, not meaning to sound as patronizing as I suspect I did.

"Who would have thought?" She continued to speak as if under her breath to herself. "I can't even do the simplest things anymore, like run to the grocery store, without it being such a huge deal, you know? I'm just so tired all the time. I don't think I've slept for weeks!"

I smiled politely and thought to myself how much she sounded like a public service announcement for postpartum depression, but thought twice about doing therapy in the checkout line.

New mothers are tired. There aren't many guarantees in this business, but that's one of them. New mothers do not get enough sleep. It's irrefutable and universal. To further obscure the picture, sleep problems cross over between cause and effect variables with respect to postpartum depression, and we cannot always speak to the direction of causality. That is, sleep disturbances can contribute to the development of postpartum depression, and they can be a symptom of postpartum depression. Either way, they require our immediate attention. Sleep deprivation and its role in postpartum depression are of utmost importance, particularly for women with a history of bipolar disorder, because insomnia can potentially induce mania, depression, or psychosis (Chaudron, 2003).

The interaction between sleep and perinatal mood disorders is significant. Starting in early pregnancy, hormonal fluctuations can interfere with sleep (Ross, Murray, & Steiner, 2005). The growing fetus can make it difficult to sleep and uncomfortable later in pregnancy, and care of a newborn typically involves numerous nighttime awakenings. These changes in sleep patterns and the associated fatigue can affect a woman's physical and mental well-being, her relationships, and her ability to adjust to the new role of mother.

During the postpartum period, one important consideration is how the baby is sleeping and what impact this is having on the mother. It stands to reason that it would be difficult to determine which caused which, but what is clear is that infant sleep disturbances and maternal sleep disturbances are related. Research shows that depressed mothers are more likely to perceive their infants' sleep patterns as problematic than nondepressed mothers (Hiscock & Wake, 2001). The researchers speculate that this could be due to the fact that depressed women are likely to suffer from impaired sleep and therefore are prone to be more awake and aware of their infants' night awakenings. Additionally, the authors consider the possibility that infants of depressed mothers may be harder to settle or more likely to waken during the night. In a randomized controlled trial, they further discovered that a simple behavioral intervention—controlled crying (France, Henderson, & Hudson, 1996)—was shown to be effective in reducing the infant's sleep problems and symptoms of depression in mothers (Hiscock & Wake, 2002).

"I just need to get some sleep," a postpartum woman may report. "Everything will be fine, if I just get some sleep."

This may very well be true. Or, it may be the last thing she says before she takes a handful of sleeping pills.

As most new mothers can attest, going too long with too little sleep can quickly turn things from bad to worse. Once a cycle of insomnia sets in and women report that they are unable to sleep even when the baby is sleeping, we have relevant diagnostic information. If a woman reports being exhausted but is able to sleep when her baby is sleeping, this is good. She may not be getting as much sleep as she'd like, and surely she is weary beyond words, but this is a different clinical presentation from the mother who reports that her baby sleeps better than she does.

Consider these two responses to the question: "Are you able to sleep when your baby sleeps?"

"Are you kidding? That's all I do when he sleeps. Crib side goes up and I'm half asleep by the time my head hits the pillow!"
"I wish I could. I lie in bed with thoughts racing around in my head, thinking what I'm doing tomorrow, wondering why I did what I did today, all the time thinking, 'I wish I could sleep.'"

Maternal sleep deprivation has proven to be an important predictive variable when studying postpartum depression. One longitudinal study that examined the relationships among infant sleep patterns, maternal fatigue, and the development of postpartum depression suggested that infant sleep patterns and maternal fatigue are strongly associated with the onset of new depressive symptoms in the postpartum period (Dennis & Ross, 2005). It further revealed that sleep patterns of the infant and the mother were associated with scores on the Edinburgh indicating that major depression was probable. The study revealed that self-reported fatigue, defined as fewer than 6 hours within a 24-hour time frame, and frequent infant crying were found to be significant variables that corresponded with EPDS scores greater than 12.

When one asks any new mother, depressed or nondepressed, how much sleep she is getting, she may respond with any number of insufficient answers:

"Not enough"

"I haven't slept at all in a month!"

"Are you serious? I never sleep at all anymore."

"I don't think I'll ever sleep again."

A new mother with depression, however, may be less likely to see the humor in this question and is more likely to respond with a more somber haziness, such as, "I don't know" or "I'm too tired to think straight." The space between wakefulness and the so-desired, but unattainable promise of sleep feels insurmountable. When she says, "I'm so tired," you can practically feel it. It's no longer just about sleep. It's about her body betraying her. It's about defeat, and it's about the shutdown of her system.

In the clinical setting, it's important that we get a clear sense of how much sleep she is actually getting. As we've seen, asking general questions will elicit unsatisfactory answers. Clinicians need to be specific:

- How many hours of sleep do you think you are getting?
- Tell me about a typical night's sleep. When do you go to bed? How many times do you awaken? Why do you awaken (baby? restlessness? panic?)?
- How much sleep were you used to getting before you had the baby?
- How much sleep do you think you need to function at your best?
- Do you have a history of any sleep problems before the baby?
- How did you sleep during your pregnancy? What factors contributed to that?
- Do you feel you could sleep if your baby were sleeping better?

Many postpartum women want to believe that sleep is the definitive answer. It appears that this would simplify things for them by normalizing the way they are feeling: *I'm not sick; I'm just tired.* However, it's important to keep in mind that most postpartum women who present with sleep impairment are, more times than not, not just having sleep problems, even if that is the only one they identify. Most postpartum women who cannot sleep when their babies sleep are also suffering from symptoms of depression and anxiety that contribute to their sleep disturbance. With acute anxiety, sleep can become the object of their obsession: *What if I don't sleep again tonight? I can't go one more night without sleep. How will I function with no sleep? How can my husband sleep through the night like this? If I go another night without sleeping, I know I'll really go crazy.* When the depression is treated, the sleep generally improves.

EVALUATE THE NATURE OF HER SLEEP DISTURBANCE

Case 1

Katherine came in 7 days after her baby was born. Her primary complaint was that she was tired, and the fatigue got in the way of almost everything she was doing. She told me she was used to sleeping 8 or 9 hours a night and would "never get used to this." She was scared she would never sleep again.

She told me she fell asleep around 10:30 p.m., then awoke with the baby around midnight and again at 3:00 in the morning. At 6:00 a.m., she would get up with her husband because "I'm up anyway" and would try to fall back to sleep after he left for work, but the baby would awaken around that time. I figured that she was getting about 6 hours of very broken sleep and, indeed, she must be tired.

"Katherine, if someone were to come in and help you through the night with the baby, would you be able to sleep?"

"Oh, in a heartbeat. Got someone in mind? You volunteering?"

This intermittent sleep pattern occurring within the first couple of postpartum weeks falls within our expected parameters and does not signal anything out of the ordinary. As long as she is sleeping, eating well, and generally feeling like herself, it is likely that she is experiencing a blues-related, baby-generated phenomenon that may not impress us clinically but nonetheless is quite disconcerting to the new mother. After our complete history, which further reinforced the initial assessment that there were no other contributing factors, we determined that we would need to fortify her support system in order to facilitate better sleeping patterns and less disruption.

After reviewing the fact that her history of depression, although noteworthy, was uncomplicated and straightforward, we discussed the details. We talked about who she could call, who was available to help out, how uncomfortable she was thinking about asking others for help, how she could reprioritize things so she could put getting rest on the top of her list of things to do, and whether she and her husband would have to readjust things so he could be helping her more.

During these early postpartum days and weeks, when so much depends on a couple's ability to adapt and settle into the demands of new babyhood, sleepless nights affect both the mom and dad. Often, the best role we can assume during these early weeks is to help give them permission to do it differently, in a manner that helps both feel supported.

Case 2

Lori said she hadn't slept well during her pregnancy and even before that:

> I've just been so uncomfortable. The whole pregnancy I've felt awful, not at all like myself. Sometimes I wonder why I got pregnant; I hate to say that, but it's true. Things were so much better before I got pregnant. That's what started this whole thing; that's when my head started doing somersaults in and out of this dark abyss that continues to swallow me up now. I get sucked into this claustrophobic hole, and it feels like I'll never get out. It's dark and lonely and scary. I can't sleep anymore. All I can do is think about how bad I feel. When I do finally sleep for a bit, the first thing I think about when I awake is how I am feeling. Is this going to be a good day, a bad day, or a day from hell? Sometimes I'm even afraid to go to sleep 'cause I'm so tired of not being able to sleep, if that makes any sense. It's like I don't want to lie there obsessing about it, so I'd rather stay up and get things done. But I don't think I can keep this up much longer. I can't function like this. I've completely lost my appetite. I have no desire to see any of my friends who are calling, and all I want to do is sleep.

She closed her eyes and made a comment I have heard a hundred times: "If I could just sleep here for an hour, it would be worth the money."

She sat with her eyes closed, soaking up the brief reprieve. We talked further about her symptoms of anxiety and depression that were complicating her sleep patterns. She was open to our discussion about how medication might help break her cycle of anxious thinking and make sleep more accessible. That sounded good to her.

When considering the nature of the sleep disruption, as with other postpartum symptoms, it's important to bear in mind the context:

- At what postpartum stage is she?
- How unusual is this pattern of sleep for her?
- Is she able to sleep when her baby is sleeping?
- What other symptoms of depression or anxiety is she exhibiting?
- What kind of support is she getting or not getting?
- What is the nature of the sleep disturbance? For example, is there an obsessive quality attached to it? Has it taken on features of insomnia leading to night after night of continuous impairment?
- Are work schedules or feeding issues contributing to the problem?
- How is this impacting her relationship?
- How does she describe the sleep disruption as it affects her partner?

In a study of sleeping patterns in new parents (Gay, Lee, & Lee, 2004), it was reported that fathers also experience sleep changes similar to those of mothers in the postpartum period. The researchers used a measure referred to as *wake after sleep onset* (WASO). Defined as an estimate of fragmented sleep, WASO is reported as the percentage of minutes awake divided by minutes in bed after falling asleep. Interestingly, fathers slept less on the whole than the mothers. They further pointed out that despite the fact that the mothers were sleeping more than the fathers, it did not necessarily follow that the mothers were less sleep deprived than their partners. Pregnant and postpartum women, particularly if they are breastfeeding, likely have greater sleep needs, as well as nutritional needs, than fathers. Furthermore, and no surprise to most of us working with this population, postpartum mothers experienced more WASO than their partners. But new fathers were found to have less total sleep than their partners, though they reported similar or better sleep quality; speculation was that perhaps they had a higher degree of sleep continuity. Regardless of objective measures, both parents did report comparable degrees of postpartum fatigue, consistent with the study by Elek, Hudson, and Fleck (1997), which documented the similarity of mothers' and fathers' reports of sleep and fatigue during both the pregnancy and postpartum periods.

INTERVENTION

Many of the major neurotransmitter systems associated with the regulation of sleep are also responsible for other functions in the brain, including those associated with psychiatric disorders (Ross, Murray, & Steiner, 2005). Women often state what we know to be an association between sleep loss and cognitive impairment: "I'm so tired I can't think." Though it may be overstating the obvious, it bears repeating that improvements in the baby's sleep patterns are associated with improvements in maternal depression (Hiscock & Wake, 2002). It follows, therefore, that clinicians should pay particular attention to the sleep patterns of the mother and the baby and determine how both may be impacting the depression.

Intervention designed to reduce sleep deprivation is imperative in our early assessment. In some cases, treating the disturbance with medication can break the self-perpetuating cycle. This is particularly appropriate if the sleeplessness presents as a middle of the night disruption, referred to as early morning wakening, since this type of insomnia is a hallmark symptom of depression. In contrast, initial insomnia, characterized by difficulty falling asleep, is often associated with anxious thoughts and ruminations that interfere with the body's ability to unwind and prepare for sleep. Postpartum women frequently describe both variations.

In addition to the actual reduction in number of hours slept, clinicians need to consider other factors. The impact of sleep loss may also depend on a woman's sensitivity to such sleep deficit as well as her ability to adapt both physically and mentally to the fragmented sleep. Some women are more affected by this than others or may be better able to compensate. And there are times when it is more than just the sleep difficulty. Loss of sleep may be complicated by an inability to prioritize or set limits, or it may be a result of a new mother's feeling overwhelmed and unable to differentiate the multiple tasks by which she feels confronted. Or, it can result from a woman's resistance to taking care of herself or her hypervigilance and inability to let go. Whatever the intricacy of factors involved, we should proceed with the notion that mothers in their offices will be tired; our job is to help them sort out the contributing factors so that we can intervene appropriately.

Sleep Tips for New Mothers and Fathers

Take a hot bath about 1–2 hours before bedtime.

Do something relaxing in the 30 minutes before bedtime, such as reading, meditating, or taking a leisurely walk.

Try not to look at the clock. Obsessing over what time it is will increase anxiety.

A light snack before bedtime can aid sleep efforts, particularly turkey or milk, which contain tryptophan, an amino acid related to serotonin, which is the brain chemical that helps regulate sleep.

Avoid fluids just before bedtime.

Avoid caffeine and alcohol.

Don't stay in bed for longer than 20 minutes if you can't sleep. Try to avoid watching TV; it can be too stimulating.

Exercise may be one of the best ways to promote healthy sleep.

Create an environment for sleep: playing soft music, providing gentle light, wearing comfortable clothes.

Listen to a tape that helps visualize sleep.

Yoga, meditation, deep-breathing techniques, and relaxation exercises all help with sleep.

CHAPTER 25

The Married State

Six months after her baby was born and one month into treatment, Stacy reported she was tired of having to ask Michael for everything she wanted. "We've been married 6 years; you'd think he'd know by now."

"Know what?" I asked for clarification.

"You'd think he'd know what I need when I feel this way."

"Why do you think he should know?"

"Because we've been through this before. He's seen me this sick. He knows the medication makes me tired. He knows I can't do everything around the house without his help. He knows I'm so worn out I can hardly stand up, and all I hear is that he's tired, too. Great. Now we're both so miserable I don't know how we're going to get out of it. We don't mean to yell at each other, but he's not listening to me, and I'm so damn tired of hearing how hard he works, when *he* gets to get out of the house and talk to grown-ups! He should try staying home with the two kids and then tell me how tired he is."

"Stacy, when was the last time the two of you sat down, with no distractions, no children, no dogs, no TV, and talked about how you were each feeling and what you need from each other?"

"I really don't know, to be honest with you." She rolled her eyes, shook her head, and smirked, as if to say it wasn't going to happen or it wouldn't make a difference, anyway.

"Look, Karen, he's always been like this; you know that. He just wants me to get better already so his life can get back to the way it was. He's used to me being in control, so now when he comes home to a jungle and everything is all over the place, he goes nuts. That's just the way it is. Always has been. Always will be."

Postpartum depression is hard on a marriage.

This is the primary reason that treatment for postpartum depression should not be limited to the mother. With a family focus, we are in a better position to monitor the relationships and ensure optimal functioning. We need to observe the family closely to ascertain whether these relationships are being adversely affected by the strain of the depression or whether they may be exacerbating areas of vulnerability. Even when husbands are not directly involved in the treatment, they should remain in the forefront of much of our work.

The quality and stability of a woman's relationship with her partner have been associated with the severity and prognosis of her postpartum depression. As a preview of the extensive research on the impact of postpartum depression on the couple, I have summarized some of the highlights relevant to clinical practice:

- Lack of social support is strongly associated with postpartum depression in women (O'Hara, 1986).
- Social support is a protective factor for childbearing women. Emotional and practical support is associated with optimal maternal mental health (Cutrona & Troutman, 1986; Gjerdingen, Froberg, & Fontaine, 1991).
- Husbands are more likely to turn to their spouses for emotional support (Cronenwett & Kunst-Wilson, 1981), so if their spouse has postpartum depression, this resource is greatly diminished. Women tend to access additional outlets for support, such as friends and other family members.
- Because husbands of women with postpartum depression report greater dissatisfaction in their marriage and feel more limited regarding parenthood (Zelkowitz & Milet, 1997), there is potential for them to distance themselves from both mother and infant.
- When a woman has postpartum depression, her feelings not only influence her perception of the baby but also can influence the father's. Research shows a mother's depression can be associated with a father's negative perception of their baby (Ventura & Stevenson, 1986).
- If the husband experiences extra stress at his workplace, he may resent the additional stress resulting from his wife's depression (Zelkowitz & Milet, 1997).
- Women with postpartum depression report inadequate communication with their partners (Paykel, Emms, Fletcher, & Rassaby, 1980).
- Women with postpartum depression feel less able to talk openly about problems with their husbands (O'Hara, 1986).
- Women who reported insufficient practical support during a crisis had a slightly increased (though not statistically significant) risk of postpartum depression. On the other hand, when women reported dissatisfaction with psychological support following a crisis, there

was a significant association with the presence of postpartum depression (Boyce & Hickey, 2005).

- Women with postpartum depression may experience negative feelings toward their husbands, regarding them as unhelpful and unsympathetic (Pitt, 1968).
- When a woman has postpartum depression, both partners report dissatisfaction with the marriage (Zelkowitz & Milet, 1997).

Clearly, we have evidence that the partner is a pivotal figure when studying a mother's depressive state. What is less clear is how we define support and whether the factors that contribute to lack of support have any causal role in the development of postpartum depression. Or, as we often see in clinical settings, does the depression take its toll on the couple and then translate into marital trouble?

CAUSE OR CONSEQUENCE?

What does support mean within this context of depression and marriage? If we ask a postpartum woman directly if her husband is supportive, it becomes clear that this can mean different things to different people:

- *My husband is my best friend.*
- *He's very good with the baby.*
- *He travels a great deal.*
- *He tries to understand, but he really doesn't get it.*
- *He thinks I should just get my act together and stop complaining.*
- *It's hard for me to tell him how bad I'm feeling.*
- *I feel guilty, so I don't ask for help.*
- *If I have to ask him to do something, it's easier for me to just do it myself.*

Most people don't expect a new mother to be overcome with feelings of ambivalence and sadness. It is disarming and confusing for partners, who anticipated a joyful experience, to find themselves unprepared to contend with the weight of an unforeseen depression.

Although the link between a supportive marital relationship and postpartum depression is well known, it is complicated:

- Depression often causes social isolation and withdrawal. Women can recoil from relationships and reject emotional connection. The intimacy can feel too raw, like touching an open wound. This is bound to affect the relationship.
- Many women are exceedingly good at continuing to cope and carry out the tasks of motherhood despite compelling symptoms of depression. Many husbands state they were unaware of the extent to which their wives were suffering.

- Many women report feeling reluctant to ask for help, whether they feel supported or not. Some say they feel guilty asking their husbands to add more to their plate, because they are working and need their sleep. Others tell us they don't think their husbands would understand. Still others presume their husbands would overreact— or worse, dismiss their cries for help.
- Expressing either disappointment or relief, some women claim they are surprised by how their husbands respond to them during the depression. Others say they expected nothing more than what they are getting; it simply reflects the degree of support they were getting prior to having the baby.

Regardless of whether postpartum depression actually causes marital dysfunction or whether a lack of support causes the depression, it is certainly easy to understand that the depression will strain any marriage, whether it is stable or troubled.

FACILITATOR OR SABOTEUR?

There are cases where marriages are stressed by the depression because the relationship itself is weak. There may be limited involvement in the relationship, or perhaps the emotional connection has been absent or impaired for some time. Partners may be unwilling to help each other or offer compassion and support during times of need. This is sad, at best, and when depression descends upon the relationship, it makes things far worse before they get better. In these cases and in cases where domestic violence is part of the picture, additional and immediate intervention is required. Recognizing that there are alternative household arrangements, in this chapter we will focus on relationships where mother and father are living together. Though there are wide ranges of socioeconomic, educational, and occupational backgrounds, the couples I refer to here come for treatment with a mutual desire for recovery from the symptoms and for balance in their relationship.

Husbands are scared. For many, this is the first time they have witnessed their wives in so much pain and so out of control. If it is not the first time, it never gets any easier to endure. They are often caught off guard and may respond with unaccommodating gestures simply because they do not know what else to do. Attention by family and healthcare professionals is predominantly directed to the mother in distress, often underestimating or discounting the degree to which the partner is troubled by her suffering. Husbands too are forced to redefine their social roles. Barclay and Lupton (1999) found that men in Western society are required to simultaneously take on the roles of provider, nurturer, and household helper. Raising additional concerns, additional research shows postpartum fathers are at increased risk for psychiatric illness if they have a depressed spouse (Marks & Lovestone, 1995).

Husbands indeed suffer when their wives are sick. They worry about the well-being of their wives and are concerned about the day-to-day management of life at home. Husbands may manifest their concern in a number of ways:

- They may hope it goes away on its own: *You'll be fine.*
- They may get mad because they don't understand: *Why can't you just take care of things and stop complaining?*
- They may inadvertently push their wives in the wrong direction: *You just need to relax. You'll feel better once you get some sleep.*
- They may make it worse: *I don't see what's so hard about staying home with a baby all day; at least you don't have to go to work!*
- They may think they are supporting but miss the mark: *Honey, you don't need medication. You're strong. You always have been. You can do this; I know you can.*
- They may be the front-line intervention and can see things are wrong before this is apparent to others: *I'm worried about you. I think we should call the doctor.*
- They may postpone intervention: *This is normal, honey. All mothers feel this way.*
- They may save lives: *I don't like the way you are feeling. I'm calling the doctor.*

One of the most effective things clinicians can offer early in treatment is acknowledgment of the couple's shared struggle during this time. Supporting the husband during the early stages can help steer him in the most productive direction. When he has a better understanding of what is going on, his wife will feel more supported. The following excerpt from my book *The Postpartum Husband* (2001) points out the contradiction that often confronts husbands when they try to offer support:

> Her moods and emotional vulnerability will get in the way of good communication for now.
>
> Here's what you're up against:

If you tell her you love her, *she won't believe you.*
If you tell her she's a good mother, *she'll think you're just saying that to make her feel better.*
If you tell her she's beautiful, *she'll assume you're lying.*
If you tell her not to worry about anything, *she'll think you have no idea how bad she feels.*
If you tell her you'll come home early to help her, *she'll feel guilty.*
If you tell her you have to work late, *she'll think you don't care.*

Here's the point: Very loving, compassionate husbands can try their best and still be perceived as unsupportive. Very loving, sympathetic, and encouraging husbands can also get tangled in the web of depressive responses and quickly feel lost, angry, or desperately confused.

Therefore, as clinicians, one of our primary tasks from the outset is to map out this possibility to the couple, to increase their awareness and prepare them for the work ahead. Tackling this on their own can potentially lead them off course.

WHAT DO WE MEAN BY "SUPPORT"?

Whether the woman is engaging in therapy alone or with her husband, this exploration of whether she is receiving and perceiving sufficient support is a critical component of the early sessions. If her partner does not accompany her to the initial sessions, I often request that he join the next session, so we can set the stage for optimal communication and support. If this is not possible for logistical reasons, the offer remains open.

My reasoning for wanting him to join one of the early sessions for a rapid assessment is multifaceted:

- I like him to meet me, so he can see who is "taking care of" his wife and hopefully instill a sense of comfort in this process.
- I like to offer him the opportunity to ask me the many questions he may have. And he will have questions.
- I like to take a peek at the couple's interpersonal dynamics and see how they relate and respond to each other.
- I like to provide information, educational bits, and instructions to both of them, so we all know we are on the same page in terms of her treatment plan.
- If he has any objections to any part of the plan, this is a good time for him to voice them. Acquiring accurate information can help to reduce his anxiety.
- If I note any problem in his understanding and acceptance of what's going on or his ability to communicate effectively with his wife, this may be a good time to address these issues and explore ways of interacting.
- Often they will bring the baby in at the same time. This provides a glance into the family dynamics and how each responds to the baby.

Attendance in sessions should be flexible to meet the changing needs of the family. If a woman's symptoms are severe, the reasons for having her husband attend an early session intensify. His response and interpretation of the situation can act as a barometer for who she was before she got sick and provide a frame of reference in terms of her baseline presentation and behavior. Some couples will elect to come to each session together.

Sometimes, a woman prefers to come to sessions alone. Often, a woman will opt to come alone until her acute symptoms improve, at which time she may feel more equipped to deal with the impact the illness has had on her marriage. As she continues to progress, clinicians might encourage her husband to join some sessions for much-needed attention to the marriage.

In *This Isn't What I Expected* (Kleiman & Raskin, 1994), we refer to support during the postpartum period as either *practical* support or *emotional* support. Practical support refers to childcare tasks, household duties, or help in ways that are defined in terms of "doing." Emotional support refers to the sympathy, empathy, or understanding that is offered during this difficult time. Some men find it easier to do one or the other. One thing is for sure: Clarity here is crucial. Women want their needs taken care of and are almost certain to set their husbands up for failure and themselves up for disappointment unless they take a closer look at what they need and how to express that.

Stacy said she felt guilty asking Michael for help: "He's so tired, too. I don't think he realizes how bad I really feel. I mean, if he did, wouldn't he know what to do? Wouldn't he just do it without me having to ask?"

Good question. At the risk of oversimplifying and overgeneralizing—not to mention sparking a gender-related controversy—let me state that (for the most part) I do believe that (most) well-meaning men prefer (need) to be told what to do when their wives are sick. This isn't to say that a husband's instincts to take care of his wife aren't intact and receptive to the problem at hand. It is, rather, that the complexities of her illness obscure the picture and can put his best efforts to the test. What may have helped her feel better in the past, when she was sad, may no longer work when she's depressed. What used to make her feel better may not be enough. She may wish that he would figure this out on his own, but he may not be able to.

Martha Manning, a psychologist and author, pursues this disconnect in a poignant exchange between her and her therapist-husband in her book *Undercurrents* (1994). Whether it is right or wrong, true or not, many men do struggle with the distinction between helping and just *being*. Manning writes, "'I don't want you to help me. I want you to be with me.' He looks at me as if he has no comprehension of the difference of those two things."

I love that line. I've seen that face on many men sitting in my office, as if saying, "I'm doing all the right things; what else could you possibly want from me?" This is where we see the illness tumbling into the marriage, pushing and pulling the love, the resentment, the utter exhaustion.

What do women want when they feel this bad? Manning (1994) goes on to say, "Just hold me, sit with me. Put your arm around me. Listen as I struggle to tell you what it feels like." With these words, she sheds light on an issue commonly associated with couples struggling through postpartum depression. It's hard for a man to sit with his wife in so much pain without trying or wanting to fix it and make the pain go away. He cannot fix this. It's hard to explain to him that not only will that not help, but it also could put a wedge in the relationship that will prolong healing and recovery. Instead, he should sit and stay with her. He should let her know he can tolerate this and that he is not going anywhere. He should make sure he finds support for himself so he can endure the long haul.

Communication between the couple may deteriorate as symptoms shuffle through their relationship. Women often say they feel pressured by the demand on them to express what they need during a time when they feel least equipped to do so. Women do indeed have to tell their husbands what they need. Yet, when they do, they may be met with frustration or apprehension. Husbands are tired, too. They are working hard and trying to understand something that may be threatening their sense of security. It's a hard time for both spouses. This can polarize them and make it less likely for either to be there for the other during this time of stress.

Women feel conflicting feelings and sometimes send out mixed messages: *I want you here, but don't get so close. I need you to help, but I don't know what I need you to do. I don't like the way I'm feeling, but I'm fine; don't worry about me.*

Husbands are exasperated and concerned and sending out the same mixed messages: *I want to help, but I don't know what to do. I'm sorry you feel so bad, but I wish you'd return to who you were before, so we can get on with our lives.*

The key here, as is in most of this book, rests with the connection—not the current relationship we see in front of us but, rather, the connection that has carried the couple throughout their marriage and sustained them during previous difficult times. The respect. The mutual caring. The ease of being together. Who were they before we met them? Did they enjoy simple things together? Did they speak kindly to each other? Did they take care of the little things for each other? Did they laugh?

When depression sets in and stress and fear occupy the minds of partners swept up by the undertow, the therapeutic process at hand shifts a bit. It is now about defining what we see; reinterpreting who they are, what they are now feeling and saying and having a dialogue about; and what steps need to be taken in order for both to feel appreciated and sufficiently supported. If each side waits for the other depleted half of the marriage to fill them up, both will be waiting endlessly for a drop of sustenance that seems nowhere to be found. This futile scenario leads to anger and withdrawal. If left to fend for itself, the marriage can split down the middle, leaving each partner hungry for attention and support.

Working with the couple, even for a session or two, can drastically reduce this fracture in the marital system. Clinicians need to attend to the areas of weakness while addressing the strengths. Men tend to be problem-solvers within the marriage, while women tend be the emotional superintendents. Understanding and working with these differences are crucial. Uniting the couple in this way can fortify each of them while adding energy to the relationship. Above all, therapy can do two important things. It can (1) provide interim support for each, thereby reducing the angst of unmet needs, and (2) enlighten the couple with attention to the problem areas and provide strategies for coping in order to maximize their functioning as a team and promote further healing.

CHAPTER 26

Bonding

Ava came to see me when her daughter was 8 months old. This was 3 months after our last visit, when she had left saying, "I'll call you if I need anything." When I originally met her, she was being treated by a psychiatrist who had monitored her during her pregnancy due to her history of depression, and the doctor had referred her to our center for counseling after the baby was born.

At that time, Ava presented with significant anxiety and excessive worrying that preoccupied her thinking. It was hard for her to think about anything other than how she was feeling. She was convinced that having the baby was a mistake and that she was not "cut out to be a mother."

It is well known to clinicians who work in this field that early parenting is not always an experience of unmitigated delight. Even without meeting the criteria for a major depressive episode, many mothers experience ambivalence and feelings of disenchantment as they advance through this critical transition period. The connection of maternal ambivalence, postpartum depression, and impaired mother–infant bonding is not entirely determined; it is not clear whether maternal ambivalence acts as a causal agent or occurs as a result of these factors. However, the concomitant relationship among these dynamics is substantial.

Bertrand Cramer (1993) explores the hypothesis that a conflictual mother–infant dyad might act as a causal agent and precipitate a depression in the postpartum period; he focuses attention on the relationship as key when considering intervention and treatment focus. This concept further elucidates Winnicott's notion of maternal preoccupation (1956), when the mother is faced with the challenge of relinquishing her own narcissistic needs in order to devote herself completely to her baby, who, as we know, has little regard for the demands this places on her time and her emotional self.

It is interesting to note the reciprocal relationship between depression and maternal ambivalence. That is, postpartum depression can give rise to significant insecurities and doubts in the new mother, impacting her relationship with her baby. Likewise, any impairment in her relationship with her baby and her ability to attach can factor into the development of a depression. Therefore, we must attend to this relationship from both the practical level (How is she managing? Is she spending quality time with her baby? Is she providing sufficient need-fulfilling attention?) and the emotional level (How does this connection feel? Is she expressing appropriate affect? Is there evidence of a mutually satisfying relationship?). Although attachment styles and potential subsequent disorders are beyond the scope of this book, a woman's concept and expectation of maternal bonding merit attention.

When I first met with Ava, she expressed feelings that ranged from indifference to repulsion at the thought of being "tied down" by her new baby. A mother's detachment such as this is often accompanied by intense guilt, which can lead to feelings of hatred toward the baby or, more commonly, toward herself.

"Thank goodness there are people in my family who'll take care of Evan," she said, staring out the window. Turning back to me, she wondered aloud, "Do you think I'll eventually bond with my baby like I'm supposed to? Do you think I can make up for lost time?"

I hope so, I privately worried, concerned with her lack of emotion. "I do. For now, let's focus on getting you feeling better and making sure your family is there for Evan. Let's see if there are ways that you *are* comfortable being with him."

It can be difficult to witness a mother disconnecting from her new baby. Only rarely have I been concerned about this behavior from a clinical standpoint. This happened when the detachment felt more characterologic and was, therefore, less responsive to intervention, more enduring, and potentially more perilous to the relationship. This was an aberration relative to what clinicians should expect to see in practice. But it warrants some explanation. Any time clinicians note affect that appears, or feels, inappropriately flat, it's worth noting and may have longer-term implications. Generally, when women with no underlying or comorbid psychological disturbance experience a postpartum disconnect from their babies, it is met with a high degree of anxiety and guilt. The absence of these emotions can signal a more complicated psychological picture.

With regard to bonding behaviors, it appears that women with postpartum depression are prone to experience feelings of overattachment, detachment, or a combination of the two. This is not always the case, but it often accompanies their set of depressive and anxious symptoms. When it does, women perceive detachment as more of a problem than overattachment, but both require our attention when we assess the interaction between mother and infant. Though it may be unsettling for some clinicians to observe and experience this disconnect, it is generally not an indication of long-term relational impairment.

One of the questions women routinely ask is whether it's okay for them to be separated from their baby while they are having difficulty functioning, or is it better for them to push through it even though they are feeling so bad? Or, interpreted another way, is it okay for them to be separated? Sometimes, hinting at a preference for this scenario occurs when a mother feels too overwhelmed. These are good questions, and the answers largely depend on the individual circumstances and a case-by-case analysis. In general, clinicians tend to default to the mother's preference and assessment of her capacity to function. Common sense dictates that it's ideal to keep mother and baby together whenever possible. Instances that might necessitate temporary separation would be if contact with her baby disturbed her significantly or if the mother–infant relationship were contributing to her state of agitation or withdrawal. In those cases, it can markedly reduce anxiety to have her baby cared for by an alternative primary caregiver, such as a close family member, either in or out of the home for a short time.

When making this assessment, clinicians should pay particular attention to what she says she wants. If being away from the baby would increase her ability to take care of herself (while her own mother takes care of the baby, for example), then this arrangement might be conducive to healing, as long as all parties are in agreement. If, on the other hand, separation from the baby, regardless of how transitory it may be, increases her guilt and agitation, this might need to be revised. Of course, this determination is best made with both mother and father present and with careful consideration of all factors, including the severity of her illness; the availability of good, reliable, substitute caretakers; and a general discussion of the pros and cons of this intervention. This is an example of one of the more difficult decisions clinicians may be forced to evaluate expediently and accurately.

As with other complex decisions, there is not always one right answer. What is right may be a combination of what she and her partner want, what resources are available, and what is in her best interest. For example, though it might be preferable to keep a woman out of the hospital whenever possible, when severe symptoms endanger her life, it becomes necessary. Likewise, it is preferable to keep a pregnant woman off psychotropic medication, if possible; however, sometimes that, too, might be necessary when symptoms warrant it. Similarly, in the ideal world, we prefer not to separate a baby from his mother for any significant time period. However, if symptoms are severe enough and if being with the baby is interfering with her recovery by escalating these symptoms, a brief time away from the baby might be the most appropriate step.

If we take a closer look at how depression specifically impacts the mother–infant relationship, we can see why it's important to consider this in clinical practice. Depressed mothers have strikingly different affect from mothers who are not depressed, which can potentially compromise their interactions with their babies. Research on this relationship (Tronick, 1989) and its link to depression has shown infants as young as 3 months are actually able to detect depression in their mothers and respond with greater distress. Researchers asked nondepressed women to imitate a depressed affect with their 3-month-old babies. The women spoke in monotonous tones, with little facial expression and less physical contact with their babies. The findings revealed that after a 3-minute exposure period to a simulated depression, the infants responded with dramatic and significant results: "The infants looked away from the mothers and became distressed and wary. Their affect cycled among states of wariness and disengagement. They made brief solicitations to the mother to resume her normal affective state." This information, while potentially disturbing for depressed mothers to hear, is further evidence of the need to treat the depression (Tronick, 1989).

Additional research (Cohn & Tronick, 1989) confirms what we see in our center. Depressed mothers can present as withdrawn, sad, and disengaged, with limited verbal or behavioral interfacing, or they can present with a more intrusive manner, expressing anger and interfering behaviors. Of particular note is another group of depressed mothers who are able to gather their inner resources enough to relate in more positive ways. The authors of the study note that this ability to find the energy to interact in positive ways with their infants and, importantly, to be able to obtain pleasure from these exchanges may be a significant marker of who may or may not be at risk for a chronic course of depression.

Therefore, if mothers can "fake" depressive symptoms, precipitating a distress response in their babies, and if the ability to muster the energy in the face of true depression is linked with better coping and possibly shields against long-term depression, can we conclude that our intervention should focus on helping mothers press forward through their depressive symptoms on behalf of the mother–infant relationship? This poses interesting possibilities in therapy, depending on the severity of a woman's illness and her ability to cope with her symptoms.

Research also shows that depressed mothers interact less with their babies and are less likely to breastfeed, play with, and read to their children (MacLennan, Wilson, & Taylor, 1996). Ava made it clear to me that she was spending minimal time with her baby. This is when clinicians must weigh their concern regarding the baby's exposure to depression versus concern over limiting the baby's interaction with his mother. Clearly, the goals are to maximize her positive contact with the baby and minimize the baby's exposure to continuous negative energy. Careful assessment of how she is doing, in regard to her relationship with her baby, is essential; bringing the baby into the session is a vital part of this ongoing assessment.

Our attention to maternal responsiveness and the impact on the mother–infant interaction leads us back to the ultimate premise that underscores much of what we do: The risk of untreated depression during the postpartum period can have a number of serious repercussions, one of the most striking of which is difficulty in the mother–child relationship.

As an undergraduate at the University of Wisconsin in Madison, where primate researcher Harry Harlow (1958) had experimented with infant monkeys, I found myself being driven to distraction by the publicity of his controversial work. As a permanent fixture in the psychology department myself, I was haunted by photographs of his research. I suspect the preoccupation that plagued me is not unrelated to my enduring interest in mother–infant relationships. If I conjure up images of his experiments, where he manufactured maternal deprivation with newborn baby monkeys to this day I feel sickly responsible for their torture. As a sophomore in college, I remember thinking how awful it was for those poor baby monkeys, and wondering what would we be able to learn from this so their suffering would not be in vain.

In one early experiment, perhaps the basis of Harlow's infamous status, after separating the baby monkeys from their mothers, he placed them in a cage with two surrogate "mothers." The first was made from wire and had a bottle of milk attached. The second was made of cloth and provided nothing more than a soft touch. The scientists put the baby monkeys into the cage and observed as they clung desperately to the cloth mother, often refusing to let go of her though they remained hungry. Some held tightly to the terry cloth mother while stretching over to suck milk from the nearby bottle attached to the wire mother. Despite the fact that the wire mother was the only one providing food, the infant monkeys became more attached to the terry cloth mother and seemed to use her as a secure base to explore their environments. This experiment challenged previous theories that viewed attachment primarily as a function of feeding. Apparently, contact and comfort were indispensable.

So, what can we still learn from these sweet monkeys? On its most simplistic level, we learn that babies, all babies, long to be cuddled and warm over and above anything else. As clinicians working with mothers suffering from depression, we need to take careful note of each one's early relationship with her baby. It is crucial to assess how, if at all, this relationship is contributing to or suffering from the depression. The crux of the matter is that both mom and baby need to be cared for, and there will be times, with severe illnesses, that mom may do better if someone else in the family takes the full responsibility of caring for the infant while her symptoms are acute. The immediate plan would then be to introduce small, manageable time periods for mom to spend time with her baby as soon as possible. In extreme cases, as noted by Murray, Cooper, Wilson, and Romaniuk (2002), particular attention to the mother–infant relationship may need to be sustained in longer-term treatment, in order to prevent ongoing difficulties.

When postpartum depression interferes with the natural course of the mother–infant relationship, it can raise alarming concerns for the new mother. "What if I never bond with my baby?" Ava went into a tailspin as her anxiety mounted: "I have to admit that I like her best when she is asleep. Otherwise, it doesn't feel good at all. She's hysterical. I'm hysterical. No one knows what they're doing. I don't think this is going to work at all."

Mothers need to be reminded that bonding is a process, not an event, and it can take time. Often, it takes much more time than anticipated. If mothers have early bonding worries, many of them state they are troubled by the perceived disconnect. This raises their anxiety and exacerbates their symptoms, leading to a cycle of rejection and subsequent feelings of worthlessness. "After all," Ava said despairingly, "if your own baby doesn't love you, who will?"

Adding to their angst can be the pressure to bond correctly, or immediately, or perfectly, as presented in the media or on the playground, or in the mind of an obsessive mother. As postpartum specialists, we may be in the best objective position to reassure a mother that bonding will indeed take place and that the best thing she can do for her baby is to take care of herself. When she is ready, we can coach her through some of the basics, such as eye contact, skin-to-skin contact, voice recognition, and the importance of facial expressions. Until that time, our goal is to minimize her anxiety about bonding by (1) confirming that it will take place as she heals, (2) reminding her that her baby is well cared for by herself and others, and (3) helping her stay focused on the present.

As noted in the work of Whiffen and Gotlib (1989), depressed mothers often perceived their infants as more difficult to care for and more troublesome when compared to mothers who were not depressed. In our center, we notice that as women progress through treatment, they typically report fewer difficulties with their babies. This could be a reflection of changes in the actual behavior of the baby, the mother's improved perception of the problems, or her ability to accommodate and cope better.

One final caveat: Studies of women with postpartum depression and their children do indicate an association between the depression and impaired infant cognitive development (Murray & Cooper, 1997) as well as an increased rate in behavioral disturbances in school-age children (Sinclair & Murray, 1998). We can see then that adverse child outcomes within this context may be related to disturbances in the mother–infant interaction. This further highlights our need to be alert to the relationship and monitor any weak areas. Lusskin, Pundiak, and Habib (2007) emphasize that when identification of disturbances in this important relationship is made promptly, early intervention can be aimed specifically at resolving these problem areas.

Maternal mood in the postpartum period has a significant influence on the baby's development and long-term outcome. In severe instances, when families are especially vulnerable or lack sufficient resources, home-based interventions or more child-focused treatment may be appropriate. Clinicians should keep in mind that a woman's parenting capacity, the joy of the mother role, and the quality of the mother–baby relationship are at issue. Our attention to this primary relationship remains a key component of this work.

CHAPTER 27

Suicidal Thoughts

The risk of untreated depression can be catastrophic. Shari Lusskin, MD, director of reproductive psychiatry at New York University Medical Center, and her colleagues (Lusskin, Pundiak, & Habib, 2007) set forth some of the sobering facts in "Perinatal Depression: Hiding in Plain Sight." In this article, the authors review the research (as cited by Oates, 2003) and report the results from *The Confidential Enquiry into Maternal Deaths* (1997–1999); they note that suicide was the leading cause of maternal death within the first year after childbirth, accounting for 28% of deaths. Lusskin (2007) further reports that the first 42 days postpartum may be the time of greatest risk. Particularly interesting to me and consistent with my clinical observation is that the victims of suicide in this review died violently, such as by hanging or jumping as opposed to taking an overdose. Furthermore, these women tended to have higher socioeconomic status, be older, and have had previous mental health issues; almost half of them had suffered from a previous postpartum hospitalization.

Suicidal ideation can be active, involving a current desire, intention, and plan to die, or it can be passive, involving a desire to die or escape the pain with no actual plan to do so. In clinical terms, this is an important distinction. To me, there is no difference. If I consider the presentation of a high-functioning woman who is managing to get through her day without anyone noticing how bad she is feeling and the words she speaks within the security of my office telling me she cannot make it through another day, I am always astounded by the incongruity.

Dana was a stunning, 5'11" African American woman whose statuesque carriage and dazzling smile distracted me from how bad she surely felt. Dana was thoughtful with her answers to my questions, looked me squarely in the eyes, and didn't offer any more information other than a brief, direct answer

219

to each question. My sense at the time was that she was being honest but not open. "Do you have a history of depression, Dana?"

"Yes. When I was 18, when I first went to college."

"How was this depression treated?"

"I saw a counselor at school. It was helpful, I suppose."

"How do you feel now, compared to how you felt then? Is this the same?"

"Oh, no. This is much worse."

"In what way does it feel worse?"

She swallowed and cleared her throat. "It's terrible, really."

I took a quick glance at her paperwork, noting that she had circled number 2 on item 10 of the Edinburgh screen, indicating that she "sometimes" had thoughts of harming herself.

"I see here that you marked that you sometimes have thoughts of harming yourself. Can you tell me about these thoughts?"

Deep sigh. "I'm not so sure it's all that different from the thoughts that everyone else has when they feel overwhelmed."

It's always interesting to me how readily women admit that they have these thoughts and make light of them at the same time.

"It's no big deal," she said.

"What kinds of thoughts are you having, Dana? Are you able to describe them to me?"

"I would never do anything to hurt myself. I'm too chicken."

I fix my eyes onto hers and let her know that I am not yet reassured.

"Sometimes I just think that my baby would be better off with someone else as his mother, that's all. Or sometimes I think it would be better if I just didn't wake up. I—I don't really want to do anything to hurt myself, but, if it just happened that way … it would be okay."

I thought again about Beth and her heartbreaking suicide. She, too, had reassured me she wouldn't do anything to hurt herself.

"Dana, do you have any weapons in your house?"

This is not always an easy question to ask. Some therapists tell me they feel intrusive asking it. These clinicians are concerned that they will insult their client, who either looks "too good" to have weapons in the house or might take offense to the question because it implies that we do not believe her when she says she will not hurt herself. However, it is imperative to acquire this information, and any weapons, pills, or other potentially lethal items that might represent a way out of her pain should be removed from the premises. From a safety standpoint, it may seem that blocking her access to these hazards is sufficient; however, the mere knowledge that they are there can reinforce her distorted thinking and lock her into a cycle of unhealthy negative thoughts.

Dana answered, "Yes."

I, too, am repeatedly surprised when I hear an affirmative reply to this question. I'm not sure why. I suppose I have some naïve presumption that people I know don't have guns in their houses. Big mistake. I said, "What's in the house?"

"My husband has guns. Five of them."

"Okay. They need to be removed from the house."

"They are locked up. I don't know where the key is."

"They still need to be removed."

"How do I tell my husband this?"

"How do you tell him what? That he needs to remove the guns or that you are feeling this bad?"

"Both!" she cried.

"Why don't we tell him together, now. You call him, and I'll speak with him, if you would like, okay?"

Dana called her husband and we took turns talking to him. He said he understood the seriousness of the situation now but had had no idea she was feeling this bad. He guaranteed that the guns would be out of the house before Dana returned home. He also agreed to remove any medications that might be harmful and to take responsibility for dispensing the medications she would need to take until she felt better.

In addition to removing temptation, getting the weapons out of the house is also a symbolic gesture. Will it stop someone from killing herself? I suspect not. But letting her know we understand how bad she feels and removing the temptation to act on those feelings, thoughts, or impulses can provide great relief. This decisive action is a way of telling her we are not going to let anything bad happen to her. Therefore, regardless of resistance and despite excuses, once she discloses thoughts of this nature, action must be taken to keep her safe.

Because postpartum depression can grip women in such an acute state of agitation, it is prudent to pay close attention to their constant attention to fleeting thoughts, however passive they may be, of harming themselves. A clinical response to passive suicidal ideation should be clear and resolute. Suicidal ideation is a symptom that requires immediate intervention, including a referral to a psychiatrist and a rapid assessment of available support persons. When a woman has active suicidal thoughts with intention or a plan, this requires hospitalization to ensure her safety. However, women with passive thoughts may respond well to a verbal safety contract and, in her presence, a phone call to her husband and to a psychiatrist regarding an evaluation. Under other circumstances, it is acceptable for the client to take the initiative to contact the psychiatrist, but in these instances, it is preferable to make the call in her presence and then instruct her to follow up with an appointment. Although it does not concern me that this aggressive approach is occasionally met with conflicting emotions for the client, I do take note of the solemn demeanor it often elicits.

Perhaps that's what we see when one merges shame and fear with enormous relief.

In addition to the clinical concerns associated with a depressed client, such as keeping her safe and keeping her symptoms from escalating, clinicians must also attend to the well-being of the baby and the additional strain this may put on the mother. Colleen, who had a history of generalized anxiety, told me that the anxiety she had been feeling since her baby was born was different and the difference was palpable. "It feels claustrophobic. Like I can't get out, there's nowhere to go, nowhere to turn. I just want to get away." Sometimes, women with postpartum depression express their despair as restless isolation. This is a red flag and should prompt a clinician to follow up with probing questions beginning with, "Are you having any thoughts that are scaring you?"

This is when clinical questions may be scripted, but clinical judgment and close observation take precedence. Again, we observe her response: the look in her eyes, the energy in her response. A woman might say, "No, I'm not having any thoughts that are scaring me" or "No, I'm not having any thoughts of harming myself." However, she may have checked a 1 or a 2 on item 10 on the Edinburgh screen, or, after deeper probing, a client might say, "Sometimes I wish I could fall asleep and never wake up" or "When I'm driving I'll think, 'If I turn the wheel just a bit too much in this direction, I can drive right off that bridge.'" The common theme is escape from the pain. This may not feel like suicidal ideation to her, but it is. Alarmingly, these thoughts can either agitate an already agitated woman, or they can oddly comfort her because she believes the distorted thought that her children would indeed be better off without her. Removing herself from the picture in an effort to protect her child from the ravages of depression appears to be one of the great incentives for suicidal thought.

All thoughts of suicide should be followed by questions designed to explore the details of her thought process. The following are some guidelines for assessing suicidality with brief annotations:

- How often are you having thoughts of hurting yourself? (*determine frequency and acute nature of thoughts*)
- Are you able to describe them to me? (*assess current level of distress and willingness to disclose*)
- Have you ever had thoughts like this before? (*history of previous thoughts increases current risk*)
- What happened the last time you had these thoughts? (*assess coping potential*)
- Does your partner know how bad you are feeling? If not, why not? (*numerous factors contribute to failure to disclose, all pointing toward potential areas of vulnerability*)
- Whom do you consider your most primary connection for emotional support? (*explore all support options*)

- Does this person know how you are feeling? If not, why not? (*explore her resistance in order to determine degree of withdrawal, level of shame, ability to reach out for help*)
- Does anyone in your family know how you are feeling? (*engaging family member provides important link when her instinct is to isolate self*)
- Have you ever acted on suicidal thoughts before? (*previous suicide attempt increases current risk*)
- How do you feel about these thoughts you are having? (*assess affective response and level of distress to confirm ego dystonic nature of thoughts*)
- Do you have specific thoughts about what you would do to harm yourself? (*assess intent and plan*)
- If you do have a plan, do you know what is keeping you from acting on it? (*assess and increase her awareness of meaningful connections to reduce feelings of isolation and despair*)
- Are there weapons in your home? (*never presume to know the answer to this; in addition to the obvious danger, weapons also serve to stimulate the overactive obsessional thought process with temptation too great to ignore. All weapons, whether locked or reported as inaccessible, should be removed from the home without delay*)
- Do you have access to medications that could be harmful to you? (*all medications she is taking or has access to should be monitored by her partner until suicidal thoughts have responded to treatment, reducing risk of temptation*)
- Is there anything else you can think of that I can do right now to help you protect yourself from these thoughts? (*gives her permission to reveal any unidentified method or related worry*)
- Have you thought about what the implication would be for your baby? (*her connection to her baby may provide a critical lifeline*)
- Do you feel able to contact me if you feel you cannot stop yourself from acting on these thoughts? (*establish a verbal or written contract for safety*)

The risk of suicide among depressed women is significantly higher during the perinatal period. While the number of suicide deaths is lower during the postpartum period than in the general population of women, suicides account for as many as 20% of postpartum deaths (Lindahl, Pearson, & Colpe, 2005). Recent media attention to suicide attempts and deaths by new mothers has raised public and congressional awareness about the potentially devastating consequences of depression during the postpartum period. It is a risk that postpartum women and their families, as well as the clinicians who treat them, must take very seriously at all times, particularly in, but certainly not limited to, the early assessment stages.

Important Points to Keep in Mind

Clinicians should be clear about their ability to help the client.

Follow up on any and all requests made—for example, removing weapons from the house.

Determine level of follow-up—for example, having her report in with phone calls to assure safety.

If a woman indicates that she is having thoughts or feelings about harming herself and/or her baby and she is unable to make a verbal contract to assure she will not act on them, she should not leave the office.

Contact family members, if indicated, in her presence.

Initiate psychiatric or hospital contact.

Immediate intervention is required if she:

> Demonstrates significantly impaired functioning

> Expresses suicidal thoughts with a developed or intended plan

> Is ambivalent about her ability to keep herself and her baby safe

> Expresses intent to harm herself or her baby

> Reports physical or sexual abuse or any unsafe living situation

> Demonstrates signs of psychosis

Clinicians should be careful not to avoid questions that make them uncomfortable.

Although suicide following childbirth is rare, Margaret Oates notes that the rates are higher than the literature has indicated in the past. She emphasizes the need for strict management in the early postpartum period to protect women at risk, particularly those with a history of a serious psychiatric disorder, and states: "Few psychiatric events are as predictable as a postpartum recurrence and they come with 9 months' warning" (2003).

CHAPTER 28

Psychosis

Jessie's husband, Rick, called the office. This, alone, should not be remarkable, but in our practice there does seem to be high incidence of more severe illnesses that correlate with contacts that are initiated by the husband. It does make sense that women who are too sick to call rely on others to reach out.

Rick called and said his wife hadn't slept in a couple of days; she was irritable and angry all the time. I asked if he was worried about her. "Not really," he replied. I asked why he was calling instead of her and also whether I would be able to talk with her. He told me she asked him to call for her and she would prefer to speak to me at our appointment. After my usual litany of questions, I asked if there was anything in particular that was troubling him. He said no, that she was just very tired but wasn't telling him much more than that. "Can you see her soon?" His words spoke of an uneasiness he had not otherwise made known.

I saw Jessie, who was accompanied by a friend, the following afternoon. I thought it was somewhat unusual and noteworthy that her husband did not come with her for this first session. That was a colossal assumption, one of many more to follow. Therapists know, on some level, to always keep an extra eye out for things we do not expect. It's never okay to become complacent in this work. Each woman and each family bring in their own stories. Our job is to remain open to them, not make presumptions, and be mindful of what each client really needs from us. Sometimes that might be clear.

Sometimes, we have no idea.

Jessie smiled on cue, sat down next to her friend, and folded her hands in her lap, awaiting my lead. Her friend, who was actually a neighbor who was worried about her, spoke up, "This is not Jessie. She's usually very upbeat, and talkative and busy, always busy. This is just not her."

I looked at Jessie. She was listening but not responding.

"Jessie, is she right? Is this not like you? Tell me how you feel."

"I'm fine. I just need to sleep. I just need to sleep." She closed her eyes.

Jessie was 10 days postpartum after an uneventful pregnancy and delivery. This was her second child. She reported a previous episode of postpartum depression after her first baby that was successfully treated with antidepressants. There was a history of questionable mental illness in her family, "Not sure if anyone was diagnosed but they should have been. Everyone was crazy." I suppose we don't ever really know what that means when we hear it.

"Anyone treated for depression or anxiety, as far as you know?"

"I don't know."

"Do you know if anyone has a history of bipolar disorder?"

"You mean like manic depression? I don't know. Probably."

"What do you mean, Jessie?"

"I mean, I don't know; I'm so tired."

We talked about what we could do to help get her some sleep. We talked about how her husband worked long hours and was not able to help much in that department. Her friend and I strategized and came up with a list of names she could call upon for help.

Toward the end of our session, I was not yet convinced that Jessie was as okay as she claimed. I was concerned about her lack of concentration and inability to focus on our discussion. I was concerned about her lack of eye contact. I was concerned that her husband wasn't there when she looked so sick to me. I asked her if she felt she needed to be in a hospital so she could get the rest she needed. She said no, she just needed to sleep.

I told Jessie I wanted to see her sooner than our typical weekly appointment because she was unable to see the psychiatrist for a few days. Her obstetrician had given her some sleeping medication and she believed that would help her catch up on her sleep. She gave me permission to call her doctor and her husband to alert them to my concerns and agreed to come back in 3 days.

Two days later, I received another call from her husband. Jessie was worse. Something was wrong. I told him he should take her to the emergency room. He said she wouldn't go, that she wanted to see me. I reminded him that we were not equipped to handle emergencies and that, if warranted, I would direct her to the hospital, anyway, so perhaps they should go directly there. She wanted to see me. I conceded and told Rick I wanted him there with her.

When they came at the appointed time, Jessie didn't look good at all. She hardly looked like the woman I had seen just 2 days before. The transformation was startling. She walked stiffly, as if on command, and sat down robotically. She stared forward, her eyes fixed on nothing.

"Jessie, you okay?" I use it when I know something is wrong or when I suspect something is wrong. I may be responding to a subtle change in someone's usual demeanor or a faint expression. Other times, I might say it when I know something is terribly, terribly wrong, like this time. Either way, the tone used when asking, *"Are you okay?"* often resonates with the *good mother* voice.

"No." Jessie's abrupt response disarmed me. I looked at Rick. He sat still and said nothing.

"What are we seeing here?" I asked again for clarification and background information.

"I don't know," he replied. *Another one. No one knows. What's going on here?* I watched Jessie carefully. She continued to sit awkwardly with no apparent awareness of her surroundings. She appeared confused but not particularly bothered by that.

"Do you know where you are, Jessie?"

"Yes."

"Do you remember meeting me the other day?"

"Yes."

Flat, odd affect. Pressured speech. One-word answers. No eye contact. Withdrawn.

"Jessie, Rick needs to take you to the hospital, okay? They will take good care of you. You'll be able to sleep, and they'll know what to do to help you feel better. I will stay in touch with them and with you. We need to do this."

"Okay."

I turned to Rick and told him to sit with her while I called the hospital closest to my office. He scooted closer to her but she remained motionless. As I sat on the phone initiating contact with the admissions department, I could see Jessie was lost within herself, as her husband sat helplessly beside her.

I honestly wasn't sure what I was seeing, but I knew she couldn't function at home this way. I followed up at the hospital inpatient unit the next day to see her.

"Why do you want to see her?" one of the charming day nurses inquired.

"I just met her the other day and directed her here for treatment because she was so sick. I thought it would be helpful for her to make the transition if I connected with her."

"Well, go ahead." She most graciously and sarcastically pointed in the direction of an empty hall. "But you'll be the only one talking."

"Can you tell me what's going on with Jessie?"

"Crazy as a fox, I tell ya. Go ahead; see if you can make heads or tails of it! I'll go get her and we'll meetcha in the library."

This was not comforting. I have not yet found a spot in our medical community that is safe for extremely ill mothers who need inpatient psychiatric care. It seems that no one really knows how to deal with mothers who are severely ill.

I'm not sure why that is.

I sat in the library amid the books and the eerie stillness. Jessie was led into the room by the nurse, who guided her to sit next to me. "Have fun." She parted with the same dispassionate words with which she had greeted me. She should get another job.

I looked at Jessie's cold eyes. I could feel her breathing. I could see her breathing. Even so, I wasn't sure she was there. She stared right through me. Her occasional blink was my only clue that she could move at all.

"Jessie, it's Karen. Do you remember me?"

No response. No movement. No blinking.

Psychosis is chilling for all involved. Sometimes women are aware that something is terribly wrong; they might try to quiet the voices in their heads or pretend they are not seeing the things they don't think they should be seeing. But most of the time the symptoms rupture any attempt to subdue them. Family members often report that "strange things are happening," like the husband who told me his wife loved the color of the baby lotion and wanted the baby's room to be that color. He later found her spreading the lotion up and down the wall. When he asked her to stop, she grabbed the baby powder and skipped around the perimeter of the room, squeezing it and squealing in delight as the puffs of powder dust filled the room. These are things people notice. Symptoms such as delusions, extreme confusion, or hallucinations cause a dramatic change in functioning that usually calls attention to an urgent problem.

I had never seen this state in which Jessie was engulfed. A catatonic state. Postpartum psychosis usually begins within 2 weeks of childbirth and often manifests in manic symptoms and confusion. The onset is usually sudden, within the first few days after childbirth, presenting with startling symptoms, including hallucinations and bizarre thoughts and behaviors (Sichel & Driscoll, 2000). Brockington et al. (1981) report that catatonia, as demonstrated with Jessie, is a less frequent manifestation during the postpartum period. They also state that almost all cases of postpartum psychosis emerge by the first 2–3 weeks postpartum. These are always emergency situations that require immediate medical intervention by a psychiatrist and probably hospitalization. Included in any thorough evaluation, clinicians should follow up and make certain that physicians have ruled out any organic component to the illness.

The stakes are extremely high. If untreated, the research shows that postpartum psychosis is associated with a 5% suicide rate (Knops, 1993) and 4% infanticide rate (Cohen & Altshuler, 1997). As Margaret Spinelli, MD (2004), poignantly notes in response to the horror of Andrea Yates's psychosis and subsequent murder of her children:

> Maternal infanticide, or the murder of a child in the first year of life
> by its mother, is a subject both compelling and repulsive. The kill-

ing of an innocent elicits sorrow, anger, and horror. It is a crime. It demands retribution. That is the law. Yet the perpetrator of this act is often a victim too, and that recognition makes for a more paradoxical response. On the one hand is the image of a defenseless infant, killed by the person he or she depended on for survival. On the other hand is the image of a mother, insane and imprisoned for a crime unthinkable to many. These competing images elicit ambivalence, if not outrage.

Postpartum psychosis is not a really bad depression. It is believed to be a separate disorder; what blurs the diagnostic picture, however, is that very severe cases of postpartum depression can present with psychotic symptoms. Most experts agree that the development of postpartum psychosis is largely a bipolar event (Sit, Wisner, & Rothschild, 2006) or major depression with psychotic features (Arnold, Baugh, Fisher, Brown, & Stowe, 2002). Other factors, such as hormonal changes (Sichel & Driscoll, 2000), obstetrical difficulties, and sleep deprivation, as well as extreme environmental stressors, have been studied as precipitating factors that may also contribute to the onset of psychosis. A comprehensive discussion on postpartum psychosis is presented by Ruta Nonacs, MD (2006), in her book *A Deeper Shade of Blue.*

Later I would learn that Jessie had told her husband she heard people talking in her head, but both of them presumed it was from sleep deprivation. He also told me he would find her sitting by a window gazing out for extended periods of time. When he asked what she was doing, she abruptly shook off her broken stare and said, "Nothing," and moved away from that spot. He reported that she was "paranoid with guilt" and told him repeatedly that God would surely punish her for being such a bad mother. Neither of them knew they should be concerned about these occurrences. Increasing public awareness is never far from my mind each time families present with such tolerance for highly disturbing symptoms.

Jessie's recovery included a short hospital stay, antipsychotic medication, antidepressants, and anti-anxiety medication. Her memory of the catatonic state was vague, but her experience with it was something neither of us will soon forget. Our therapy began when I sat beside her in the silent hospital library, trying unsuccessfully to reach her, and continued aggressively on an outpatient basis twice a week until she felt more organized in her thinking and better able to cope. When she felt ready, she brought her baby in to our sessions so she could reacquaint herself with her sweet daughter, which felt comforting and rewarding to both Jessie and me.

SCREENING FOR PSYCHOSIS

Should we screen for postpartum psychosis? Absolutely. We should ask about history of bipolar illness and a family or personal history of postpartum psychosis, all of which put the client at greater risk (Sit et al., 2006). We should also ask the questions that are hard to ask.

One way to ask is: *Sometimes women with depression can have strange experiences, like hearing voices or feelings that others are trying to harm them or make them do things they don't want to do. Have you experienced anything like that?*

Women often tell me one of their greatest fears is that they will "snap" and become psychotic. "What if I can't help it and I end up doing something horrible to my baby?" Understanding that postpartum psychosis and postpartum depression with obsessional intrusive thoughts are two different illnesses is crucial. It's important that the clinician be clear about this distinction so an accurate assessment can be made.

When screening for postpartum depression, healthcare practitioners should be aware of distinguishing responses. If the mother, for example, states she is having thoughts of hurting her baby, she should be asked if she has an intention, desire, or impulse to hurt the baby.

As we discussed in chapter 19, it is important to distinguish between postpartum psychosis and obsessive–compulsive symptoms. Women with intrusive thoughts or OCD symptoms are extremely disturbed by these thoughts. Their level of anxiety is so high they will typically avoid objects or places that reinforce this anxiety. Women with psychosis, however, experience no such distress and are unable to differentiate what is real from what is a manifestation of their delusions (Brandes, Soares, & Cohen, 2004).

If a clinician is worried about the well-being of a client and believes she may be suffering from psychotic symptoms, a complete assessment is essential in order to ensure her safety and the safety of her baby. Included in the assessment should be questions about:

- Any delusions
- Any hallucinations (particularly auditory that may be telling her to hurt the baby or herself)
- Differentiating scary thoughts from obsessional thoughts
- Variable sleep patterns

Also included in the assessment should be questions about her history of bipolar illness, previous psychosis, or family history of these disorders. If there is concern about psychotic symptoms, other family members should be engaged in the therapeutic process for further assessment and a discussion of her motivation for treatment and compliance. This is an emergency situation that requires immediate medical attention.

A mother who has lost touch with reality is a concept that is difficult to grasp. This is why the attention–grabbing headlines of sensational postpartum psychosis stories are so disturbing. The bizarre nature of the symptoms and behaviors associated with psychosis is incomprehensible to those who are thinking in a rational, organized way. For mothers who cling to the edge of sanity, there can be no greater fear. As clinicians, we need to ask the right questions. We cannot presume to know how scary their scary thoughts are or whether or not they will act on them. Further questioning is critical. It is our duty to learn about this debilitating illness so we can intervene properly and expeditiously.

CHAPTER 29

Motherself

I firmly believe that the mother–daughter bond is designed by nature to become the most empowering, compassionate, intimate relationship we'll ever have. How is it, then, that when we go back to that well to be refilled, the result is so often disappointment and resentment on both sides?

Christiane Northrup, MD
Mother–Daughter Wisdom:
Understanding the Crucial Link
Between Mothers, Daughters, and Health

"How old are you now?" I asked Liz, who had been coming to see me since her 6-month-old was born.

"Thirty-one. I'll be 32 in February."

I think it's painfully endearing when young women still *count up* to their next birthday. It always makes me feel so old. "So, you have about 8 more years until you're done."

"Done what?"

"Done being angry at your mom."

Liz looked at me inquisitively with a hint of guilt, as if caught with her hand in the cookie jar. "What do you mean?"

From what I could see, Liz and her mom had been battling for control for years. Sometimes, she told me, they found themselves laughing, with a sort of anxious awareness, when they clashed in a particularly absurd way, like arguing over the right way to cut a grapefruit. Many of their exchanges, however, involved unspoken competition, leaving both feeling misunderstood, angry, and unappreciated.

The mother–daughter relationship has received a great deal of attention from the popular press. Additionally, the academic community continues to examine this relationship, suggesting that a poor relationship with one's mother is associated with psychological distress (Barnett, Kibria, Baruch, & Pleck, 1991). It cannot be disputed that this arena has huge implications for the postpartum women, particularly those who are specifically struggling with their transition into this new role of mother. For the purpose of this book, however, we will focus on how this influential relationship can simultaneously obstruct and enlighten the work that lies ahead. Briefly stated, the relationship that our clients have with their mothers will impact their own feelings, attitudes, and behaviors with respect to mothering. That's a given. Regardless of whether the relationship is intact or impaired, inspiring or irritating, it will categorically affect the way our client feels about being a mother.

This is the relationship from which we learn what it means to be a mother, for better or for worse. In another wonderful book by Martha Manning, *The Common Thread: Mothers and Daughters* (2002), we are reminded that even women who proclaim to love their mothers deeply respond with great anxiety about turning into their mothers. She mocks this lovingly, when she points out that no one responds to the accusation of "becoming just like your mother" with an earnest "Thank you."

In *This Isn't What I Expected* (Kleiman & Raskin, 1994), we explored this subject in chapter 13, "Working Through Intergenerational Issues," which walks a woman through exercises that help her come to terms with some of the more common concerns, such as:

In what specific ways would you like to repeat your mother's pattern of mothering?
In what specific ways do you hope to differ from your mother's style of mothering?

If the relationship was or is good, these questions will serve to stimulate deep thought and personal introspection. If the relationship was or is damaged in some way, these questions might be anxiety provoking and good material for therapeutic exploration.

AMBIVALENCE

The birth of a baby can trigger an emotional landslide that can keep a woman in a constant state of contradiction. When we speak of ambivalence in terms of postpartum women, we refer to two categories that are distinct yet overlapping: ambivalence toward the baby and ambivalence toward the role as mother. In chapter 26, we saw how the concept of maternal ambivalence, as with other emotional states associated with postpartum depression, can be both a precursor to or a consequence of the illness.

How does her relationship with her own mother affect her feelings about being a mother? Here, again, ambivalence is part of the picture. Manning (2002) describes this paradox with precision: "We want our mothers to love us perfectly, completely, and unconditionally. We want them to love us as they did at first sight when we were newborns. At the same time, we expect them to treat us with all the adult respect to which we feel entitled by virtue of our age and experience." Ah, don't we all, as clinicians and as children of our own mothers, know this to be true?

Women who are trying to cope with depression and a new baby can express this ambivalence in a myriad of ways; it can be expressed with anger, grief, anxiety, humor, resentment, guilt, or apathy, just to name a few. Any and each way it presents, it is there, sometimes screaming aloud and, at other times, hidden within the fixed state of the woman's inertia. It is an understatement to note that a client's relationship with her mother is paramount to our clinical work. Without intending to insult the great minds who have expounded on this original concept throughout the years or the clinicians reading this book, it cannot be overemphasized how crucial this relationship is to the postpartum woman in therapy. What's important here is that clinicians understand it within this context.

Liz wondered why I was putting a time frame on her identified anger and why, of all things, I had said 8 years.

"You'll be 32 next month, right? So you have 8 years until you're 40."

The grimace on her face reflected her horror."

"Forty?! Oh, Lord."

"That's when you'll be done." I continued. "You have between now and then to do the work you need to do with this anger and the feelings of discontent regarding your mother."

She still didn't like the implication that she had to do this on my time table, as she joked, "I have to be in therapy till then?"

"No. But when you are 40, you won't want to do this anymore. By that I mean it will feel less important for you to stay angry with your mother. And it will feel better to move past it."

Liz was confused. She thought therapy was the place where she could talk about all these unpleasant feelings of anger toward her mother and other disenchanted relationships. She thought she was free to complain about how her mother always expected her to do everything perfectly and continued to criticize her to this day. She thought this was the place where she could vent about her mother's unrealistic expectations of her and how she had to constantly prove herself worthy to her own mother.

I reassured her that this was, indeed, that place and that we would do just those things. She could talk about how she felt, cry about it, work it through, and come out the other end feeling more comfortable with herself and her mother, regardless of how damaged the connection may have felt at one time. She could continue do this work in here with me, or she could do it on her own, but either way, I suspected, she would be done with most of that work by the time she was 40. Not because she had to be done by then, but because she would want to be.

Obviously, 40 is an arbitrary number. It's an abstract delineation, another illusion of control. It creates a boundary for a seemingly immeasurable task: coming to peace with mom so a woman can focus on herself as mother.

Essentially, the stages of this work are:

Ambivalence → Anger → Grief → Letting go → Forgiveness

The rationale for this work is uncomplicated: *You will feel better as a mother if you can move beyond these issues with your own mother, whether they are resolved or not.* This may appear controversial or overly simplistic at first glance. Certainly, a psychoanalyst would prefer that she do this work on a daily basis lying on a couch and not stop until the unresolved issues are, indeed, resolved. Others might agree that this work could take years (are we ever really finished?) but insist there are strategies of intervention that can expedite the process. Still others might claim it is a function of a client's state of mind and if she modifies the way she is thinking, she is halfway home. Regardless of the theoretical basis, most experts agree that, first, clients have to feel the feelings that are getting in the way. Only after clients are able to let them in and feel them can they let them go.

Therefore, clinicians must teach the client to endure the ambivalence. In doing so, we guide her through the darkness of her anger. We help her transform the anger into the sadness that accompanies unmet emotional needs. We help her see that releasing her grip on these emotions feels better than holding on. Finally, we help her understand that accepting things she cannot change can lead to forgiveness.

When we talk about forgiveness in this context, we refer to a client's capacity to let go. We remind her that forgiveness does not mean that what someone else did, whatever that may be, is okay. Rather, it's about deciding that she will no longer hold someone else accountable for how she feels. *Because when we forgive people,* we reiterate, *it doesn't mean we like what the other person did, or why they did it. It means we are no longer going to hold someone else responsible for how we feel.* Forgiveness can make room for new, untainted visions of motherhood, a reservoir of pure emotions from which to draw. This, in the long run, is a much healthier place to be. Working toward true forgiveness can be short-term or very long-term work. In any case, it is work that should, at least, be identified in later sessions, whether the client ultimately engages in that process at that time or not.

MOTHERSELF

Are we ever really done trying to please, or become like, or improve on, or distance ourselves from our own mothers? I often joke about wanting to call my mother whenever something wonderful happens in my life. But it's no joke. Apparently, I come by this honestly. When my then 72-year-old mother was visiting her 92-year-old mother in California, she found herself at the crux of this issue. She was coming out of the shower, wrapping a towel around herself, when her mother came into the bathroom to get something. Observing my mother drying herself, my grandmother cried out with her German flair, "Vat are you doing?"

"I'm drying myself," my mother coyly responded, reporting to me later that she felt, oh, about 4 years old.

"You mustn't use the towel until you dry off with the washcloth first. Otherwise, the towel gets too wet. See? Then you can use the towel again."

At first stunned into compliance, my mother then snapped herself out of automatic pilot: "Mom, I'm 72 years old. I know how to dry myself after a shower."

A second passed. Catching sight of the ridiculousness of the moment, both bent over in spontaneous laughter.

Thus, aside from the inescapable truth that I am destined to a comparable lifelong pursuit of maternal acceptance, the story illustrates an important point: Women can't help it. No matter how hard they try and how long they persevere, they may still find themselves crushed by their own unrelenting need for approval by their mothers, whether this is based in current or past reality or not. And so, as we witness this inevitable ambivalence with our clients, we validate that.

Despite the fact that this appears to contradict my flip proclamation that this work should be done by age 40, we need to remind each woman that this ambivalence is natural. We should confirm that this quest is genuine and, arguably, a primal urge of sorts. At the same time, clinicians should encourage the client to break free from it, helping to reduce her anxiety and focus the work on her new self, her motherself.

"Motherself" is a word I use to describe a woman's new identity as a mother, after she integrates who she expected herself to be, including all the good and the bad that comes with that. Pure motherself recognition comes only after there is adequate separation from perceived or real expectations of who she thinks she "should" be. And that takes work. Similar to all good therapy, this work is best achieved after the client has sufficient symptom relief. Only then can the postpartum woman tolerate the range of feelings and memories, those that are pleasurable and those that are painful.

This newfound self develops nicely in the presence of a loving *good mother* therapist who can remain objective and help the client differentiate her needs from her mother's needs as well as provide the maternal framework in which she can feel protected and safe to explore the issues. When postpartum women achieve or reclaim a sense of self during this tumultuous time, they are better equipped to emerge with confidence and a solid belief in who they are. Learning to accept and embrace their ambivalent emotions regarding their own mothers enables them to have greater insight into themselves as mothers.

If we presume our clients' mothers really did do the best they could, as we often proclaim, shouldn't that be good enough at this point? Shouldn't we help our clients impose the same constructs when referring to their mothers' mothering as they do to their own? After all, don't all mothers, including ourselves, ultimately hope that our children will forgive the mistakes we are surely making? If we cannot forgive our mothers, can we expect our children to forgive us?

CHAPTER 30

Prevention?

Postpartum depression cannot be predicted or prevented with absolute accuracy. Even so, prediction and prevention could be improved if healthcare practitioners were more vigilant about screening and taking risk factors into account. Though significant gaps remain in the research regarding screening and prevention of this illness (Dennis, 2004), as we discussed in chapter 12, the reliability and validity of available screening tools have been well established (Cox, Holden, & Sagovsky, 1987).

We know that early identification and treatment for postpartum depression are associated with better outcomes (Campagne, 2004). Healthcare professionals who are in contact with women before and during pregnancy should routinely educate women and alert them to the possibility of depression. At the same time, women need to fully disclose any prior history that puts them at risk or any current concerns they may have. Women tell me they had "no idea this could happen" to them. Some feel betrayed by the medical community, claiming they should have been informed.

Despite improved training and educational programs for the medical community, one frustrating hurdle to prevention persists. There are women who have very few risk factors, or at least present that way at first, who ultimately exhibit full-blown depressive episodes. Furthermore, because some factors, such as postpartum blues (especially if severe), have been shown to contribute to the onset of postpartum depression (Cox, Connor, & Kendell, 1982), clinicians need to pay close attention to all variables that are known to put a woman at risk This practice is essential when treating her during pregnancy and throughout the postpartum year.

When considering prevention, a primary focus should be on those things that healthcare practitioners can do before or during pregnancy to prepare women; this should be followed by the initiation of timely support. One pilot study (Zlotnick, Johnson, Miller, Pearlstein, & Howard, 2001), referred to in chapter 8, revealed that women receiving public assistance were less likely to experience postpartum depression when they participated in weekly prenatal survival skills classes. These particular classes focused on increasing support and parenting skills and used a brief interpersonal group therapy–oriented intervention. These findings suggest that women who are financially disadvantaged could decrease their risk of developing postpartum depression and greatly benefit from this type of 4-week group support. One might generalize that the success of this intervention would apply to other populations of women as well and inspire similar programs.

PREGNANCY SUPPORT

Although many postpartum advocates continue to significantly influence the healthcare practice guidelines, in reality, as clinicians, our authority in this endeavor may be best exerted in direct practice with our clients. Prevention of postpartum depression, on this smaller scale, calls to our attention those factors that put women at risk for postpartum depression before or during pregnancy. In this way, clinicians can do their part to contribute to this effort to help reduce a woman's risk for postpartum depression.

Therapists who have been in practice for a while understand that when the therapist/client relationship is meaningful and intact, the likelihood is high that this client will return to this same therapist in the future, if further support is needed down the line. At our center, we have a pregnancy support program in place to help meet the needs of women who are at risk for postpartum depression. This program, as is true for most of what we do, was developed in response to what our clients were telling us they needed.

Our "Risk Assessment During Pregnancy" (Kleiman, 1999) is not a diagnostic tool. As we've seen, risk factors do not cause postpartum depression. If, however, women are aware of what factors make them vulnerable to depression, they are more likely to mobilize their resources and better protect themselves. This is something we complete in a session together, so we can go over those factors a client feels place her at greatest risk, whether she has experienced a previous postpartum depression or not.

RISK ASSESSMENT DURING PREGNANCY

☐ I was not happy to learn I was pregnant.
☐ My partner was not happy to learn I was pregnant.
☐ I have had a previous episode of postpartum depression and/or anxiety that was successfully treated with therapy and/or medication.

☐ I might have experienced symptoms of postpartum depression following previous births, but I never sought professional help.

☐ I have had one or more pregnancy losses.

☐ I have a history of depression/anxiety that was not related to childbirth.

☐ I have lost a child.

☐ I have been a victim of the following:
- Childhood sexual abuse
- Childhood physical abuse
- Physical assault by someone I know
- Physical assault by stranger
- Physical assault during this pregnancy
- Sexual assault by someone I know
- Sexual assault by stranger

☐ There is a family history of depression/anxiety, treated or untreated.

☐ I have a history of severe PMS.

☐ I have experienced suicidal thoughts or have considered doing something to hurt myself in the past.

☐ I do not have a strong support system to help me if I need it.

☐ I have a history of drug or alcohol abuse.

☐ People have told me I'm a perfectionist.

☐ During this pregnancy, I have experienced some emotions about which I am very concerned.

☐ I feel sad.

☐ My relationship with my partner is not as strong as I'd like it to be.

☐ My partner and I have been thinking about separating or divorcing.

☐ I am not likely to admit it when I need help.

☐ During the past year, I have experienced an unusual amount of stress (e.g., move, job loss, divorce, loss of loved one)

☐ I have little interest in things that I used to find pleasurable.

☐ I am having anxiety attacks.

☐ Sometimes I worry about things so much that I can't get the thoughts out of my head.

☐ I am bothered and frightened by thoughts that I can't get out of my mind, especially about my baby's well-being.

☐ I have thoughts of hurting myself.

☐ I have thoughts of hurting my baby.

☐ I am more irritable and/or angry than usual.

☐ I just don't feel like myself.

☐ Sometimes, I feel like I can't shake off these bad feelings no matter what I do.

☐ I'm afraid if I tell someone how I really feel, they will not understand or they will think something is really wrong with me.

Women who have experienced a previous postpartum depression are at particular risk. Because this previous episode is one of the greatest predictors of a subsequent postpartum depression, it is helpful to review the prior experience and course of treatment as having a central role in the planning of another pregnancy. In my book *What Am I Thinking: Having Another Baby After Postpartum Depression* (2005), the importance of helping women become stronger, more effective consumers and advocates for their own best healthcare is discussed. The focus is toward empowering the reader by guiding her through her previous experience and treatment of depression to help her determine what worked best as well as what still needs to change. It is pointed out that with proper preparation and planning, along with a healthcare team that is mobilized on her behalf, interventions are likely to minimize the impact of an ensuing depression, should it surface.

Laying the groundwork is essential. Our clients will be better prepared, less anxious, and in a stronger position to cope with whatever transpires if they have information and strategies on hand. There is work that needs to be done. The work involves detailed preparation, teaching women how to be good consumers of the healthcare system, and careful analysis of their previous history and treatment. This is another example of how postpartum therapists transgress from traditional therapeutic directives on behalf of comprehensive care. To illustrate: Making a phone call to a doctor who doesn't respond with compassion is difficult, especially when a new mother is feeling helpless. She needs to hear why this is important and she needs to hear how we can help her do that. Whether it's a crash course in assertiveness training or role-modeling the dialogue that she can imagine or write down for later use, the focus needs to be on helping her take care of herself when she feels unable or unwilling to do that.

Tanya was 34 years old and had been married for 6 years to a man she had always told me made marriage fun. As she was leaving her final session with me, she proclaimed with a grin of certainty, "Oh, you'll be hearing from me!"

Some 2 years later, Tanya's response to her second pregnancy came across loud and clear in her phone message:

> Hi, Karen, it's Tanya. Remember me? I told you I'd call when I got pregnant. So, the good news is, I'm 2 months pregnant. The bad news is I'm scared to death. I feel fine right now, but I wanted to call to see what you think I should do, you know, about after the baby comes and everything. So call me as soon as you get this message.

Tanya had been doing well. She seemed comfortable with her new decision to stay at home and loved being a mother, an emotion she was convinced she was not capable of at the height of her illness. Her previous treatment included the gold standard: antidepressants and psychotherapy. She responded well to both, and her decision to wean off the antidepressants, after a year of taking them, went without incident. She had hoped to stay off antidepressants during the pregnancy.

I reviewed our protocol over the phone to Tanya:

> If you're feeling good during your pregnancy, we can wait a bit, but let's plan on meeting soon so we can map out a plan of action. After that, if you continue to feel good, we'll set up a time to meet at least one time before your last month of pregnancy, with you and your husband, so we can review the postpartum plan. If at any point during this pregnancy you don't like the way you are feeling, let me know and you will come in at that time. Either way, we'll meet a couple of times before you deliver to verify that we are all on the same page and safeguard against any deviation from our plan.

Preferably, these two sessions that would take place during the pregnancy would include her partner.

When given the option, most women decide to come in sooner, rather than later, so they can alleviate their initial anxiety by developing a blueprint for intervention. This blueprint includes discussions among her, her husband, and me, in addition to any prescribing or adjunctive healthcare practitioner she might contact. Because Tanya had a history of previous postpartum depression, we would discuss previous treatment and options for this subsequent pregnancy and beyond, in the hopes of lowering the risk of another episode.

Not all women we treat for postpartum depression return for support during subsequent pregnancies. But increasingly more women, as well as their treating physicians, are seeing the value of maximizing the support during pregnancy in preparation for the postpartum period. The rationalization for augmenting support during pregnancy and monitoring mood prior to delivery for women with a history of postpartum depression is compelling:

1. Women with prior history of depression or family history of a mood disorder are at increased risk for postpartum depression (Moline, Kahn, Ross, Altshuler, & Cohen, 2001).
2. After the initial episode, women who have had postpartum depression are at risk for both postpartum and nonpostpartum relapses of depression (Cooper & Murray, 1995).
3. The strongest predictor for postpartum depression is a previous episode of postpartum depression. Although there are differences in recurrence rates, it is generally agreed that at least one third of the women who have had postpartum depression have a recurrence of symptoms after a subsequent delivery (Wisner et al., 2001).
4. Women are also more vulnerable to postpartum depression if they have been depressed during pregnancy (Moline et al., 2001).
5. Psychotherapy during pregnancy can reduce the risk of illness during the postpartum period (O'Hara, 1995).

6. Research has found an association between prenatal and postpartum depression, citing only half of the women with postpartum depression as new-onset depressions (Gotlib, Whiffen, Mount, Milne, & Cordy, 1989).
7. Sixty percent of women with bipolar disorder have a relapse after childbirth (Cohen, Sichel, Robertson, Heckscher, & Rosenbaum, 1995).
8. Research has shown that prophylactic antidepressant treatment reduced the recurrence of postpartum depression (Wisner & Wheeler, 1994).

The rationale behind having the client come in for a session *early* in the pregnancy, even if she is not symptomatic, includes:

1. If she hasn't been in therapy for a while, it is helpful to get a baseline assessment of how she is now doing, relative to what we know from our past relationship.
2. It is important to ascertain any changes that have taken place in her personal and emotional life as well as medical and physical status and ways that this might impact how she is feeling and coping.
3. It is helpful to reassess the marital relationship as well as other areas that may signal declining support or otherwise put her at greater risk.
4. If a woman is at risk for postpartum depression, prophylactic treatment, including supportive intervention, will decrease the likelihood of a full-blown episode and certainly reduce its impact, should it emerge.

Some women continue in therapy, from one baby to another, with no hiatus. Others may have been away for a number of years. When resuming work with a previous client, there may be times when it feels the work can continue right where it left off. Other times, clinicians may need to start again at the beginning. Or, it may be the case that so many years and events have transpired between the last visit and the current one that the only place from which to start is now. Whatever the point of intervention, the goal is the same: integrating what she has learned with what she still needs to know, in order to fortify her resources and help her feel confident about the pregnancy and postpartum period. That may include therapy, or it may not.

Keep in mind that advance planning for the postpartum period will:

- Reduce anxiety
- Enable her to mobilize resources
- Enhance communication of the issues by providing her and her partner time to explore and discuss options
- Restore a feeling of control

Recommendations for different treatment options will depend on a number of factors, primarily her history, the severity of her previous illness, and her response to the course of treatment. In our center, we have found it most helpful to be very direct and specific during these planning sessions. *What worked for you? Why was that helpful? What didn't work? Why not? What needs to be changed? What have you learned that you need to do differently?* These questions should be directed to both the client and her partner and refer to an assortment of issues such as medication, therapy, support systems, babysitters, sleeping patterns, division of labor, mothers, and mothers-in-law. We want to encourage a candid dialogue that carefully analyzes the client's previous experience so we can effectively replicate what worked and modify what did not.

At this point we utilize two tools of intervention:

1. Note to Self
2. The Postpartum Pact

Tanya loved the Note to Self. Her insight brought her to the point where she was well aware of all the things she needed to do for herself when she started feeling bad. The problem was, as she pointed out, "When I feel bad, I don't remember, or I don't feel like doing what I need to do, or I don't care." She told me about her worry that she wouldn't always feel as good as she feels now; "what if" she sank rapidly despite her best preparations? "It's as if right now, I know, but who knows how I'll feel after I have the baby? I know what signs to look out for, but I'm afraid once I'm in the middle of it, I won't know what to do."

Sometimes, in the fog of depressive thinking, women might not see what we think they could see, if they were thinking clearly. Symptoms get in the way.

The Note to Self is a made-up script, composed by the two of us together, relying on words from the healthy part of her self to the part that may struggle in the future. It reflects the strength of conviction emerging from a woman who has recovered. It is a voice that will resonate with her self if she becomes drained and weakened by depressive symptoms—as if the depressed self is separate, somehow, and might need the wisdom that only the current, healthy voice can articulate. The format can be as individualized as the content, but the gist is this: She will want and need a reminder of all that she has learned. The process of writing it together will be an empowering one, and sharing it with her partner ("give this to me if I start feeling bad") will increase her sense of control over the unknown.

The Postpartum Pact (see appendix) is a second tool that reinforces her ability to intervene on her own behalf. It is an agreement that reviews specific concerns and potential areas of risk that couples are encouraged to sit down and review together in preparation for the postpartum period. This process will effectively engage her partner and go far to reduce her feelings of isolation and anxiety.

This preparation work is implemented in the hopes of protecting the woman from the symptoms of depression. With postpartum depression, a previous episode sensitizes a woman to the development of future episodes after subsequent pregnancies. Therefore, it is best to prepare for the possibility that she might get it again. In this way, we tell her, she'll be prepared, and if symptoms do emerge, she will be armed and in a better position to intervene effectively. We know that early intervention augments recovery. If we presume that she might get depressed again, all involved will feel more prepared and in charge of the situation.

As pointed out in the concluding chapter of *What Am I Thinking: Having Another Baby After Postpartum Depression* (2005):

> Despite the timeless image of the perfect pregnancy and idealized portrayals of a new mother and her baby, women with a history of postpartum depression know there is a darker side to motherhood that is sometimes ignored, sometimes sensationalized, and usually misunderstood. Let's face it, it's something many healthcare practitioners and many women and their families would prefer not to talk about. Postpartum depression falls into that category of magical thinking: *If I don't think about it, maybe it won't happen.* It doesn't work that way and even if you know that, it can still be tempting to hope it just doesn't happen again.

Women don't like to think about getting depressed again. They don't like the idea of sinking without a lifeline, either. Because there can be long-term consequences of postpartum depression for women, their partners, and the baby, preventive measures are warranted. The more knowledge a woman has, the less she will fear the unknown. The groundwork presented in this chapter will help relieve her apprehensions and strengthen her resolve as she moves forward. The therapeutic work and practical intervention will help her weave together her understanding of how her previous depression impacted her life, her marriage, her family, and her spirit.

CHAPTER 31

Burnout, Boundaries, and Other Pitfalls

One of the questions that prospective students of The Postpartum Stress Center's training program are asked is: *What do you consider to be your greatest personal strength regarding this work?* Many, if not most, reply with reference to their compassion for others and their ability to empathize. The next question on the registration form is: *What do you consider to be your greatest personal weakness regarding this work?* Most reply with something akin to "I tend to get overinvolved or enmeshed if I'm not careful." Here we can see how a clinician's greatest asset can also contribute to one of the most prevalent occupational hazards.

Burnout. Psychotherapists are all too familiar with the concept of burnout. It is a complex concept with well-established descriptions in the world of psychology. For our purpose here, I will provide an overview of the concept within the context of psychotherapy, but my primary purpose is to refer to the specific demands of working with this particular population of postpartum women.

EMPATHY AND BURNOUT

If empathy is a great protector of the connection between therapist and client, it is also the greatest offender relative to burnout. It is, as we have seen, both a blessing and a curse for the sympathetic soul engaged in a helping profession. I remember coming face-to-face with this during my graduate internship, some 30 years ago. Naïve and forever trusting, I was thrust into the innards of a state mental hospital, a square, brick building with cold, desolate hallways, locked down for maximum security, for the sake of the "patients' best interests." On my first, and an unforgettable day, I entered a secure wing of the building where I was assigned and was inundated by curious, wayward patients coming up to me, for no reason other than to prove they were as mad as I feared they'd be. One told me he was there because his station on the Milky Way was overcrowded and as soon as they relocated, they would send for him. He really did have foil antennas on his head. Another grabbed my breast and stood motionless, smiling a Cheshire cat grin. I, too, stood frozen beside him.

Overwhelmed by my horror and inexperience, I scanned the room for guidance of some sort, glancing over to the nurses' station, better known as "the drug stop." I have no intention to be judgmental or exaggerate for melodramatic purposes. But if my memory serves me correctly, when I searched for support, I found four or five obese, middle-aged, weary-looking women sitting behind the desk, either talking to each other, or doing something else of little consequence. I recall being struck by the incongruity of the picture, with the patients roaming aimlessly and the staff sitting by, oblivious to it all. Of course, my impression could have been wrong, but I don't think it was. I remember thinking how difficult this work must be, day after day, when boundaries between what's real and what's not are blurred and challenged. I remember witnessing how strenuous it must be to prevent a physical brawl between two or more robust men when both are hearing voices and seeing things that aren't there. I learned how disheartening it was to work hard at helping someone change and grow, only to discover that what you say or do makes no difference whatsoever.

I also learned that these nurses had been working in this institution for many years. And sometimes this is just what happens. The paradox presented in my head was this: *If you care too much, the work feels painful and unrewarding. If you don't care enough, you are protected from the pain and you are ineffective.*

Maslach, Schaufel, and Leiter (2001), who have written extensively on this topic of burnout, refer to it as a syndrome of emotional exhaustion, accompanied by cynicism, avoidance, or distancing behaviors. When further describing how it is most often manifested, the researchers point to exhaustion as its central quality. According to Maslach el al. (2001), there are personality qualities that are correlated with degrees of burnout:

1. People who have an external center of control, thereby attributing achievements to others or to chance, are more likely to experience burnout.
2. Those who have an internal locus of control and the ability to attribute events and achievement to their own efforts and capabilities are better protected.

3. There is an association between people who cope with stressful events in a passive, defensive way being more prone to burnout compared to those who deal with the stress in an active way.
4. Individuals with low self-esteem may be vulnerable to burnout.
5. Individuals who are "feeling types" as opposed to "thinking types" are more subject to burnout.

The last item in this list is where the problem lies. While experts promote the value of empathy as the connecting force of all good therapy, if we, as clinicians, are not mindful of the mechanisms involved and monitor our own work along the way, we are vulnerable to varying degrees of fatigue and burnout. When we are working, listening, thinking, making decisions, and guiding, we are also feeling. It is important that we remain self-aware and honest about what we are feeling. Equally important is our ability to pay attention to any internal signals of discomfort in our bodies and to respond with self-nurturing measures or other action that might ease the discomfort.

BOUNDARIES

Sometimes these internal signals of distress stem from boundaries that have been weakened. We might, for example, be getting too close, projecting our experience onto our client's, or reenacting a personal trauma. Boundaries in clinical practice are established to create a safe and reliable arena within which our work takes place. The ability to self-regulate our emotional state is crucial. The need to protect ourselves from overinvolvement and, at the same time, preserve the integrity of our work warrants a discussion on why maintaining boundaries is essential:

- Clear, consistent boundaries provide a structure for many clients that can be a healing factor in itself.
- The therapeutic setting is where we model healthy boundaries in order to contain the affective experience.
- Mismanagement of boundaries can diminish therapeutic effectiveness and increase the likelihood of countertransference issues intruding into the process.
- Paying attention to our own needs should be a constant, self-critical analysis in the service of our client's best interest as well as our own.
- If we ignore our own needs in the service of our client, we run the risk of
  - Resenting our client
  - Our client's growing to resent us
  - Experiencing trauma by proxy

"Vicarious trauma." "Compassion fatigue." These are two terms used to describe what can happen to persons in helping professions who are essentially secondary witnesses to the trauma of their clients (McCann & Pearlman, 1990). If clinicians are caring people, how do we adjust this level of caring so we don't blur the boundaries? How do we care enough but not too much? How do we fine-tune our compassion so it echoes the emotion of the moment without risking a deluge of sudden sensations? How much is just the right amount? How do we stay true to our intention and still protect ourselves,while we remain objective and effective?

Margaret Rand, PhD, a perinatal psychologist, addresses this in her article "Self, Body and Boundaries" (Rand & Fewster, n.d.):

> People with a clear sense of their own boundaries are able to claim their own physical space, identify and embrace their own feelings, be spontaneous, say their real "yes's" and "no's," process information effortlessly, and make decisions appropriate to their own needs while remaining sensitive and responsive to the needs of others.

As if in perfect harmony with our notion of a sanctuary, or holding environment, and other gifts from Winnicott (1963) that we have woven into the postpartum domain, Rand refers to the mother–infant relationship when alluding to boundaries. Further explicating this concept is the work of neuropsychoanalyst Allan N. Schore (1994), who reminds us that the ability to identify behavioral boundaries actually begins early in infancy within a securely attached relationship, such as the primary alliance between mother and child. At the risk of oversimplifying concepts that far exceed my intellectual grasp, an infant eventually learns to monitor "cycles of arousal and relaxation," which eventually leads to emotional self-regulation.

Schore (1994) goes to great lengths and impressive neurobiological detail to describe an infant's attachment to the mother, which, he says, is based on the mother's healthy response and support of the infant's autonomic nervous system cycles as well as the mother's ability to regulate her own emotional states.

Here is where we see Schore's (1994) work and Rand's (n.d.) emphasis on the body–mind–spirit connection merge with our craft. Rand makes the parallel between the mother/infant relationship and the therapist/client relationship and tells us that when we attend to our bodily sensations and can, presumably, control our affect and adjust to those of our clients, we gain understanding and insight into our reactions. In other words, if we are attuned to our own emotional state and can regulate that appropriately, we will enhance the therapeutic alliance by monitoring our (healthy) response and modeling self-regulation and emotional management.

Many therapists tell me they can relate to this on a physical level. When we feel a strong emotional response, in unison with our clients' strong emotional expressions, on occasion it can be felt in our body, somewhere, usually encompassing our chest, our heart, and our breathing. Those moments of concentrated empathy are at the core of connectedness, but they are also the moments we must be on guard to shield ourselves from emotional overexposure. We protect ourselves by (1) being aware; (2) understanding the meaning of our reaction; (3) monitoring it with a physical response, such as deep breathing, if necessary; and (4) expressing it if or when appropriate.

PROTECT YOURSELF

Burnout is often accompanied by symptoms such as fatigue, inattention, and irritability and can be experienced by seasoned therapists or those new in the field. It is a natural response to the chronic emotional strain when working closely with other human beings, especially when they are troubled (Maslach, Schaufel, & Leiter, 2001).

So what can we do about it?

1. Take advantage of professional consultation and supervision on a regular basis.
2. Stay connected with other helping professionals who are working with you to reduce the isolation and enhance the multidisciplinary approach.
3. Make sure to stay up to date with good clinical practice techniques, including risk management, ongoing continuing education, changing laws, and other factors that will impact practice guidelines.
4. Follow our own good advice by staying involved in outside activities that can provide healthy outlets.
5. Set limits. This applies to family and work.
6. Listen to bodily cues. Clinicians must remember to make their own needs a priority, especially when feeling depleted.
7. Do not underestimate the value of informal peer consultation. Call a colleague. Stop someone in the hall. While remaining true to terms of confidentiality, get support, advice, or a new perspective.
8. TLC: Eat well, rest well, laugh often.

Perhaps the best way to avoid burnout is to maintain a sense of balance: balance between how much we give and how much we need, between our family and our work. Just as we say to our mothers in therapy that the best way for them to take care of their babies is to first take care of themselves, we must heed our own counsel. We must invest in ourselves, in order for our lives to be balanced and our work to be meaningful. Drawing attention to the factors that compromise our efficacy and our ability to remain objective is an ambitious, but necessary, task. Above all, we must remember to honor our deeply held principles that drive our work by staying attuned to our own physical and emotional states. Only then can we truly and unselfishly begin to master the therapeutic process.

PART 4

The Healing

CHAPTER 32

The Umbilical Factor

Mothers are fonder than fathers of their children because they are more certain they are their own.

Aristotle

Great thinker that he was, I imagine Aristotle meant no disrespect when he put forth the preceding tidbit of philosophy, and neither do I by referring to it. I must admit, however, it resonated strongly and transported me to July 18, 1984. This is when I delivered (such an active word for such a passive position; I instead say I was lying there motionless, sedated, and strapped down with my abdomen split open when they pulled out) my first baby. I remember being overcome by one single thought that occurred to me at that moment, which I still find curious and slightly troubling to this day. Let me explain.

Pregnancy is surely a shared event on many levels, but most men and women alike will attest to the fact that growing a baby inside one's belly is an experience that is hard to fully realize unless one has experienced it oneself. I opt not to probe the psychoanalytic and feminist theories of penis and womb envy, although I admit these concepts intrigued me long before I ever thought of my own motherliness. For our purposes in this chapter, we will focus on the unique alliance between a pregnant woman and her baby: a sacred union that can both burden and empower a new mother.

This early experience of oneness with the growing baby has inspired great writers, artists, researchers, and philosophers for centuries. Its uniqueness as a female experience has no equivalent in the male world. It can be, for some women, a self-absorbing period of specialness, marked by feelings of privilege and prestige. For other women, it can be an unpredictable and emotional passage fraught with anxious concern. Whatever the experience for each individual, it is one that holds unparalleled meaning and value.

For me, pregnancy was something about which I felt both anxious and determined. I was keenly attuned to each developing phase and stage (my husband says I could feel my baby's hair growing) and felt quite comfortable merging my newly married self with that of this unknown precious baby inside me. As pregnancy progressed and my baby and belly enlarged in unison, it felt as if every fiber of my being braced for motherhood. I held my breath and waited.

After a couple of failed epidurals and a preparation that felt perfectly scripted but far too medicalized to assist my maiden journey into motherhood, my baby emerged. Yanked out of a *how-do-they-get-a-baby-out-of-that* 4-inch incision, my baby was whisked quickly into the arms of someone other than me, and I remember hearing these words, which still echo in my head, as my devoted and fretful husband sat close, his head next to mine. Immediately, as they tugged our baby out of my belly, the thought that raced in my head about my husband was: *Whatever life has in store for us, whatever happens to you and me, I can tell you one thing right now for sure. ... This is way more my baby than it is yours.*

That's not exactly what I meant, but it's what I felt at the time.

Fortunately, some 25 years later, the subject has not come up again. Nevertheless, what evolved from that moment was the indisputable realization that women's bodies connect them to their babies in ways that, perhaps, men might never be able to fully understand.

My family and I do continue to make jokes about my umbilical cord, like when my first child was looking at colleges and I told him that my umbilical cord could only extend out to a 5-hour driving time radius. I stretched out my arm with a sweeping motion to demonstrate from point of origin, my belly button, out to some unknown campus, 5 hours' driving time, tops. My son knew I was kidding and that I would support any decision he would make. He also knew I was quite serious, and that I was not then or anytime in the near future going to accept his growing up and away with grace.

Recently, he moved out of our home and into his own, strangled by his overprotective mother's ambivalence and excited about his burgeoning independence. My sister phoned from states away: "So ... I hear you cut the cord."

They say there are no nerves in the umbilical cord, so cutting it is not painful for the mother or the newborn. Maybe that's true at birth, but some 20 odd years later, it's another story altogether.

The umbilical cord. It's a tube that connects a developing fetus to the placenta, and its chief function is to transfer nutrients and oxygen to the fetus and return waste products to the placenta from the fetus. It's hard to ignore the likeness to a mother's primary and unending function of providing nourishment and absorbing the scraps left behind. The ultimate irony here is that the blessing of this vital attachment is only matched by the burden it places on mothers who struggle with depression.

Elizabeth first felt this tug when her baby was only a couple of months old. She was doing well and, for the most part, probably could have adjusted unremarkably to her new life with baby if it weren't for the fact that she and her husband had recently moved to the Philadelphia area, thrusting her into unfamiliar places far away from the support of her family. She had no history of depression but had seen a counselor in the past for support when she found herself in the throes of major life transitions. She had shown that she was good at taking care of herself but often worried that she didn't know how much was too much in the "doing" department and wondered if having a baby would send her spinning into a panic. She had stopped working as a sales representative to stay home with her son. Always sure of herself and decidedly comfortable with the choices she had made in her life, Elizabeth suddenly felt out of control.

"I don't know what I'm doing. I turn around and everything I just did is undone. I keep going forward and end up in exactly the same place, getting nowhere. Why do I have to do it all? Why do I have to do it *all*? Why am I always the only one who does it all?"

"What is it that you're doing so much of?" I asked, trying to tease out the fatigue from the whining from the depressive thinking from something else unknown to me.

"I don't know," she pondered, made uneasy by the sound of her own words. "I do not know. All I know is that I keep doing the same thing over and over and I'm angry that I'm doing so much laundry and so much feeding and so much bathing. Jesus, can't someone else feed the baby? I mean, it's not like I'm breastfeeding or anything. When I tell Adam to go make a bottle he asks, 'How much? Where? Now? What if he's not hungry? Then what do I do?'" She smacks her hand atop her head, bracing it from spiraling right off the rest of her body.

I waited patiently, trying to decide if she was exaggerating or not.

"Okay, so he'll feed him a bottle once in a while, but really, I practically have to hand it to him."

"How would you like it to be?"

"I'd like him to make a decision about the baby without asking me how to do it."

"You would?" I asked, recalling a session past where she reprimanded him for diapering their son the wrong way. The tabs were too tight around the waist, I think. "Are you sure you'd prefer him to do some of these things by himself?"

"I think so." Elizabeth waits for my response. "Why wouldn't I?" she asks, with all the healthy skepticism of a confused and overwhelmed mother.

"You tell me. What is it that you really want from Adam?"

"I want his help. I really want his help. I want him to do it but … okay, so I want him to do it my way, don't I? It's hard for me to sit back and let him do it the way he does it, 'cause he does it wrong."

He does it wrong. Ah. Here we go. The mommy–daddy battle of who knows best. Mommy often wins by default. Daddy is often okay with that. Mommy wants that to happen but then resents it.

At the risk of overgeneralizing, the contradiction in terms is this: Women feel overwhelmed and feel they need to do it all. Women want to do it all. Women can't do it all. They resent doing it all. They don't want to admit they can use the help. They don't like or know how to ask for help. They get sick doing it all.

It's as if there is a built-in, inflexible expectation that, as a "good mother" or "good-enough mother," a woman is *supposed* to do it all, in keeping with primal instincts, maternal and otherwise. If she doesn't, she is flawed, imperfect, or, worse, a bad mother. Daphne de Marneffe (2004) talks about a woman's sense of prerogative in this role of primary parent in her book *Maternal Desire*. In it, she explores this paradox of women wanting and resisting this central role and how it often comes in conflict with their attempts to do this collaboratively with their partners.

"Why do I always have to be the one to decide what to bring in the diaper bag when we go out? I know it sounds silly, but, seriously, why do I have to be the one?" Elizabeth continues.

"Because … "

She sat waiting for what she hoped would be my well-thought-out words of wisdom.

"Because … you're better at it?"

"I'm better at what? Knowing what to put in the diaper bag?" she smirked.

"Well, yes, so to speak. If we see the diaper bag as a symbol that stands for everything you do that you wish your husband could help you with, then yes, don't you think, when you get right down to it, that you're better at it? Isn't it easier to do it than to fight about it or wait for him to do it, so you can then redo it the way you want it done?"

Believe me, I'm all about asking for help. This is even truer when women are balancing babies and depression. But I also believe that women should not waste precious energy in power struggles. As unpopular or controversial as this stance may prove to be, I believe that women are better at some things than men. I also believe that men are better at some things than women. Learning this and accepting it as true can smooth trouble spots and save marriages.

This may be profoundly incompatible with feminist thinking, but it is often at the crux of early negotiations when adjusting to parenthood. Mothers and fathers need to be taught that competing for participation points or who's doing a better job, regardless of whether it's in or out of the house, will get no one anywhere fast. Division of labor requires fine-tuning and good instincts.

Delegating roles, accepting limitations, and learning how to let go are essential for both parents.

The umbilical factor is a term I apply when describing some of the things that are hard to put into words that women, quite often, do better than men. When my son was days old and most content screaming at my breast, I did what I now tell mothers never to do. I brought him into bed with me to nurse, to sleep, to nurse again, and perchance to sleep again. Hour after sleepless hour and scores of ear-piercing wails later, my husband would awaken for work long before darkness gave way to the morning sun. He would turn to me, cast his eyes on his newborn son sleeping peacefully at long last, and burst with pride: "Honey, did the baby sleep through the night again last night?"

This is an example of the umbilical factor—or lack thereof.

There's a wonderful and wise comedian named Rob Becker (2008), whose Broadway-smash show elucidates some of the more entertaining differences between men and women. His humor is upfront and obvious, but his awesome accomplishment is how he intersects the gender gap by revealing clichés that not only make us laugh but also make us think. He ends the show with a message something like this: If men understand how women think and women understand how men think and we all understand that there *are* real differences and these differences need to be cherished and respected, relationships will thrive.

The umbilical factor is just a way for me to remind mothers that some things are not worth fighting over. This is especially true if she is feeling tired, overworked, underappreciated, and weary. The postpartum period is a time when both parents are competing for attention, purpose, and connection. Roles are being challenged and contested. One of the ways we can help soothe the commotion is to remind each or both to relinquish this competition and defer to each other's areas of strength. Even if it feels unbalanced at times. Sometimes teams work best when it's not always 50/50. Sometimes players sit on the bench and are pulled in to play when the timing is just right. At times, they strike out. Other times, they knock the ball out of the park. Couples who struggle for power might see this as surrender. It's about collaboration and compromise. It doesn't matter who's right or who's wrong. It doesn't matter who does more or who works harder. What matters is that couples work together, each listening to what the other wants and needs and continuing to do his or her best, to do his or her part.

CHAPTER 33

The Bracelet

It is in the space between inner and outer world, which is also the space between people—the transitional space—that intimate relationships and creativity occur.

D. W. Winnicott, 1951

When all the best theories and evidence-based research fall short of the perfect intervention, there is always magic. And if you *believe* ... it works.

Much of what I do in practice with postpartum women is based on a fundamental belief that the greatest power comes from within our clients and the ability to channel that power into personal connections. One prerequisite for connecting and establishing meaningful relationships is an individual's sense of self, often experienced as *do I feel lovable or worthy of this relationship?*

Implicit in the study of postpartum depression is the mother's crisis of confidence with respect to her budding relationship with her infant. *How can I take care of my baby if I feel so bad? Will I be able to do this? What if I make a mistake? What if I'm too sick? What if I'm just too tired?*

Trish was too tired. For 28 years she had been working hard to take care of her family. She was the "gifted child" singled out by parents who were too busy focusing on other things to take care of her. Distinguished psychoanalyst Alice Miller explores this concept in her book *The Drama of the Gifted Child* (1981) and reminds us that "experience shows that in the long run there is only one weapon available against mental sickness: emotional discovery and acceptance of the truth in our individual and unique childhood history."

Trish didn't think she was coming to therapy to talk about her parents. She was debilitated by intrusive thoughts and persistent anxiety. Her husband was worried about her because she wasn't "functioning as well as she usually does." She was exhausted and didn't know how she was going to be able to care for her baby. She thought she was tired because she was only getting 4 or 5 hours of sleep each night. I thought she was tired because she had little reserve left after spending a lifetime worrying that she might make a mistake and something terrible would happen. Because terrible things *did* happen.

Once, when Trish was 8, she found her mother lifeless in bed after taking too many sleeping pills. Alone and frightened beyond description, Trish knew to call an ambulance and her mother spent the next couple of weeks away from her in a hospital where "I wasn't allowed to see her." Trish would later learn that this was not her mother's first suicide attempt. And it would not be her last.

When she was 10, Trish would skip home from school to an empty house because "Mom and Dad had a business to run. It wasn't easy for them, though. We never seemed to have enough money and they were always fighting about business. It just seemed like they couldn't get it right. I felt sorry for them." Another time, when Trish was home alone with her little sister, she found her crying and bleeding from a nasty bicycle fall she had taken. Trish, only 10 or 11 at the time, called mom at work, who instructed her to go next door to a neighbor for help. She did.

When Trish was in high school, her father called home saying he needed her to take him to the hospital because he couldn't breathe and was having chest pains. This wasn't the first time she had been asked to do this. "Where's Mom?" she asked, and was told mom needed to stay at the shop to keep an eye on the business. Trish sat with him in the emergency waiting room for hours awaiting the diagnosis she had heard before; dad was treated for a panic attack and sent home.

I was struck by Trish's attentive and loyal references to her parents despite their emotional unavailability and inappropriate expectations. She was not done taking care of them, even as we spoke.

Referring to the sexual abuse by a beloved teacher, Trish recalls her mother's dismissive words as she walked out of the house, pointing to Trish's bedroom., "Oh please, don't be ridiculous. You're overreacting; now make sure your room is clean when I get home." Trish seemed to take this all in stride: "What can you do? This is just the way it is. The way it's always been. Living with two parents who were depressed all the time became a way of life for me. They didn't have much time to take care of anything else."

I asked her how her parents responded when she didn't feel good, as a child. "What if you were too sick to go to school; what did mom do?"

"She would tell me that I needed to decide how sick I was. Was I able to go to school or did I have to stay home?"

"How old were you when you were asked to make that decision?" I asked, thinking to myself how hard that is, even for an adult. It's one of those silly questions adults continue to ask themselves when they don't feel well: *Am I too sick to go to work? Am I sick enough to stay home?*

"I don't know; I was in elementary school; I was little. It was always that way, though, throughout school."

"So how did you decide? Do you remember?"

"Well, I guess I thought that I had to be pretty sick to stay home 'cause I didn't want to be home by myself. My parents would be at their shop, so I usually decided to go to school feeling sick." Trish's mood shifted; she sat quietly, choked by her words. "I don't think I was ever sick enough to stay home." She paused to clear her throat, "How sick did I have to be?"

I could tell Trish wanted to cry. It's a look that's hard to describe; it's something that can be felt. It's a look of quiet panic in fear of total disintegration, as if not crying will keep it all intact. All of it: all the years of going and doing and taking care of everyone and everything, no matter what—whether or not she was too busy, too tired, or too scared. Trish must have learned, early on, that crying didn't help. She knew it wouldn't get her very far and she needed to save her strength, so she learned to stop crying. It was hard for me to imagine that she had held it all together for so long that, even now, here with me, overwhelmed with emotion, she was unable to free herself and cry.

"I was never sick enough," she repeated.

We sat together in the brilliance of that sacred space that never fails to underscore how valuable this work is and how important it feels to me. It's a feeling that cannot be matched by any other professional experience. It's an energy that truly and quite genuinely connects the two of us. I gently brought Trish's eyes back to mine and said to her softly, with conviction, "You're sick enough now, Trish."

In 28 years, this might have been the first time she'd heard anyone tell her it was okay for her to take care of herself, which implied it was also okay to let someone else take care of her. She didn't have to be the only strong one anymore. She didn't have to fix it for everyone else. She didn't have to make all the pain go away. She could just be sick for a while and feel bad, and sad, and whatever else she needed to feel. And just when I thought she would surely cry, she smiled.

I returned the smile curiously, inviting her to explain her composure. "What? Tell me about the sweet smile on your face."

The sparkle in her eyes was not what I expected. "In a weird way it feels good to feel so bad, d'you know what I mean?" she giggled.

"I do."

The tears cascaded down her flushed cheeks. "Oh, my God, I'm sorry," she said, making excuses for what she surely felt was a loss of control.

"Sweetheart, it's okay. It's really okay. This is good. It means you don't have to hold it all in anymore. It means you don't have to do this all by yourself. You don't have to fix everything right now, and you don't have to feel bad all alone anymore."

"Thank you," she whispered, staying true to her respectful manner.

This is often the point where I break out the magic bracelet.

"You're very welcome, Trish," I said as I twisted around in my chair, taking hold of my black velvet box, a box I had purchased at Marshall's for $7.99 that now overflows with enchanting powers. "Do you believe in magic?" I typically ask, raising my eyebrows and nodding my head slightly, prompting an affirmative response. I usually hear something like "No, not really" or "Oh, yeah, sure, uh-huh. I believe in magic" as they read my cue that there is only one right answer to this question.

Trish giggled like a child hungry for a treat. "Of course I believe in magic."

"Good," I asserted with certainty, "then it will work."

I brought the box to my lap, placing the palms of my hands on top of it, knowing full well at this early stage of our work together that I was starting to look a bit eccentric, but I felt confident that she would go along for the ride. I opened the box so it faced her, displaying an assortment of colorful power-bead bracelets. These are fabulous elastic beaded bands radiating hope and the promise of good things to come. There are rose quartz, tiger eye, opalite, and jade. There are amethyst, moon stone, and smoky agate. There are snowflake obsidian and all kinds of other gems of which I have never heard. They are inexpensive (dare I say imitations of genuine jewel stones?)—like Cinderella's pumpkin, at rest until the spell releases their power. When I opened the box of bracelets in full view of Trish, the magic cast forth.

"Ohhhhhhh, wow. How pretty." Like a child with too many choices to make at the ice cream parlor, she leaned closer to me to get a better look.

"Pick one that you like," I instructed her, "and give it back to me for a minute." I love this moment. Some women grab the first bracelet in the pile and hand it to me. Others pick up one of interest at a time, inspect it, put it back and continue this until they find their perfect match, one that would go with anything they would decide to wear. Trish picked the soft jade. "I love this," she said as she handed it to me.

"It is beautiful, and it looks good with your eyes," I confirmed, never missing a fashion opportunity. It's part of the magic, connecting on a more surface level that speaks to her weakened feminine state aching for validation and a hint of beauty. I held the bracelet in my closed palm.

"Here's how it works. First we give the bracelet some information that is unique to you, what you need from it." I open my palm and look at the bracelet while I'm touching it with my other hand and speak deliberately and slowly:

> When you wear this bracelet, Trish, it's going to remind you that it's okay for you to be sick right now, that you are getting good help and you're doing all the right things to feel better. You don't have to do everything perfectly right now. It's okay for you to take the time to

take good care of yourself. You don't have to feel guilty about this. You don't have to work hard to fix it all by yourself.

Her eyes filled with tears that she fiercely held back with each blink. I put the bracelet on my wrist to demonstrate, pausing after each sentence.

Are you familiar with the rubber band trick to help minimize negative thoughts? You put a rubber band around your wrist and when you become aware of negative self-talk, you pull the band and let it snap back. It will sting and serve as a slightly negative consequence and reminder that will do two things. First, it allows conscious behavior to intercept the negative thought pattern by making you aware of what you are thinking, how you are thinking, and how often that is happening. Second, it sends a pain impulse to the brain and, from what I understand, it's hard to experience pain and obsess at the same time, so for the instant, it tricks your brain into not obsessing or thinking negatively.

Trish continued to follow my roundabout explanation intently.

So you wear this bracelet. And when you're driving, or working, or worrying, or finding yourself in the midst of busy work and your mind starts to wander back to old patterns of negative thinking, and your eye catches a glimpse of the bracelet, it will signal your brain to stop thinking that thought. You'll pick a sound bite, like "it's okay," and as soon as you see the bracelet, you say to yourself, over and over, "It's okay. It's okay." You take a deep, long breath and refocus. It's okay. Do you understand? It's a way of soothing yourself. So when you start thinking you don't deserve to get help or you're not sick enough or you should spend your time worrying about someone other than yourself, you'll see the bracelet and say to yourself, "It's okay. I'm okay; all is good. I'm doing the right thing. I'm taking care of myself. I will feel better again."

Trish sat quietly following my lead.

Now, here's the magic part. In order for the bracelet to work, you have to empower it. I can tell it what to do, but it won't work unless *you* empower it. So when you leave my office and have a quiet moment to yourself, maybe in the car before you leave, sit with the bracelet in your hand, close both hands around it, and then, tell it what you need it to do for you. Say it out loud or say to yourself and tell the bracelet, *I need you to remind me that everything is going to be okay. That I'll feel better again. That it's okay for me not to feel good now and I can let others help me. Everything is going to be okay.*

I looked directly at Trish and continued. "And then it knows what to do. And it works." I handed the bracelet to her eager hands with a final whisper of caution, "Don't tell anyone about it or what it does; it won't work as well." I winked, as I trivialized the grand display of supernatural force surrounding us. I am forever intrigued and touched by the seriousness with which each and every woman responds to this intervention.

"Thank you." She put it on her wrist.

"Don't forget to empower it."

"I won't."

I'm not sure if women actually wear the bracelet every day or if they dutifully put it on just prior to coming to their session with me, but I often notice it on their wrists. Some come in proudly reporting, "It works!" Others wear it and say nothing. But I take notice every time I see it on their wrists.

THE TRANSITIONAL OBJECT

In the spirit of Winnicott and his focus on dependence and separation within the context of the mother–infant relationship, here again we see how the therapeutic relationship parallels that of the mother–child relationship. Often paralyzed by the anxiety of moving forward into the mothering role, the therapist is perceived as an anchor, a sustainer during this fragile period. This illusion of omnipotence, as put forth by Winnicott (1956), enables the therapist to provide a safe space within which the mother can begin to heal and, ultimately, separate from, as she reenters the world between her and her baby.

In this way, the bracelet, much like the proverbial soft blanket, becomes an object of "us," transforming the "you" and "me" into a space of overlapping language. Nothing needs to be said in words, but the gift represents the words of the good mother, *I know you can do this. I can help you along the way. This will remind you that everything will be okay, even when I am not with you.* This message, in Winnicott's terms (1951), eases the transition to separateness and launches her into the ever widening environment of her self, with her baby.

On a perhaps more superficial, but no less important level, the bracelet is pretty. It is a sweet, smooth-to-the-touch object of femininity. During a time when self-care is not top on their list of things to do, postpartum women crave the simplicity of this object of beauty. Simply put, it feels good and it looks good to them. And when they find a quiet place to connect with it and empower it with their own words, revealing their innermost need for strength and direction, they begin to transform the therapist's power into their own. This is when the real magic begins.

CHAPTER 34

Therapy Exposed

The meeting of two personalities is like the contact of two chemical substances; if there is any reaction, both are transformed.

Carl Jung

"I was talking to my mother right before I came here today," Carrie stated 2 minutes into the session. "She asked me how it's going in therapy and I told her I liked coming here, and I thought it was helping. She said, 'It sounds like she's taking good care of you.' I said, 'Yes, she is.'"

"How did that feel to you, Carrie?"

"I think it was okay," she said, with hesitation. After pausing, she continued, "I mean, but, shouldn't I be getting this stuff from my mother? Instead of you?" as if composing a line for this book.

"What do you mean?" Therapists are often inclined to ask questions to which we think we know the answer. Most of the time, though, there are as many answers as there are women we ask.

"I dunno. I feel gypped, cheated. I guess I just keep thinking my mom should be the one who takes care of me; that's silly, though," she laughed nervously.

"Why is it silly?"

"'Cause. I'm 30 years old! Why would I want my mother to take care of me?"

"Good question. Why would you?" I smiled, thinking about the previous week when I was lying flat on my office floor, after a back injury of unknown origin suddenly made it impossible for me to sit, stand, walk, or breathe. There I lay, helpless and motionless, but managed to squirm to my cell phone

267

so I could at least pass the time with some meaningless chit chat. Fortunately, my day was over and all I needed to do was get home, so after a pathetic plea to my husband to come scoop me up, I called my mother. Why? Because she was 900 miles away and could do nothing to help but say, "Awwwwwww" or "Oh, no" or something else equally consoling.

Yes, I think that's why.

It's a mommy thing.

Imagine someone who never got that good stuff growing up, who was followed by the bottomless abyss into adulthood. Many factors may have conspired to obscure the picture, but, surely, women who have been robbed of this entitlement, as Carrie alluded, may spend much of their lives looking for something to fill that deep hole. They are looking for approval, love, acceptance, and nurturing. Fantasies of being smothered with kisses are cast aside and in their place is the backdrop of an enduring ache for connection. If a woman seeking such approval entered therapy while teetering on the edge on a life transition that felt unachievable, she would, most certainly, hope to find something to fill that hole.

Of course, she may not know that at the time.

"Carrie, do you think you're too old to want your mother to comfort you when you don't feel good?"

Her childlike smile emerged; perhaps she was embarrassed to hear the words spoken out loud. "Yes, I'm too old," she asserted. "Besides," she continued, "it's silly because that's just not who she is. I still think one day I'll wake up and she'll be that kind of mother."

"What kind?"

"You know, the kind that you see in TV commercials and movies. That mom who's baking cookies when the little girl skips home from school, and they giggle together with the essence of love spraying throughout the air and blah, blah, blah."

Many women carry with them the illusion of the perfect mother, whether they feel they were sufficiently loved or not. It's an illusion that is oddly comforting and stands juxtaposed against their budding vision of themselves as mothers. So they ask themselves: *Will I be a mother like my own mother? Will I be a better mother? Can I expect to be as good or as bad? Am I doomed to repeat all of her mistakes? How do I know how to do this?*

It's hard to be a mother on many levels.

There simply is no pleasure in rushing a nauseous child to the bathroom, praying for perfect aim. There is no gratification in a clean house when the urge to maintain order is driven by the fear of a return to childhood chaos. There is no relief when 4 hours of sleep come with one eye open in anticipation of the certain and startling cry. When they are healthy, women learn how to be mothers the way we learn lots of things, by doing it. They learn by doing their best and by making mistakes.

When they are sick with depressive thoughts, they learn, in part, by talk-ing to us.

THERAPEUTIC AND MATERNAL POWER

Once again we reexamine Winnicott's (1963) concept of the "good-enough mother" and adapt it to our therapy with new mothers.

Imagine a basic exchange between two adults and how it would feel to hear the response to the question "What do you need?"

I'm tired; I'm scared; I can't sleep; I can't eat; I can't stop crying; I can't do any-thing; I'm dying; I'm totally and utterly useless.

Now imagine how most caregivers would respond if these needs were attached to an infant or someone else's child. Imagine the hasty reaction to fix, feed, hold, comfort, console, and restore to health: *Let me find you a bed and dry your tears. Let me chase away your fears, offer you some food, and help you reclaim your strength.* Not everyone will have this response, but most readers of this book presumably would.

Winnicott (1956) views the constant, but often imperceptible, inter-actions between the mother and baby as central to the development of the infant's widening world. Infancy is characterized by *illusions of omnipotence* and, while this phenomenon is not an indicator of good mental health in later life, these feelings directed toward the primary caregiver are necessary to proper infant development (Winnicott, 1956). Satisfying these basic needs is a prerequisite for moving forward.

This is where we see our role as therapist glide into Winnicott's influential framework of thinking. During an initial assessment, we exhibit two simul-taneous objectives (Winnicott, 1956): (1) immediate attention to the fragile state of the client's physical and emotional needs (maternal preoccupation) and (2) the establishment of ourselves as experts who can facilitate symptom relief and recovery (illusion of omnipotence). Admittedly, the use of the word *omnipotent* is a stretch, so I'll explain to avoid misinterpretation. The parallel is this: The message to our client who is scared and suffering must be clear and straightforward. It is one that I refer to repeatedly throughout this book: *I know what this is and I know exactly what steps to take to help you feel better.* If clinicians cannot conceptualize themselves as experts who are confident about their ability to help her, strategies may be rejected and the effectiveness of therapy will weaken. Thus, as therapists and as experts, we are obliged to listen and to believe in what she is telling us; at the same time, we must keep the larger picture in sight. As all good mothers try to do, we must attend with keen responsiveness in a state of unselfish awareness.

I remember waking in my hospital bed 2 days after my C-section think-ing that today was the day of glory. I could eat solid food today! Fleeting thoughts of my new son, who had spent the night under fluorescent nursery lights, were replaced by delightful images of a Wendy's hamburger with extra pickles. What began with ice chips and ended with chicken bouillon and Jell-O over the past 2 days had left me hungry for the juiciest and junkiest food I could find. My husband was only too happy to indulge my craving and hurried to the street below. Other women might have wanted diamonds to honor this passage; I wanted Wendy's.

I could smell the sweet aroma of my unhealthy choice coming around the corner and felt like a teenager backstage coming face-to-face with a rock star. I quickly unwrapped the burger, and before I knew what was happening, I heard the unmistakable voice of my newborn hollering for his mother. What a tease. What an awful shame. My sacred moment of bliss had been abruptly interrupted by the call of motherhood and throbbing breasts. My instantaneous, though appalling, response was, *okay he's just going to have to wait.*

At that moment, with the unexplainable magic of split-second maternal instincts, I sighed and thought to myself: *This is the first of many more (the rest of my life?) sacrifices I will make on behalf of my children.* I remember the feeling in my chest; I can almost still feel it. It was as if my body physically substituted my hunger and desire from one object to the other. Though it doesn't seem quite fair to balance my baby with my burger, the realization of my needs' taking second place not only felt new to me, but it also felt quite doable and quite right. It felt like home.

As a mother, I continue to balance this equation, shuffling my needs with their needs and deciding whose needs come first, and when and why. Now that both children are adults, I suspect mine should come first. But they don't.

For a therapist, it is always the client who comes first. There is no *me* in this equation. It is very clear. It is very important. In this way, once again, we become the good mother.

ESTABLISHING THE CONNECTION

As the client moves through the early stages of this therapeutic alliance, she should be given messages that match those implicit in Winnicott's work—*you are not alone; you know where to find me; let me know if you need anything; let me know if something changes*—thus establishing early stages of intimacy, trust, and communication. This is not to suggest we adopt the strictest interpretation, representing ourselves as models of maternal self-sacrifice. But if we consider the fact that this mother in therapy experiences unbearable isolation and worries she will be dismissed if she lets anyone know how bad she is feeling, we are bound to respond in ways that may dare to cross conventional therapeutic boundaries. This is what drives me to modify some of the guidelines I was taught in graduate school. Therefore, in our center:

- She can call me if she needs me.
- I may call her before our next scheduled appointment if I am worried about her.

- If she is acutely ill, I will ask her to check in with my voicemail and leave me a message so I can hear how she's doing.
- I will answer her questions directly and not respond with psycho-babble innuendos.
- I will touch her with a soothing pat if I sense this will be comforting as she is entering or leaving my office.
- If she fails to show up for a follow-up appointment, I will call to make sure everything is okay.
- I will let her know if I'm worried about her in a voice that is both confident and empathetic.

In this work, we offer solace. Then, we stay in this comfortable space with her, in that therapeutic and healing zone, until she feels healthy and prepared to move forward without us. This parallels the way in which Winn-icott frames a mother's primary role. This role, according to Winnicott (1956), entails creating the illusion of being all-powerful, in order to provide early comfort and need fulfillment, and then creating the disillusion that steadily launches the child into a world that is separate from mother. The disillusion in therapeutic terms is the exchange between the "me" and the "you." Or, as understood from our perspective: *I'll help you do this while you are so ill by empowering you and fortifying your resources. It will feel like it's coming from me, but it's not. I am facilitating the process; you are doing the work.*

How do we explain all of this to the woman who presents these complex psychological constructs in perfect form, as Carrie did?

How do we put into words what this is, when she may already know it and feel it?

"We have lots to talk about regarding you and your mother, if you want to do that at some point. For now, are you okay with how this feels? Is it okay with you that your mom is your mom and what we are doing here is different? We can keep those things separate and still work on them, both at the same time. Do you know what I mean?"

"I do," she replied. "I'll just come here for that good stuff you always talk about."

"Well, I know this raises issues for you and I know you have some hesita-tion about it. That's okay. It makes sense that you would be ambivalent about this, doesn't it? For now, what I'd like to do is focus on your feeling better. As you get stronger and your symptoms are under control, we will come back to this and take a closer look at some of the issues it raises for you. Are you okay with this for now? You and me?" I ask, gesturing out to her, then back to me.

"You and me? Here? Oh, yeah." She laughed out loud with assurance and conviction. "I wouldn't pay you so much if it didn't feel so good!"

I returned the smile and thought to myself that it's not really funny, and it's very, very true.

CHAPTER 35

Finding the Power to Heal

I have been blessed by the companionship of a man who makes me laugh on a daily basis. If he does this with intention, I would say he does it with perfect execution. But because I believe he is totally oblivious to his capacity to entertain me at the oddest times—such as at 3 in the morning, after I've rudely awakened him because I couldn't sleep—I'd say I'm a very lucky woman.

There are things in life that help us get through. For some people, these riches are magnificently incorporated into their lives through their environment or through just plain good luck. For others, they are intrinsic to their nature, finding goodness wherever they are and wherever they look. Sometimes wonderful things happen fortuitously, and sometimes they happen after great determination. Generally speaking, most people have to work at attaining these riches, these healing moments—especially during difficult times.

What may not be innate for many can be learned. It is about acquiring new skills and learning to open oneself up to the possibility that something yet untried can be integrated into an existing set of strategies and make things feel better.

THE BUTTERFLY

There's a sweet saying that has been plucked from the chamber of anonymous authors and found its way into popular culture and right into my heart: *Just when the caterpillar thought the world was over … it became a butterfly.* The large, blue, square-shaped magnet that displays these words is posted at home and at work, as an ever-present reminder to me and to those around me that good things are going to happen.

I love the image it conjures up, and the message is one that holds particular meaning to someone who is besieged by despair. The implication that change does not come to pass overnight is unthinkable to someone who is anxious for instant relief. Transformation, in nature or in recovery of one's body and soul, takes place after untold periods of time, hard work, pain, and discomfort. When healing does take place, it is, indeed, a metamorphosis.

Butterflies are amazing creatures that can take our breath away. How many of us have found ourselves sitting outside in a warm sunlit spot catching a glimpse of a butterfly who was diligently trying to avoid us? Or, what about being blessed by a rare occasion of contact with such a creature who, for reasons unknown, decides to settle somewhere on our body, tickling our knee or perching on our arm? When that happens, we stop breathing for a second. *Don't move,* we think, lest we lose this precious moment of connection too divine to really understand. We stop and gaze at the loveliness of it all.

In my work with postpartum women, I rely on butterflies as an icon of good things to come and joy that is possible and within reach. This belief that good things can still happen, perhaps unfathomable to our client in the earliest sessions, will eventually be endorsed by women who secretly long for it.

When discussing butterflies with clients, I tell them there are some people in this world who seem to be surrounded by butterflies. Good things just seem to happen to them. People are attracted to them. Positive energy emanates from them. This is not something you can see, of course, but most who are tuned in can feel it.

Some women respond to this notion with objection, reminding me that they just are not wired that way. I agree that it's hard to find the butterflies in one's life if it's not a natural tendency. Try convincing any pessimistic thinker that all she has to do is think optimistically! We know it doesn't work that way. But if I didn't believe on some fundamental level that people could change the way they think and the way they behave, I couldn't do the work I do.

So we look for butterflies. One could make the argument that it's a cognitive intervention and that we are helping our clients engage in a process of reframing their negative thinking. This would be true. I prefer to think of it as increasing their awareness and tapping into their own unsung potential for healing and self-renewal. *There are butterflies all around us,* I continue; *we just have to look for them.* This is hard to do when everything appears dark and menacing but important for us to say, nonetheless. Looking for butterflies when our client feels like her world is crashing around her is an instruction that might, quite frankly, infuriate her. Yet, what we are doing is instilling the early stages of hope and providing a hint of reassurance that it will not always feel this way. As treatment progresses, looking for butterflies gets easier.

If a woman isn't sure what this means, I will help her, but most of the time, women bring their butterflies right to the session:

"Sitting in the grass with my 3-year-old looking for four-leaf clovers."

"The look on my toddler's face yesterday when she saw her first balloon."
"A cloudless, crystal blue sky."
"My husband taking my hand and squeezing it tight when I least
    expected it."
"The smell of home-baked cookies when I passed the corner bakery."

What *is* a butterfly? It's a moment of pure joy. It's an instant in time when everything feels right. It's a thing, or a look, or a feeling. It's a sense or an energy that grabs us from behind, often when we are not looking. Most of the time, it is fleeting. Sometimes, it rests right in front of us. We cannot see it if we do not look for it. If we aren't mindful, we will miss it, and it will be gone. If we find it, it's exquisite.

"GOOD THINGS ARE GOING TO HAPPEN"

These words are hand-painted on a ceramic plaque that hangs on the wall in our waiting room. In part, it's decorative, but in truth those of us who work there secretly expect subliminal rejuvenation. It's part of the magic.

Most would agree that positive emotions help buffer individuals against negative outcomes, both psychologically and physically. Again, we must make allowances for temperaments and personality types that are more inclined to think positively or negatively and admit that adjusting thinking patterns to this extent is not an easy undertaking. Still, the implication for clinical practice is that we can present this as an option and a goal for those who feel inclined or motivated to move in this direction.

Optimism, or the anticipation of a good outcome, has been specifically associated with adaptation, while pessimism, particularly during stressful times, has been determined to have a negative impact on an individual's psychological health (Scheier & Carver, 1992). Whereas it may be intuitive that during periods of greater stress, an optimistic outlook would help one feel and cope better, in a study by Grote and Bledsoe (2007), it is suggested that it also protects against depressive symptoms.

Grote and Bledsoe (2007) support the notion that optimism during pregnancy is protective against the emergence of postpartum depression, and the authors suggest that optimism can be enhanced by helping clients develop constructive coping strategies. They also make the excellent point that pregnancy may provide a good time to discuss some of these strategies because pregnant women tend to be motivated to make changes that will improve their health before the birth of their babies (Cowan & Cowan, 2000).

The prospect of enhancing resilience is intriguing. Why do some people cope better than others? And if we explore this, can we use what we learn to help some cope better than they might if left to their current resources? Years ago, when I was first studying postpartum depression, I familiarized myself with some of the characteristics linked to positive adaptation so I could observe this in our clinical practice. The interesting part was not whether women who possessed certain traits would ultimately recover better but, instead, that if we enhanced these qualities associated with resilience or nurtured them in therapy, recovery might be smoother. And at the very least, it might be *perceived* by women as smoother.

Think about it: Helping her perceive her recovery as smoother, whether or not it's proceeding as desired by her, can be almost as valuable as any tried-and-true intervention. This is demonstrated when we see a woman who is significantly more ill adjust to her symptoms and course of treatment better than a woman who may not be as sick. "Better" is more than just a judgment call based on a clinician's interpretation of how she is doing. It is also not a coincidence that women who perceive their recovery process as better feel better, whether they are actually progressing at the desired rate or not. *It feels better to feel better,* I often say. As ridiculous as that may sound, it means that even when recovery is impeded or taking longer than our client might like, it feels better for her if we can help her focus on things that feel good.

Taylor, Lichtman, and Wood (1984) paid particular note to this area of individual adaptation to traumatic events or serious illness. One of the more striking results of their research was with women diagnosed with breast cancer. Their objective was to identify resources that could assist these women in their return to their previous level of functioning after going through this traumatic event. Throughout the interviews, Taylor et al. heard stories of lives that had changed, many for the better. Some reported that they had a new sense of themselves as stronger and more resilient. Others commented on their desire and ability to rearrange priorities and make time for things that were most meaningful to them. Additionally, social relationships, particularly with family and close friends, had been enhanced. Blaming others for their illness or attributing it to external or uncontrollable causes was associated with poor adjustment (Taylor, 1983).

In this study, confirmed by additional work by Taylor, Kemeny, Reed, Bower, and Gruenewald (2000), it is reported that many of the women expressed the belief that they could personally control the cancer and stop it from returning. Other women were adamant that they had been cured, even though medical records indicated that the illness was progressing. The researchers were stunned by this result and concluded that even when these beliefs were contradicted by medical evidence, the women holding these beliefs were no worse off; they concluded that the positive illusions appeared to have protective psychological effects.

Taylor et al. (2000) suggest that stressful experiences can be associated with positive consequences such as finding new meaning in life, developing improved coping skills, and reevaluating personal priorities. Furthermore, their work highlights the notion that when perceptions are characterized by a positive sense of self, a sense of personal control, and an optimistic (even unrealistically optimistic) vision of the future, they reveal personal resources that help individuals cope and deal with intensely stressful events.

This association between psychological beliefs and mental health is demonstrated in the postpartum population when we hear some clients reveal how the depression has changed their lives for the better in some ways, how their marital relationship is stronger, or how they are now better able to take care of themselves. This is not the case for all women, but what can be learned from the ones who do report a stronger sense of self?

In line with the research on individual adaptation to trauma, there are characteristics that have emerged as restorative elements for women recovering from postpartum depression. Although to date there is no rigorous study of this application to postpartum women, the value of strengthening these attributes as part of their treatment should be evident. "Characteristics of Positive Postpartum Adaptation" is inspired by Carver, Scheier, and Weintraub (1989) and their research on coping strategies. It is a compilation of qualities we have determined, at our center, to be associated with a more positive adjustment to the illness of postpartum depression, as well as its course and treatment.

CHARACTERISTICS OF POSITIVE POSTPARTUM ADAPTATION*

1. Positive reinterpretation and personal growth
2. Active coping
3. Planning
4. Seeking social support
5. Humor
6. Ability to accept and trust current state
7. Rearranging priorities
8. Insight
9. Capacity for or interest in intimacy
10. Self-expression
11. Spiritual search

RESILIENCE

Resilience is the capacity to recover from stress, adversity, or misfortune. A person's vulnerability to stress and capacity for resilience and/or recovery are complex and can be understood as contributing to depressive illness as well as providing protection from it. Are we able to look at a woman's personality type and unique characteristics to determine how we can best tap into her reserve resources and maximize her adaptive capability?

---

* ©1999 by The Postpartum Stress Center (Adapted from the work of Carver, Scheirer, & Weintraub [1989]).

If clinicians are aware of the personality strengths and weaknesses of the client that were present before the onset of the illness, it enhances the overall picture and offers valuable information for therapeutic intervention. As we traverse this uncharted terrain with each client, we listen to the cues and watch for signs of who she is and who she was before. Not always, but occasionally, when we stay present with open eyes, we can see a woman sparkle with hints of virtues that will help her navigate the healing process.

If we review the list of characteristics of positive postpartum adaptation, we can imagine, for example, how the therapeutic alliance might address each specifically—how we might, for example, teach coping strategies, encourage social networking, assist and expand her personal reflection as it relates to her experience, and help her adjust her expectations or engage in proactive planning. Sometimes, it is helpful to review this list with the client, creating a dialogue of what she thinks her areas of strength are and which ones she hopes to cultivate. When the timing is right, this discussion can be extremely fruitful as well as encouraging for her, as we focus on identifying and enhancing resilience.

It is well established that stress generates more stress. A major stressor like a depressive illness can produce additional stressors, such as financial issues, relationship concerns, or isolation from social support—all of which may then exacerbate the illness or intensify the symptoms. The physical and psychological impact of this enormous amount of stress on the body and heart and soul of a woman drives much of what we do. It follows, then, that one of our goals in working with postpartum women should be to foster resilience. There are several reasons to believe that if we tease out the characteristics that appear to be associated with a more positive outcome, we can augment recovery by decreasing their perceived helplessness and increasing adaptive functioning.

EMPATHY

Empathy refers to the ability to identify with and understand the emotions, thoughts, or beliefs of another. It lies at the heart of every psychotherapeutic relationship. Most therapists are quite familiar with this concept from an academic standpoint as well as their own personal perspectives. As we've noted, most therapists find themselves drawn to this work partly because of a highly developed sense of empathy.

In one notable study by **Marci, Ham, Moran, and Orr** (2007), researchers interested in the psychobiology of empathy monitored the physiological and emotional responses in both the clinician and client during psychotherapy sessions. As defined by **Marci et al.** (2007), the sharing of positive emotions, as well as the physical arousal that accompanies it, contributes to the empathic connection during therapy. Throughout videotaped therapy sessions, clients and therapists were monitored to register their physiologic responses. Interestingly, during moments of high positive emotion, both clients and therapists had similar physiologic responses. Furthermore, higher levels of shared responses led to a greater perception of and higher ratings by the client regarding the therapist's degree of empathy. Simply put, when the therapist joined the client and matched a level of mutual emotional response, the client perceived (and rated) the experience as more meaningful. Finally, it was pointed out by the study's lead author, Dr. Carl Marci, that there was less physiologic agreement when the therapist was speaking, as opposed to listening, suggesting that clinicians are more likely to achieve true empathy when they are listening rather than talking.

As we return to the world of D. W. Winnicott, we come full circle in our examination of how best to describe and maximize this reciprocal journey between the therapist and the postpartum woman. Psychoanalyst Margaret Little (1993) describes Winnicott's capacity for empathy in her essay "Psychotherapy with D. W. W.," as she recounts her own psychoanalysis with him:

> He did not defend against his own feelings but could allow their full range and, on occasion, expression. Without sentimentality he was able to feel about, with and for his patient, entering into and sharing an experience in such a way that emotion that had been damned up could be set free.

Through the words of Margaret Little (1993), Winnicott reminds us that the power to heal women with postpartum depression comes from within them and within us. Our ability to engage them in a process of self-exploration, combined with their motivation and readiness for this challenge, can result in the lessening of symptoms and a burgeoning sense of control. Our open-mindedness and willingness to trust what we are hearing and feeling from all people, including ourselves, will facilitate the recovery and healing of the postpartum woman. In being open, we become more authentic. As Winnicott (1963) stated, "The analyst is *holding* [original italics] the patient, and this often takes the form of conveying in words at the appropriate moment something that shows that the analyst knows and understands the deepest anxiety that is being experienced, or that is waiting to be experienced."

When we effectively adapt to our clients' needs and communicate genuine affect, we can create the metaphorical holding environment that Winnicott put forth. Ultimately, it is this capacity to establish and sustain an empathic connection between ourselves and our clients that nourishes our good-mother role and allows our clients' true self (Winnicott, 1960) to emerge.

THE EXPERT

Perhaps our greatest resource to promote healing that comes from within us is presented in seemingly contradictory terms. We are, indeed, experts who know nothing. Each woman brings to us her own history, struggle, perspective, and resources. We must project authority on this subject yet remain open to that which our clients reveal to and need from us. As we listen with an impartial ear, we set aside our emotional reactivity and desire for a quick fix and return to a state of calm presence. We must simply be there. Mark Epstein (1995) is a psychiatrist and author of *Thoughts Without a Thinker,* an inspiring book that I highly recommend that all clinicians read. In it, he blends the contributions of great psychoanalytic influences, such as Freud and Winnicott, with his study of Buddhist scholars, and he weaves the combined principles superbly within the context of the psychotherapeutic experience for both the clinician and the client. Epstein describes the use of silence in therapy:

> When a therapist can sit with a patient without an agenda, without trying to force an experience, without thinking that she knows what is going to happen or who this person is, then the therapist is infusing the therapy with the lessons of meditation. The patient can feel such a posture. This is most important during the patient's own silences, for when he falls silent, he is often just about ready to enter some new and unexplored territory. The possibility of some real, spontaneous, unscripted communication exists at such a moment: but the patient is, above all, sensing the therapist's mental state to see whether such communication will be safe.

Our ability to sit with, listen to, and tolerate a mother's anguish and ambivalence will create the foundation for her capacity to work through it. Epstein (1995) makes reference to Freud's original (1914) definition of "working through" resistance "to overcome it by continuing, in defiance of it." Implicit in this reference is the notion that the best way out of a negative feeling or experience is to know that it's there and allow it to be and to experience its unpleasantness. It's hard to tolerate pain whether it is our own or our clients'. Our society is sometimes quick to numb or medicate pain, and, despite our best intentions, sometimes we unintentionally judge those who have trouble moving beyond severe emotional pain. But when there is great loss, deep pain is inevitable. Accepting this inevitability forces us to sit tight with it and encourage our clients to do the same. In time, understanding their pain will lead to greater self-awareness and insight.

As postpartum specialists, we are granted an esteemed position of expertise, one that entitles us to speak with authority and, at the same time, create an environment that is conducive to psychic comfort, change, and personal growth. This can be accomplished by our secure hold of a new mother's vulnerability and all the imperfection that entails. The postpartum woman aching from untold anguish may or may not be aware of what is keeping her from feeling better at any moment in time. It may be the wrong medication or it may be a bad marriage. Ideally, in our presence, she will learn how to access resources both outside and within herself. She will learn how to bring about resolutions and settle for nothing less. She will learn that she can, if even for a split second, imagine the glorious return to her former self. That is when she will begin to believe in the possibility of finding peace with her motherself, her new normal, as she integrates who she was with who she is now.

CHAPTER 36

Recovery Revealed

"How did you know Dad was the man you wanted to spend the rest of your life with?"

My darling daughter, in pursuit of her own interpersonal harmony, if not perfection, never failed to honor me with her detailed attention to my life and my choices while she was growing up. Feeling obliged to offer the best answer, the exact, right answer, the answer that would help shape her wandering heart and soul into the excellence for which she strived, I replied, "You just know."

It was the best I could come up with. She looked at me inquisitively, with her typical suspicion of my touchy–feely proclamations. "What do you mean? How did you just 'know'?" she asked insistently.

"Well, I'm not sure, exactly. But somehow, after years of good instincts, scores of life experiences, both negative and positive, intuitive know-how, and a strong sense of who you are and what you need, something happens. Something clicks into place and everything feels right. Then you throw in a little bit of good luck, good timing, and a general belief in the order of the universe, and there you have it. You just know."

Clearly, she had no idea what I was talking about and either secretly hoped that she, too, would develop a comparable comfort zone amid the frenzy of teenage angst or perhaps (and far more likely) was thinking her mother was again spouting psychobabble nonsense. Either way, I knew what I meant.

Sometimes, in life, you really do just know.

When one of my therapy students asked, "How do you know when therapy is working?" I responded with similarly vague confidence, "You'll know." There are some things you just cannot teach. One either learns it on his own, at some point in one's life or professional career, or one may never learn it. It's like finding a good babysitter. Some people mistakenly believe that a younger babysitter is not as responsible or as "good" as an older, more experienced one. I say, if someone is good, she is good at 14. And if she is not good—that is, does not have good instincts with children or is not passionate about the work she is doing—then it's likely she won't be any better when she is 19. A teenager can learn how to warm up a bottle or change a diaper. But if she doesn't want to be there or isn't comfortable playing and laughing with your child, she won't be a good babysitter, no matter how old she is.

To be sure, one cannot entrust the success of the therapeutic process based on our good instincts. Obviously, that would lead to inferior work, and, what is more, we cannot forget that some clinicians have better instincts than others. Not everyone will just *know* when things are working well. Even seasoned therapists miss it.

So how do we really know? Beyond the good instincts, it is a combination of hard work, relationship expertise, and the application of good, solid, evidence-supported theories. Sometimes, we can actually see it working, as in a look in her eyes. Sometimes, we can hear it, as in something she says. Sometimes, we can feel it.

Sara was 32 years old, married to a fabulously warm and attentive man who accompanied her to her first session when she was 2 months pregnant with their first baby.

Her depressive symptoms were impressive, marked by a lack of motivation; slow, deliberate speech; and a loss of pleasure in all activities that had previously enriched her life. She reported poor eating, sleeplessness, a distinct disconnect from her husband, and isolation from other meaningful relationships. She had a history of suicidal thoughts and a tendency to shut down completely when she felt overwhelmed with symptoms. She either functioned exceedingly well or not at all.

Still, she appeared remarkably comfortable sitting in my office, expressing symptoms of significant impairment. This contradiction always intrigues me. After we exchanged obligatory clinical declarations (hers: why she was here; mine: how I could help), I followed up on my observation of her discomfort.

"You okay?" I asked Sara.

"I'm fine," she smiled, seemingly both grateful and annoyed that I had asked. What a silly question to ask, she must have thought, sitting here in the office of a psychotherapist who specializes in the treatment of depression.

When someone responds with "I'm fine," I'm never really certain what they are saying or how they would like me to proceed. Nonetheless, I rarely accept it as an answer, if I sense something different.

"You're 'fine'?" I repeated. She looked anxious and sad, but I had no frame of reference with which to compare. During an initial session we are forced to weigh our "good instincts" with everything we may know, or not yet know, about who she is and who she was before she felt so bad. We need to be careful not to judge or leap to conclusions that may prove misguided.

"I'm *fine*," she asserted with deliberate emphasis, which I interpreted as "don't ask me again." So I didn't.

At least, not at that moment. I waited until she felt a bit safer. Then, I did ask.

"Sara, how are you feeling right now? You scored a 20 on this Edinburgh screen. Are you familiar with this tool?"

"Well, I know that it means I'm depressed. But, Karen, this is not a new state of being for me. In fact, I'm quite at home with the way I feel. Ted dragged me in here today—he's so sweet, isn't he?—because he's worried; I'm not sure why. I suppose it's because I'm pregnant, and he's right. I mean, it's not like I'm going to do anything to harm myself or our baby. He doesn't like to see me sad. He just thinks I should feel better."

"Do you? Do you think you should feel better?"

Sara sat still. She had a captivating manner about her. I would ask her a question and she would stop to think. When she was thinking, she would sit up tall, close her eyes, and breathe deeply. I could feel her listen to my words while she cautiously pondered what she was feeling and what she wanted to say. She crossed her feet and folded her hands together with deliberate execution. Then she slowly rocked forward and back again, inhaling deeply through her nose before she spoke. I was beginning to understand what she was saying when she told me she was so used to being depressed that it was no longer an undesirable state. I didn't quite believe it to be an accurate reflection of how she felt, but I understood what she was telling.

"I'm not sure," she whispered, as she opened her eyes and looked into mine.

There was no doubt that I needed to know more, but her ambivalence was screaming out to me. Sara wasn't sure if she deserved to be there or feel better, but she was certainly going to do the right thing for her baby.

I later learned how hard Sara had worked most of her life to keep herself from "spiraling rapidly down and out beyond all recognition." Years of therapy had brought her to this conclusion: Therapists were nice. They meant well. They tried hard. But no one could really understand who she was or made a difference in how she felt. It was a waste of time. "No offense," she'd tease with a smile.

"None taken," I'd smile back.

Sara was a perfectionist who held herself to harsh scrutiny on a moment-by-moment basis. She believed that others would be overly critical of her behavior, as taught to her by her punitive stepfather, which left her strangled by unrealistically high standards of performance, overwhelming guilt, and feelings of inferiority. As a consequence of these maladaptive beliefs, Sara was constantly seeking approval and relief from her own unforgiving attitudes.

After months of working together and her transitioning from pregnancy through the postpartum period, Sara learned to rely on the therapeutic relationship as one that would, perhaps for the first time, not criticize or reject her. It took her a long time to trust this collaboration, and her vulnerability was never far from the surface. But in time, she was able to experience the shift from unrealistic beliefs about herself to more realistic and adaptive beliefs, resulting in symptom relief and inner strength.

Months into our treatment together, Sara walked into my office with an unfamiliar flair. She sat purposefully and perked her posture up, awaiting my greeting.

"Good morning, Sara." I couldn't help but notice her quiet eagerness, almost impatience, as if she had something exciting to share with me. "You look good." I jumped at the opportunity to compliment her.

"I do?"

"You do." We smiled.

"How do you feel?"

"I feel good," she remarked, with hint of cautious optimism.

Her delivery of speech was different on this day. As I often do, I found myself simultaneously distracted and absorbed by the process of how she was looking and sounding, rather than specifically attending to the content of what she was saying. She spoke of her relationships with her husband and her son and how fabulously they had been living life with renewed enthusiasm. I continued to look at her face while she spoke of hiking adventures and sipping pomegranate juice with her son when they became too weary to climb further.

"You really look good today, Sara. You look different. Your eyes look different."

"Really? What do you mean?" She seemed a bit embarrassed, as if I could see inside her, exposing something private and personal.

"I'm not exactly sure. I can see something in your eyes that wasn't there before." I continued, speaking slowly, "It's a sparkle, of sorts, as if your eyes are open, almost as if you can see things differently. I can hear it in what you are saying, and I can actually see it in your eyes."

"Really? Tell me more," she snuggled back into the comfy couch and took great pleasure in what she interpreted as a flattering remark. She relished the glory of my tribute to her hard work. "Oh, do tell. ... " She closed her eyes and soaked in my words, as if quenching an eternal thirst.

When our session came to an end, Sara approached my desk, as she had done for months, and sat to write her check. She looked up at the photograph of my children on my desk and asked, "Is this a new picture?"

"No. It's always been there."

"Oh." She turned to finish writing the check and handed it to me. She turned to the picture again and then back to me. She saw me smiling. "Oh. Wow. It's always been there? Hmmmm ... interesting." She replaced her checkbook into her handbag and moved toward the door.

"My eyes are open," Sara mimicked my words as she sauntered out.

"Indeed, they are."

THE HEALING BEGINS

One of the markers that distinguish postpartum depression is the variable nature of the clinical course. Although mood fluctuation is normal within the postpartum period, as a woman begins to recover from depression during this time, she may be especially unsettled by the vacillation the recovery process can present. Just when she starts to think she is feeling better, she may experience a return to an earlier level of heightened anxiety or other disturbing symptom. Though recovery will vary from individual to individual, it is common to hear women say, "I had 3 good days in a row; then, out of nowhere, I felt consumed by anxiety and sadness again. I thought I was getting better; what's happening?"

During the first months of the postpartum period, feelings are emotionally charged and heightened by the demands of caring for a new baby. Often I find myself reiterating what seems so obvious to me but is lost in the chaos of the moment: *You are exhausted. You are hormonally, biologically, and physically compromised. You are sleep deprived. You are recovering from both childbirth and a major depressive disorder.*

Sometimes, they forget this. For this reason, it is necessary to remind them:

- *Take it slow:* It is common for postpartum women to be eager to return to their previous level of functioning as quickly as possible. It is helpful for the clinician to articulate this in order to identify her impatience, but further clarification is needed. Slow, incremental improvement is better than a rapid return to normal functioning, which may set her up for a crash later on down the road.
- *Do not expect too much too soon:* Postpartum women are often frustrated and discouraged by the pace of recovery. Sometimes this is due to their perfectionist inclinations that urge them to recover with swiftness and precision. Other times it may be because they are restless and fear that the longer it takes, the harder it will be to get back to who they were. It's as if their life at home is moving forward without them, and they must hurry to reunite for fear that they will lose momentum and remain off course. Here again, we must restate the value of letting go of how they *think they should be* recovering. We must also reframe what healthy objective expectations of recovery look like and help them modulate accordingly.
- *Do not overextend:* There's laundry to be done and marriages to work on. The list of things to manage ranges from the ridiculous to the sublime. From diapers to sanity. The tendency to overdo is tempting for all. Reassure clients that everything that needs to be done will get done and that overexerting themselves is likely to intensify their exhaustion and sabotage their recovery.
- *Expect intermittent bad days or slight regressions in progress:* Because of the additional stressors during this time, recovery can be quite a

bumpy ride. Alerting clients in advance and reinforcing this message as needed can reduce their expectations and ease lingering concerns that their recovery is not *good enough*.

• *Guilt will get in the way:* Postpartum depression and guilt are one of the absolutes of this work. Mothers feel guilty because they are doing too much or too little, they are working outside the home, or they are working as stay-at-home moms and not bringing in additional income. They feel guilty because they are breastfeeding or because they are bottle-feeding. Or, they are not reading to their children enough, or not hand-grinding their vegetables, or teaching the children a foreign language. The list never ends. Because guilt will be exacerbated during depression and recovery, it is helpful for clinicians to accept the fact that it will be present. Trying to talk a mother out of feeling guilty or trying to help her see that it is getting in the way is, quite frankly, useless. Her guilt is embedded into this process, and our best response is to understand that, identify it to her so she knows it is something we expect and see all the time, and put it out there as something that can accompany this process, whether we attend to it or not.

Guilt is a waste of her energy. Our job is to help her use that energy in more positive directions. Focusing on the guilt will be disempowering and unproductive. As she continues to recover, the guilt that is symptom driven will lessen. A derivative of this guilt may emerge further along as she returns to a healthier state and longs for the time lost during the depression. At those times when she blames herself for her illness and her loss, it is best to remember that grief is at the heart of this pain. Her guilt will subside as she moves through stages, by mourning the loss and reclaiming her sense of self.

Often we are asked by our clients how long postpartum depression lasts. Postpartum depression can last for weeks or many months, depending on a number of variables, such as course of treatment, severity of symptoms, and external stressors. This is another example of a question that arises early in treatment that doesn't have a clear answer and is, more times than not, anxiety driven. Although it is a valid concern, the best response is to address the anxiety rather than attempt to predict the unknown course a client's illness will take. A vague response, such as *it may be weeks or months*, will provide an overview of what she might expect and help suspend any expectation of a quick fix.

Recovery from postpartum depression is a process, one that can take on as many forms as there are women going through it. Sometimes, it is crystal clear, with striking clinical presence. Most of the time, it is understated, with slow, steady, incremental progress. Either way, it is often something that clinicians will detect before the client recognizes it in herself. We've seen that it may be a look in her eyes or the words she uses to describe how she is feeling. It may be the way she holds her baby or the care she took getting dressed for the day. Identifying these early steps toward recovery, however inconsequential they may appear at first glance, will reinforce the healing momentum and strengthen her staying power. Telling her she is getting better by revealing the subtle or observable shifts toward recovery will fortify her belief that the hard work is paying off and that she will find her way back to her self.

CHAPTER 37

The Search for Meaning

Sara continued to make good progress in therapy. After months of alternating between scars from her past and untapped visions of her future, she was beginning to settle nicely into a place she hardly knew. Every once in a while, she would wiggle like a child uncomfortable in new clothes—brand-new clothes that someone else had bought for her: a "I-know-it looks-good-but-I'm-not-sure-it's-my-style" kind of wiggle. She wasn't yet sure if she liked how any of this felt yet. It's not exactly that she liked feeling depressed. It's more like she was so used to being depressed for much of her life that she was now both exhilarated and apprehensive about how things would go from here.

Sara told me about her rare and uncharacteristic shopping excursion at the mall that morning, which clearly had invigorated her.

"Like my new shoes?" she asked mid-session, showing off her slip-on clogs lined with plushy fleece by pointing her toes in my direction.

"I do. I love them. How cozy and comfy they look."

"They are. I can't remember the last time I bought a pair of shoes." She smiled, sharing my acknowledgment of her long-overdue indulgence.

"So you're feeling good, huh?" I thought the hike in the Poconos she had told me about was nice evidence of her revived emotional state. But buying a pair of shoes? I'm not sure she ever would have done that prior to therapy.

"I am." She continued to sit up proudly. "But I have a confession to make." She inhaled slowly as she often did, before speaking. "Earlier today when you asked how I was feeling, and I said 'good,' remember that? Well, ... actually, I didn't want to say it then, but ... truthfully. ... " She lowered her voice, as if to guard the delicateness of her words. "I feel ... great." She gave me a full-tooth grin—something, I suspect, that had not graced her face for most of her lifetime.

What a gift for a therapist.

"Sara, it's so good to hear you say that. And so good to know you feel that. Do you know what kept you from telling me you felt great earlier?"

"Of course I do. I wanted to leave room for suffering."

If suffering is going to have any meaning to our clients, our greatest task is to help them put it in some kind of context that makes sense to them. This journey in search of meaning is best tackled after symptom resolution has been achieved or is well on the way. Making sense out of an emotional trauma is a facet of healing that can have far-reaching implications for the rest of our clients' lives and their ability to cope in the future.

Viktor Frankl, a neurologist and psychiatrist, wrote an autobiographical account of his experiences as a prisoner in Auschwitz in his powerful book *Man's Search for Meaning* (1959). He describes, in horrific detail, the tormenting days in a concentration camp prompting his philosophical exploration of who survived such torture, and why.

Therapists may be quite familiar with this book. I recall going to a conference on eating disorders years ago and the speaker began her presentation by telling the audience of clinicians that at each initial session, she hands a copy of this book to her new client, asking her to read it before returning to the next session. She makes it mandatory. Anyone who has read the book knows why.

Frankl (1959) refers to a universal drive for meaning in one's life, often precipitated by suffering, and inspired by a quest for existential purpose. He notes that when we are stripped of everything "except, literally, our naked existence," it compels us to make sense out of the experience. Our sheer survival may depend on it. He speaks of suffering:

> There was plenty of suffering for us to get through. Therefore, it was necessary for us to face up to the full amount of suffering, trying to keep moments of weakness and furtive tears to a minimum. But there was no need to be ashamed of tears, for tears bore witness that a man had the greatest of courage, the courage to suffer.

Although no comparison to this extreme torture is intended, women with postpartum depression do experience a similar feeling of nakedness. They describe a core self that is left excruciatingly exposed, defenseless, and unprotected from the ravages of depression. As they proceed through treatment with initial symptom relief, the urge to make sense out of the experience may be equaled by their hunger for renewed strength. The coexistence of these desires often creates the impetus for powerful therapeutic work, a stepping stone to full recovery.

Thus, as Frankl (1959) models for us and advocates on behalf of all who suffer, we find ourselves somewhat obliged to help our postpartum clients strive for meaning to their suffering. Therapists who have practiced in this field for some time know that this is often a natural course of therapy, one that does not entail prompting from us. The motivation to find meaning in an illness that deprives a mother of precious time with her baby is a driving force for many postpartum women who remain in therapy.

Whether this pursuit is therapist led or self-initiated, the context is best understood within the framework of Shelley Taylor's trauma work (1983), referred to in chapter 35. It's a framework that adapts nicely to our postpartum work and one that should guide the later stages of recovery. Understanding Taylor's three principles of cognitive adaptation—(1) the search for meaning, (2) gaining a sense of mastery, and (3) the process of self-enhancement—provides the foundation for a deeper understanding of how the depression has impacted our clients. It also may explain how many of them move through recovery, proclaiming an enriched sense of self.

1. *The search for meaning*: This refers to an understanding of why the event occurred, as well as lessons learned. The principle here is that attributing a purpose to the event helps an individual regain a sense of organization and comprehensibility in one's life (Taylor, 1983). In our work with postpartum women, the event would be the depression itself, and/or the associated loss of self, and/or the loss of the early relationship with the infant.

   Coming to terms with depression is not a simple undertaking. It can be said, categorically, that a particular woman may never really know why her depression emerged at any given time. The search may even lead to more questions than answers. Still, it is the very search itself from which springs forth a wealth of material upon which our clients may draw. We may be able to help them come to their own conclusions in this matter; they might have an epiphany, such as "I think this happened to make my marriage stronger." Or, they may experience a subtle acceptance: "I hope I've learned how to take better care of myself." Some women say that their experience with postpartum depression has given them a new mission in their lives and say they feel compelled to help others who may experience postpartum mood disorders.

   One way to do this is by starting support groups or engaging in community support services in other ways. I have known many women who have recovered from postpartum depression (calling themselves "PPD survivors") who have gone back to school to obtain a graduate degree in counseling or a related field so they can pursue a career in helping others through this. The passion with which they follow their desire to make this happen is impressive. Many say they have no choice: This is their calling; they say that perhaps they got sick so they could see how it feels and now help others. This is one example of what we mean when we talk about a search for meaning.

2. *Gaining a sense of mastery*: Again, we review the experience, which takes into account the illness itself, symptoms, treatment, course, impact on family functioning, and recovery process, as well as how she now feels about the experience. What can be done differently? What can she do to change the way she feels about it? Here, the focus is on maximizing her sense of personal control and reducing feelings of helplessness. Some of this takes place as an analysis of the preceding weeks, but most of the emphasis should concentrate on the here-and-now so she can reconstruct a sense of control. Justifiably, it's hard for a woman to imagine any positive outcome arising from such anguish, but her ability to do so will go far to fortify the healing that is taking place.

3. *Process of self-enhancement*: Previously plagued by negative thoughts, our client's focus should now turn to areas of empowerment and coping strategies. As she considers the coping skills she used to manage the internal and external demands of the stress of motherhood and depression, she can begin to emerge with renewed empowerment. Self-evaluation and the process of discovering which attributes have contributed to her recovery will boost self-esteem and add value to her experience. Any or all three of these adaptive themes may be initiated by the client or the clinician. In either case, we must remain attuned to this part of the process as her attempt to put closure on the open wound.

LESSONS LEARNED

As we attempt to balance what has been learned with that which remains unexplored in this final phase of work with the postpartum woman, it brings to mind the paradox of holding on and letting go. Each of us tends to recoil from unpleasant experiences and do our best to avoid them. If it is purported that our soul is strengthened through suffering, then part of our responsibility to our client is to help her surrender to that which she cannot, or should not, change. Winnicott (1956) spoke of this lesson when he referred to the mother's failure to meet all of her child's needs as the baby develops, thereby fostering independence as she loosens her hold on his environment. Similarly, if we can teach our client to endure the losses incurred through her experience with depression and accept the disappointment in herself she will inevitably bear, true healing can begin. In the end, isn't it really about helping her come to terms with who she is, depression and all?

It is always difficult to face difficult emotions. When these pressing emotions rest side by side with the spectacular life changes that accompany new motherhood, it is particularly challenging. As a postpartum woman in therapy wrestles with why this happened and struggles to uncover the lessons learned, we encourage her to immerse herself in the voice of depression. If she listens carefully, she can find pathways to greater self-awareness and tolerance.

CHAPTER 38

The Quintessential Mother

When all is said and done, much of what we do as postpartum specialists rests largely on what it means to be a mother. If it didn't, we would be able to apply any theory of depression and treat postpartum women as we would anyone else with depression, whether there were a baby in the picture or not. Many mental health practitioners are currently doing this. It may be enough in some instances, but from where I sit, it feels immensely inadequate.

Imagine a woman besieged by haunting thoughts and unspeakable sadness associated with an opportunity in her life she has waited for and idealized for months or years. Consider the woman who does not, for a moment, regard these negative feelings as symptoms; rather, she believes herself to be appallingly flawed and unworthy of the esteemed mother role.

As therapists who specialize in the treatment of women with postpartum depression and anxiety, we are honored by this unique position that each and every woman we see sanctions. As we discussed in the early pages of this book, she may or may not want us there initially, peering into her oozing wound. But as the dynamics of the therapeutic process take hold, we find a comfortable spot in this sacred space between her and ourselves. We are alone together.

As all therapists know, this process can be filled with extraordinary satisfaction as well as great pain. When we do it right—that is, sufficiently absorb ourselves to the exclusion of everything else at that moment—it can be all consuming. Postpartum women, who are simultaneously recovering from physical demands as well as suffering the panic and outrage that mothering is not coming "naturally" for them, are propelled, along with us, into this therapeutic alliance. It is, as we have seen, this connection that will ultimately promote healing.

Other experts from various disciplines have identified this universal need for new mothers to be cared for during the postpartum period. In popular literature it is referred to as "mothering the mother" or "nurturing the nurturer," primarily referring to the thrust of attention that postpartum women are entitled to and require for optimal functioning. When we add depressive symptoms and the breakdown of all expectations into that mix, we see how postpartum therapists take on a role that distinguishes them from therapists who do not specialize in this area. It's hard to ignore the impact of sleep deprivation, hormonal fluctuations, feeding and bonding issues, physical exhaustion, and the transition to motherhood. These are just a few of the changes that remain in the background with each step we take.

The occupational hazards of this work are similar to those of any therapeutic relationship; depressive symptoms can be invisible, yet scorching at the same time. We must constantly be on the lookout for what is not being said and must protect ourselves from the elaborate expressions of untold heartache and profound grief. If a therapist is isolated in private practice, the value of good supervision cannot be stressed enough. Having the opportunity to connect with other therapists who are familiar with this work is a great gift, and there is absolutely no downside to it. Group settings are nice for this, and individual supervision is a plus for additional support and guidance. What matters most is that clinicians find a comfortable and reliable setting within which they can identify and explore the issues raised while doing this specialized work.

"IT'S OKAY"

I suspect that most clinicians have a beloved children's book that resonates for them to which they occasionally refer or pull off the bookshelf and read aloud to their clients. I have several favorites, but the two I read most often to my postpartum women are Judith Viorst's *Alexander and the Terrible, Horrible, No Good, Very Bad Day* and Crescent Dragonwagon's *Will It Be Okay?* Reading a good book to a client can serve a couple of purposes. First, it leads them into a more dependent posture, of sorts, which might help relax any opposition they may have to the process. The role of mother reading a storybook to her child is too obvious to ignore, but frankly, it can really work wonders to set the stage for the relationship to unfold. The second reason for reading these or other relevant books is equally obvious: They have fabulously important messages. I presume that most therapists reading this book are familiar with *Alexander.* Those who are not should buy the book, read it to their own children if they have any, and then put it on a bookshelf in their offices for easy access.

Will It Be Okay? (Dragonwagon, 1977) may be a less familiar book. It was brought to my attention by a colleague who worked with me at a local mental health agency in the early '80s, who candidly spoke of her own mother issues. She showed me the book and told me how nice it would be to have had a mother like the one depicted in this story. I also remember how sad it was to listen to her reveal layers of unresolved grief after 50 years of trying to make sense of her relationship with her mother. Later, when I was working with postpartum women, I rediscovered the book sitting on a back shelf and read it again.

Will It Be Okay? tells the sweet story of an uncertain child, beset by normal growing pains, who goes to her mother for reassurance. The message is clear: Things will not always go the way you want them to. When you are disappointed, you have more power than you know to make things better. When things are really unbelievably bad, you can still find ways to make it okay. And if you have internalized the consistent love of a nurturing mother figure, whether it's your own mother, your therapist, your grandmother, or yourself, no matter what happens, it will be okay.

The mother in this story is, of course, the quintessential mother. She has all the right answers, to be sure, but what she does best is support her daughter by providing tools. They talk about being alone, being hated by friends, being scared, being hurt, and feeling unloved. What mother hasn't snapped a patronizing response, "Don't worry, everything will be fine," only to realize it had zero impact on the child's fear? Here, instead of simply telling her daughter that everything is going to be okay, she tells her how to make it okay, by suggesting alternative behaviors or images that can help ease the anxiety:

> "But what if there is thunder and lightning?"
> "You sit at your window
> and watch the rain beating down
> over the houses and fields
> in the dark night.
> You see how special it is,
> because the lightning
> shows the rainy sky and countryside and all the city.
> You pay attention
> because the loud thunder is calling you,
> saying:
> Look, look!
> The world is receiving a deep long drink!"

As the mother in this book is devoted to her child's emotional well-being, so, too, we follow a similar path as we teach, guide, support, and care for the postpartum woman who comes to us for help. The beauty of our therapeutic relationship is that while we escort her in and out of what she already knows but may not yet realize, we transcend our own personal agenda and she remains our sole focus. We take our own life experience, mix it in with everything else we have learned, and serve it up with other bits of wisdom, as we share the space with a woman desperate for answers and relief. We sit and we listen to the cries of fear, the thunder and the lightning. We acknowledge and reassure. Then, we tell her what she might do, how she might make it better, how she can reframe, endure, or survive this. We guide her, we show her, or we wait for her to discover it on her own in our presence. However it comes to light, we let her know she does not have to suffer alone anymore.

The end of the short book concludes with a reference to the child's fear of the mother's dying. In response, the mother superbly recounts all of the book's lessons in one evocative passage, as she ties it all together in the form of the perfect transitional object. The author's opening and last lines of the story are words that inspire my response to a client's similar recurring query:

"So will it be okay?"
"Yes, my love, it will."

This quick read about a mother and her young daughter captures the essence of what we do in therapy with a postpartum woman. I suppose it's part of the reason this work feels so good. Our work is immeasurably rewarding and transformative for both the client and the clinician, as it parallels the childhood fantasy of the perfect mother.

We make use of this space by predominantly modeling unconditional acceptance and tolerance of all emotional states. Clinicians should never underestimate how good that feels to the client. If they never received that from their own mothers, it will feel strangely appealing. If they did receive it from their own mothers, it will feel like a warm blanket.

Lastly, remember that postpartum women who come seeking our assistance know what they need from us; they just don't always know that they know. Though I strongly encourage ongoing training, excellent supervision, and constant access to current information and literature, bear in mind that each woman who comes and sits in front of us will teach us what we need to know to help her. They are our greatest teachers. Listen to them. Ask them what they need. Listen carefully to what they say, but also take note of what they have not yet said. Above all, let them know that, amid the frenzy of the postpartum highs and lows and the social and medical communities who instill impossible expectations, there are still people who are tuned in to how they feel and take this very seriously. Tell them there are things they can do to feel better. Tell them that sometimes good mothers get sick. Tell them they will not always feel this way and that they will, indeed, feel like good mothers one day soon. Tell them it will be okay.

Appendices

A. OUR POSTPARTUM PACT*
(To be reviewed by couple prior to delivery)

We are reading this together because I need your help. It's possible that after the birth of our baby, I might not feel well. Because I'm at risk for depression again, we need to be alert for some of the signs so we can take care of things right away. I need to trust that you will be observant and candid about what you see and what concerns you. You need to trust that I am a good judge of how I am feeling.

In the event that my symptoms interfere with my ability to determine how I am feeling or what is best for me, it is crucial that you solicit help from our family, our friends, my doctor, and my therapist. We both know that it is better to be overly cautious than to assume things will get better on their own.

I need you to tell me now that you understand how important all of this is and that you are prepared to act accordingly. Knowing this will give me great comfort. These are questions that may help you determine how things are going after our baby is born. They may not all apply to us, but they will provide a general outline for us to follow. As we review each point together, we will highlight those that feel particularly relevant to our situation so we don't miss a thing. If any feeling or experience that we went through has been overlooked, we will discuss that together and add it to the pact. After our baby

---

* Excerpted from *What Am I Thinking? Having a Baby After Postpartum Depression* by Karen Kleiman, 2005.

comes, I will depend on you to go over these items a number of times at various stages because things can potentially change.

Here's what I need you to look for:

- Am I acting like myself?
- Is there anything I am saying or doing that seems out of character to you or not like my usual self?
- Am I too worried, too withdrawn, too talkative, too euphoric, too exhausted, hyper, too unhappy, too uninterested?
- Do I seem confused?
- Am I crying all the time?
- Am I eating the way I usually do?
- Am I taking care of myself the way I typically do?
- Am I spending time with the baby?
- Am I reacting appropriately to the baby?
- Do I seem too worried or too detached regarding the baby?
- Am I less interested in things that used to interest me?
- Is my anxiety getting in the way of doing what I need to do?
- Do I seem preoccupied with worry or fear that seems out of proportion to you?
- Do I resist spending time with people who care about me?
- Do I seem too attentive or concerned with the baby's health?
- Am I having trouble sleeping, even when the baby is sleeping?
- Am I overly concerned with things being done perfectly, with no room for mistakes?
- Are you noticing that I am isolating myself even though I am fearful of being alone?
- Am I too angry, too irritable, too anxious, too short-tempered?
- Am I having panic attacks, where I say I can't breathe or think clearly?

Here's what I need you to listen for:

- Am I saying anything that scares you?
- Do I say that I think something is wrong?
- Do I say I just don't feel like myself?
- Am I telling you I can't or don't want to do something that surprises you?
- Am I telling you I want leave or stop all this or hurt myself?
- Am I asking you for things I don't usually ask for?
- Am I saying I'm too scared or too tired or too unable to do what I need to do?
- Am I asking you to stay home with me all the time?
- Am I telling you I can't do this without your help?
- Am I expressing feelings of inadequacy, failure, or hopelessness?

- Do I keep asking you for reassurance or ask to you to repeat the same thing over and over?
- Am I complaining a lot about how I feel physically (headaches, stomachaches, chest pains, shortness of breath)?
- Am I telling you we made a mistake and I don't want this baby?
- Am I blaming everything on our marriage?
- Am I worried that you'll leave me?
- Do I tell you that you and the baby would be better off without me?
- Am I afraid I will always feel this way?
- Do I tell you I'm a bad mother?

Here's what I need you to do:

- Check in with me on a regular basis, several times a day. Ask me how I'm feeling and ask me what you can do to help.
- Enlist our friends and family to help whenever possible during the early weeks. Even if I resist, please insist that it's better for me to accept the help.
- Remind me that I've been through this before and things got better.
- Help me, even if I don't ask.
- Insist that I rest, even if I'm not able to sleep.
- Make sure I eat, even if I'm not hungry.
- Spend as much time caring for the baby as you can.
- If you are the slightest bit worried, encourage me to contact my doctor and therapist. If I protest, tell me that you will call them for me and come with me to the appointment.
- Remind me that even if everything's okay, it may be helpful and reassuring to make an appointment so that we know for certain.
- Take a walk with me.
- Help with the baby during the night. If you're not able to, please make sure someone else is there to help so that I don't get sleep deprived, which would make everything worse.
- Trust your instincts if you are worried or you think something needs to be done differently.
- Talk to me. Tell me what you're thinking.
- Sit with me. Stay close even when there's nothing to say.
- Help me get professional help.
- Help me find the joy. Help me stay present and appreciate the little things. Help me find and feel the butterflies, the giggles, the hugs, the sunshine, the belly laughs, the smiles.

Here's what I need you *not* to do or say:

- Do not assume I am fine because I say I am.
- Do not leave everything up to me if I am feeling overwhelmed.

- Do not use this time to work harder or later or longer if I need you at home during the first few weeks.
- Do not tell me to snap out of it. I can't.
- Do not let my resistance or denial get in the way of what we need to do.
- Do not tell everyone how well I'm doing if I'm not doing well.
- Please do not tell me I am strong and can do this without help if I need help.
- Please do not sabotage any effort I might need to make to seek treatment, such as resisting medication or pressuring me about the financial strain.
- Do not complain about the cost of treatment.
- Do not pressure me to have sex while I'm feeling so bad.
- Please do not do anything behind my back. If you are worried, let me know. If you want to call my doctor, let me know you are doing this.
- Do not forget to take care of yourself during this time.
- Make sure you are eating well, resting as much as possible, and finding support for yourself from friends and family.

Here's what I need you to say:

- Tell me you will do whatever I need you to do to make sure I feel healthy.
- Tell me you can tolerate my anxiety, my fears, my irritability, my moodiness.
- Tell me you are keeping an eye on how I am feeling so things won't get out of hand.
- Tell me you love me.
- Tell me I'm a good mother.
- Tell me it's okay if things aren't perfect all the time.
- Tell me you are not going to leave me, no matter what.

Here's what I need you to remember:

- I'm doing the best I can.
- Sometimes the big things that seem scary at first aren't as scary as more subtle things.
- For instance, if I have an anxiety attack or snap at you, even though it's upsetting, it may not be as troublesome as if I'm isolating myself in the bedroom and quietly withdrawing.
- If you're not sure about something regarding how I am feeling or how I am acting, please ask for help and tell me you will call my doctor or therapist.
- If I become symptomatic, chances are things will not get better on their own.
- Do not underestimate how much I appreciate the fact that I know I can count on you during difficult times.

Things we need to add to our list:*

1.
2.
3.
4.
5.

* ©2008 by The Postpartum Stress Center (www.postpartumstress.com)

B. PPSC SUICIDE ASSESSMENT FOR A POSITIVE EPDS SCREEN*

Note: All clinicians administering the Edinburgh screen should ask the following questions to every patient who answers item 10 (the thought of harming myself has occurred to me) with a 1, 2, or 3. These questions are in no particular order and have not been validated in any way. It is recommended that these or similar questions be part of the initial clinical interview when triaging a woman with postpartum depression.

- ☑ How often are you having thoughts of hurting yourself? (*determine frequency and acute nature of thoughts*)
- ☑ Are you able to describe them to me? (*assess current level of distress and willingness to disclose*)
- ☑ Have you ever had thoughts like this before? (*history of previous thoughts increases current risk*)
- ☑ What happened the last time you had these thoughts? (*assess coping potential*)
- ☑ Does your partner know how bad you are feeling? If not, why not? (*numerous factors contribute to failure to disclose, all pointing toward potential areas of vulnerability*)
- ☑ Whom do you consider your most primary connection for emotional support? (*explore all support options*)
- ☑ Does this person know how you are feeling? If not, why not? (*explore her resistance in order to determine degree of withdrawal, level of shame, ability to reach out for help*)
- ☑ Does anyone in your family know how you are feeling? (*engaging family member provides important link when her instinct is to isolate self*)
- ☑ Have you ever acted on suicidal thoughts before? (*previous suicide attempt increases current risk*)
- ☑ How do you feel about these thoughts you are having? (*assess affective response and level of distress to confirm ego dystonic nature of thoughts*)
- ☑ Do you have specific thoughts about what you would do to harm yourself? (*assess intent and plan*)
- ☑ If you do have a plan, do you know what is keeping you from acting on it? (*assess and increase her awareness of meaningful connections to reduce feelings of isolation and despair*)
- ☑ Are there weapons in your home? (*never presume to know the answer to this; in addition to the obvious danger, weapons serve to stimulate the overactive obsessional thought process with temptation too great to ignore. All weapons, whether locked or reported as inaccessible, should be removed from the home without delay*)

---

* ©2008 by The Postpartum Stress Center (www.postpartumstress.com)

☑ Do you have access to medications that could be harmful to you? (*all medications she is taking or has access to should be monitored by her partner until suicidal thoughts have responded to treatment, reducing risk of temptation*)

☑ Is there anything else you can think of that I can do right now to help you protect yourself from these thoughts? (*gives her permission to reveal any unidentified method or related worry*)

☑ Have you thought about what the implication would be for your baby? (*her connection to her baby may provide a critical lifeline*)

☑ Do you feel able to contact me if you feel you cannot stop yourself from acting on these thoughts? (*establish a verbal or written contract for safety*)

Important Points to Keep in Mind

- Be clear about your ability to help her.
- Determine whether hospitalization is required.
- Contact family members, if indicated, in her presence.
- Initiate psychiatric contact.
- Follow up with any and all requests (e.g., weapons out of the house).
- Determine level of follow-up (e.g., "report in" phone calls to/from patient to ensure safety).
- Do not avoid questions that make you uncomfortable.

C. PPSC SYMPTOM LIST*

Please check all that apply to how you are feeling.

- ☐ Can't fall asleep at night
- ☐ Unable to sleep, even when baby sleeps
- ☐ Wake up several times during the night
- ☐ Wake up early and can't go back to sleep
- ☐ Sleeping too much
- ☐ Tired all the time

_____

- ☐ Overeating
- ☐ Eating less than usual
- ☐ Unable to eat
- ☐ Nauseous
- ☐ Butterflies in stomach
- ☐ Losing weight
- ☐ Gaining weight
- ☐ Craving sweets
- ☐ Forcing myself to eat
- ☐ Unable to force myself to eat
- ☐ Eating too much junk food
- ☐ Caffeine in my diet
- ☐ Alcohol in my diet

_____

- ☐ Tightness in my chest
- ☐ Difficulty breathing
- ☐ Feeling of impending doom
- ☐ Nervousness
- ☐ Hot/cold flashes/chills
- ☐ Anxiety
- ☐ Panic attacks
- ☐ Dizziness
- ☐ Chest pain
- ☐ Shakiness
- ☐ Palpitations

- ☐ Heart skipping beats
- ☐ Numbness
- ☐ Restlessness
- ☐ Shortness of breath
- ☐ Feeling separate from my body
- ☐ Headaches
- ☐ Diarrhea
- ☐ Vomiting

_____

- ☐ Irritable
- ☐ Fearful
- ☐ Sad
- ☐ Angry
- ☐ Hopeless
- ☐ Inadequate
- ☐ Dependent
- ☐ Helpless
- ☐ Withdrawn
- ☐ Frustrated
- ☐ Worried
- ☐ Overwhelmed
- ☐ Guilty
- ☐ Worthless
- ☐ Uninterested in pleasurable things
- ☐ Lack of energy
- ☐ Exhausted

_____

- ☐ Scary thoughts about my baby
- ☐ Scary thoughts about myself
- ☐ Scary thoughts about others I love
- ☐ Thoughts of harming myself in some way

☐ Thoughts of harming my baby

☐ Negative, intrusive, repetitive thoughts or images

☐ Afraid to tell anyone my thoughts

☐ Racing thoughts keep me up at night

☐ Fear that I'm going crazy

☐ Fear of losing control

☐ Difficulty concentrating

☐ Difficulty making decisions

☐ Memory loss

☐ Crying all the time

☐ Uncomfortable being with baby

☐ Overattached to baby

☐ Unable to cope

☐ Detached from baby

☐ Nervous about ability to care for baby

☐ Afraid to be alone with baby

☐ Overly attached to my husband

☐ Detached from my husband

☐ Loss of sexual interest

☐ I feel worse in morning

☐ I feel worse in afternoon

☐ I just don't feel like myself

☐ This isn't who I usually am

☐ I am worried about the way I am feeling

☐ Others are worried about the way I am feeling

☐ I just want to run away

☐ I wish I didn't have to be here

☐ I'm afraid I'll never feel better

☐ My child and husband would be better off without me

☐ I don't think I can do this by myself

☐ I have felt this bad before

☐ Confused

☐ This is the worst I have ever felt

D. PPSC INITIAL SESSION INSTRUCTION PAD*

THE POSTPARTUM STRESS CENTER   610.525.7527
Please call us if you or your partner have any questions

Things to take care of before you do anything else...

postpartumstress.com

☐ Call Doctor for meds: _____

☐ Antidepressant: _____

☐ Anti-anxiety? _____

☐ Sleep aid? _____

☐ Call PPSC with info from doc _____

☐ Eliminate caffeine & alcohol _____

☐ Let your partner know how bad you feel _____

☐ Get thyroid checked _____

☐ Adjust support network to facilitate sleep _____

☐ Breastfeeding issues: _____

☐ Other: _____

E. PPSC PHONE ASSESSMENT*

Key points to keep in mind:

- Source of referral?
- Weeks/months postpartum? pregnant?
- First pregnancy?
- Why are you calling? What are you feeling? (specific as possible, try not to suggest symptoms, assess level of distress and urgency for treatment, evidence of vegetative symptoms or rapid decompensation)
  - Listen to quality, tone, pace of voice
  - Listen to words chosen
- How long have you been feeling this way? Have you ever felt this way before?
  - History of depression/family history
  - Previous therapy/treatment? What worked, what didn't work?
- How consistent are the symptoms? Do you ever have days when you feel better?
- Are you having any thoughts that are scaring you?
- What have you done in response to these feelings? (call doctor, talk to partner, try to ignore it, read self-help books, etc.; assessment of initial coping skills)
- Breastfeeding or bottle-feeding? How is it going? (assessment of mom's early response to any feeding-related difficulties)
- What is your baby's name? How is _____ doing?
  - Listen carefully to mom's report of how baby is doing
  - Verbal response can be strong indicator of attachment issues
- Support network: What is your husband's name? How's _____ doing? Is he worried about how you are feeling? Other family member available for support? (special attention to relationship with mother or loss of mother)
- Assess level of motivation for treatment (doctor told me to call, anxious for symptom resolution, information only; denial? resistance?)
- Offer reassurance of your ability to help her
- Provide information for early coping
- Outline steps for appropriate self-care
- Remind her to make taking care of herself a priority
- Validate her feelings
- Give her permission to call if her symptoms worsen or if she is troubled by anything
- Remind her that her partner can feel free to join the first session or to call if he has concerns
- As always, take any thoughts of suicide, however passive they may be, very seriously and assess whether she should be seen by a psychiatrist *before* she sees you, if circumstances warrant that.

---

* ©2008 by The Postpartum Stress Center (www.postpartumstress.com)

F. EDINBURGH POSTNATAL DEPRESSION SCALE (EPDS)*

Name_____   Today's Date_____

Please circle the answer which comes closest to how you have felt in the past 7 days.

1. I have been able to laugh and see the funny side of things.

   0   As much as I always could
   1   Not quite so much now
   2   Not so much now
   3   Not at all

2. I have looked forward with enjoyment to things.

   0   As much as I ever did
   1   Somewhat less than I used to
   2   A lot less than I used to
   3   Hardly at all

3. I have blamed myself unnecessarily when things went wrong.

   0   No, not at all
   1   Hardly ever
   2   Yes, sometimes
   3   Yes, very often

4. I have been anxious or worried for no good reason.

   3   Yes, often
   2   Yes, sometimes
   1   No, not much
   0   No, not at all

5. I have felt scared or panicky for no good reason.

   3   Yes, often
   2   Yes, sometimes
   1   No, not much
   0   No, not at all

6. Things have been too much for me.

   3   Yes, most of the time I haven't been able to cope at all
   2   Yes, sometimes I haven't been coping as well as usual
   1   No, most of the time I have coped well
   0   No, I have been coping as well as ever

* J. L. Cox, J. M. Holden, and R. Sagovsky, Department of Psychiatry, University of Edinburgh.

7. I have been so unhappy that I have had difficulty sleeping.

   3 Yes, most of the time
   2 Yes, sometimes
   1 Not very often
   0 No, not at all

8. I have felt sad or miserable

   3 Yes, most of the time
   2 Yes, quite often
   1 Not very often
   0 No, not at all

9. I have been so unhappy that I have been crying.

   3 Yes, most of the time
   2 Yes, quite often
   1 Only occasionally
   0 No, never

10. The thought of harming myself has occurred to me.

   3 Yes, quite often
   2 Sometimes
   1 Hardly ever
   0 Never

TOTAL SCORE: _____

Scoring   A score of 10 may require a repeat assessment, as depression symptoms *may* be present. A score of 12 indicates that depression is likely and further assessment by a trained healthcare provider is recommended. If any number other than 0 is circled for item number 10, further assessment is required right away. Please contact your healthcare provider immediately. The EPDS is an assessment tool and should not override clinical judgment. A comprehensive clinical assessment should confirm the diagnosis.

References

Abramowitz, J. S., Schwartz, S. A., & Moore, K. M. (2003). Obsessional thoughts in postpartum females and their partners: Content, severity, and relationship with depression. *Journal of Clinical Psychology in Medical Settings, 10,* 167–174.

Alexander, F., & Ross, H. (Eds.). (1952). *The impact of Freudian psychiatry.* Chicago: University of Chicago Press.

Allen, J., Schnyer, R., Chambers, A., Hitt, S., Moreno, F., & Manber, R. (2006). Acupuncture for depression: A randomized controlled clinical trial. *The Journal of Clinical Psychiatry, 67*(11), 1665–1673.

American Academy of Pediatrics. Breastfeeding. Retrieved January 31, 2008, from http://www.aap.org/healthtopics/breastfeeding.cfm

American College of Obstetrics & Gynecology. (1999). Patient education pamphlet. Washington, DC.

American Psychiatric Association. (2004). Postpartum onset specifiers. In *Diagnostic and Statistical Manual of Mental Disorders* (4th ed.). Washington, DC: American Psychiatric Publishing, Inc.

Appleby, L., Warner, R., Whitton, A., & Faragher, B. (1997). A controlled study of fluoxetine and cognitive–behavioral counseling in the treatment of postnatal depression. *British Medical Journal, 314,* 932–936.

Armstrong, K., & Edwards, H. (2003). The effects of exercise and social support on mothers reporting depressive symptoms: A pilot randomized controlled trial. *International Journal of Mental Health Nursing, 12*(2), 130–138.

Arnold, A. F., Baugh, C., Fisher, A., Brown, J., & Stowe, Z. N. (2002). Psychiatric aspects of the postpartum period. In *Women's mental health: A comprehensive textbook* (1st ed.). New York: The Guildford Press.

Barclay, L., & Lupton, D. (1999). The experience of new parenthood: A sociocultural analysis, *Journal of Advanced Nursing, 29,* 1013–1020.

Barnett, R., Kibria, N., Baruch, G., & Pleck, J. (1991). Adult daughter–parent relationships and their associations with daughters' subjective well-being and psychological distress. *Journal of Marriage & Family, 53*(1), 29–42.

Beck, A. T., Rush, A. J., Shaw, B. F., & Emery, G. (1979). *Cognitive therapy of depression.* New York: Guilford.

Beck, C., & Gable, R. (2002). Postpartum depression screening scale. Western Psychological Services. Los Angeles, CA. Retrieved January 18, 2008, from http://www.wpspublish.com.

Beck, C. T. (2001). Predictors of postpartum depression: An update. *Nursing Research, 50*(5), 275–285.

Beck, C. T. (2004). Post-traumatic stress disorder due to childbirth: The aftermath. *Nursing Research, 53*(4), 216–224.

Beck, C. T. (2006). Postpartum depression: It isn't just the blues. *American Journal of Nursing, 106*(5), 40–50.

Becker, R. *Defending the caveman.* Retrieved January 18, 2008, from http://www.defendingthecaveman.com/

Berle, J., Aarre, T. F., Mykletun, A., Dahl, A., & Holsten, F. (2003). Screening for postnatal depression. Validation of the Norwegian version of the Edinburgh Postnatal Depression Scale, and assessment of risk factors for postnatal depression. *Journal of Affective Disorders, 76,* 151–156.

Bloch, M., Schmidt, P. J., Danaceau, M., Murphy, J., Nieman, L., & Rubinow, D. R. (2000). Effects of gonadal steroids in women with a history of postpartum depression. *American Journal of Psychiatry, 157*(6), 924–930.

Blum, L. (2007). Psychodynamics of postpartum depression. *Psychoanalytic Psychology, 24*(1), 45–62.

Boyce, P., & Hickey, A. (2005). Psychosocial risk factors to major depression after childbirth. *International Journal for Research in Social and Genetic Epidemiology and Mental Health Services, 40,* 605–612.

Brandes, M., Soares, C. N., & Cohen, L. S. (2004). Postpartum onset obsessive–compulsive disorder: Diagnosis and management. *Archives in Women's Mental Health, 7,* 99–110.

Brockington, I. F. (1996). Puerperal psychosis. In *Motherhood and mental health* (pp. 200–284). Oxford: Oxford University Press.

Brockington, I. F., Cernik, K. F., Scholfield, E. M., Downing, A. R., Francis, A. F., & Keelan, C. (1981). Puerperal psychosis. Phenomena and diagnosis. *Archives of General Psychiatry, 38*(7), 829–833.

Bruch, H. (1974). *Learning psychotherapy.* Cambridge, MA: Harvard University Press.

Buist, A., & Janson, H. (2001). Childhood sexual abuse, parenting and postpartum depression—A 3-year follow-up study. *Child Abuse and Neglect, 25*(7), 909–921.

Burt, V. K., Suri, R., Altshuler, L., Stowe, Z., Hendrick, V. C., & Muntean, E. (2001). The use of psychotropic medications during breast-feeding. *American Journal of Psychiatry, 158,* 1001–1009.

Campagne, D. M. (2004). The obstetrician and depression during pregnancy. *European Journal of Obstetrics, Gynecology and Reproductive Biology, 116,* 125–130.

Campbell, S. B., & Cohn, J. F. (1991). Prevalence and correlates of postpartum depression in first-time mothers. *Journal of Abnormal Psychology, 100,* 594–599.

Carver, C. S., Scheier, M. F., & Weintraub, J. K. (1989). Assessing coping strategies: A theoretically based approach. *Journal of Personality and Social Psychology, 56*(2), 267–283.

Chambers, C. D., Hernandez-Diaz, S., Van Marter, L. J., Werler, M. M., Louik, C., Jones, K. L., et al. (2006). Selective serotonin-reuptake inhibitors and risk of persistent pulmonary hypertension of the newborn. *New England Journal of Medicine, 354,* 579–587.

Chaudron, L. (2003). Postpartum depression: What pediatricians need to know. *Pediatrics in Review, 24*(5), 154–161.

Chaudron, L., Szilagyi, P., Kitzman, H., Wadkins, H., & Conwell, Y. (2004). Detection of postpartum depressive symptoms by screening at well-child visits. *Pediatrics, 113*(3), 551–558.

Cohen, L. S., & Altshuler, L. L. (1997). Pharmacologic management of psychiatric illness during pregnancy and the postpartum period. In *Psychiatric Clinics of North America Annual of Drug Therapy* (1st ed., pp. 21–61). Philadelphia, PA: Saunders.

Cohen, L. S., & Rosenbaum, J. F. (1998). Psychotropic drug use during pregnancy: Weighing the risks. *Journal of Clinical Psychiatry, 59*(2), 18–28.

Cohen, L. S., Sichel, D. A., Robertson, L. M., Heckscher, E., & Rosenbaum, J. F. (1995). Postpartum prophylaxis for women with bipolar disorder. *American Journal of Psychiatry, 152,* 1641–1645.

Cohn, J. F., & Tronick, E. Z. (1989). Specificity of infants' response to mothers' affective behavior. *Journal of American Academy of Child and Adolescent Psychiatry, 28,* 242–248.

Cooper, P. J., & Murray, L. (1995). Course and recurrence of postnatal depression. Evidence for the specificity of the diagnostic concept. *British Journal of Psychiatry, 166*(2), 191–195.

Cooper, P. J., & Murray L. (1997). Prediction, detection and treatment of postnatal depression. *Archives of Disease in Childhood, 77,* 97–101.

Corral, M., Kuan, A., & Kostaras, D. (2000). Bright light therapy's effect on postpartum depression. *American Journal of Psychiatry, 157*(2), 303–304.

Cowan, C. P., & Cowan, P. A. (2000). *When partners become parents: The big life change for couples.* Mahwah, NJ: Lawrence Erlbaum.

Cox, J. L., Connor, Y., & Kendell, R. E. (1982). Prospective study of the psychiatric disorders of childbirth. *British Journal of Psychiatry, 140,* 111–117.

Cox, J. L., Holden, J. M., & Sagovsky, R. (1987). Detection of postnatal depression: Development of the 10-item Edinburgh Postnatal Depression Scale. *British Journal of Psychiatry, 150,* 782–786.

Cramer, B. (1993). Are postpartum depressions a mother–infant relationship disorder? *Infant Mental Health Journal, 14*(4), 283–297.

Cronenwett, L. R., & Kunst-Wilson, W. (1981). Stress, social support, and the transition to fatherhood. *Nursing Research, 30,* 196–201.

Cutrona, C. E., & Troutman, B. R. (1986). Social support, infant temperament, and parenting self-efficacy: A mediational model of postpartum depression. *Child Development, 57,* 1507–1518.

Deglin, J. H., & Vallerand, A. H. (2003). *Davis's drug guide for nurses* (8th ed.). Philadelphia, PA: F. A. Davis Company.

de Marneffe, D. (2004). *Maternal desire.* New York: Little, Brown and Company.

Dennis, C. L. (2004). Prevention of postpartum depression. Part II: A critical review of nonbiological interventions. *Canadian Journal of Psychiatry, 49*(8), 526–538.

Dennis, C. L., & Ross, L. E. (2005). Relationships among infant **sleep** patterns, maternal fatigue, and development of depressive symptomatology. *Birth: Issues in Perinatal Care, 32*(3), 187–193.

Dennis, C. L., & Ross, L. E. (2006). The clinical utility of maternal self-reported personal and familial psychiatric history in identifying women at risk for postpartum depression. *Acta Obstetricia et Gynecologica Scandinavica, 85*(10), 1179–1185.

Doskoch, P. (2001). Which is more toxic to a fetus—Antidepressants or maternal depression? *Neuropsychiatry Reviews, 2*(5) Retrieved January 18, 2008, www.neuropsychiatryreviews.com.

Dragonwagon, C. (1977). *Will it be okay?* New York: Harper & Row. Retrieved January 18, 2008, from www.Dragonwagon.com

Dugoua, J. J., Mills, E., Perri, D., & Koren, G. (2006). Safety and efficacy of St. John's wort (hypericum) during pregnancy and lactation. *Canadian Journal of Clinical Pharmacology, 3,* 268–276.

Dunn, A. L., Trivedi, M. H., Kampert, J. B., Clark, C. G., & Chambliss, H. O. (2005). Exercise treatment for depression: Efficacy and dose response. *American Journal of Preventative Medicine, 28*(1), 1–8.

Eberhard-Gran, M., Eskild, A., & Opjordsmoen, S. (2005). Treating mood disorders during pregnancy: Safety considerations. *Drug Safety, 28*(8), 695–706.

Eberhard-Gran, M., Eskild, A., & Opjordsmoen, S. (2006). Use of psychotropic medications in treating mood during lactation. *CNS Drugs, 20*(3), 187–198.

Elek, S. M., Hudson, D. B., & Fleck, M. O. (1997). Expectant parents' experience with fatigue and sleep during pregnancy. *Birth, 24*(1), 49–54.

El-Mallakh, R., & Karippot, A. (2002). Use of antidepressants to treat depression in bipolar disorder. *Psychiatric Services, 53,* 580–584. American Psychiatric Association.

Epperson, C. N. (1999). Postpartum major depression: Detection and treatment. *American Family Physician, 59*(8), 2247–2259.

Epstein, M. (1995). *Thoughts without a thinker* (pp. 187–188). New York: Basic Books.

Epstein, S. (1991). The self concept, the traumatic neuroses and the structure of personality. In D. Ozer, J. M. Healy, & R. A. J. Stewart (Eds.), *Perspectives on personality* (Vol. 3A). London: Jessica Kingsley.

Evans, J., Heron, J., Francomb, H., Oke, S., & Golding, J. (2001). Cohort study of depressed mood during pregnancy and after childbirth. *British Medical Journal, 323,* 257–260.

Fergusson, D., Horwood, J., & Ridder, E. (2006). Abortion in young women and subsequent mental health. *Journal of Child Psychology and Psychiatry, 47*(1), 16–24.

Fleming, A. S., Klein, E., & Corter, C. (1992). The effects of a social support group on depression, maternal attitudes and behavior in new mothers. *Journal of Child Psychology and Psychiatry, 33,* 685–698.

Flores, D. L., & Hendrick, V. C. (2002). Etiology and treatment of postpartum depression. *Current Psychiatry Reports, 4,* 461–466.

France, K. G., & Henderson, S. M. (1996). Fact, act, and tact: A three-stage approach to treating the sleep problems of infants and young children. *Child and Adolescent Psychiatric Clinics of North America, 5,* 581–599.

Frank, J. B., Weihs, K., Minerva, E., & Lieberman, D. Z. (1998). Women's mental health in primary care. Depression, anxiety, somatization, eating disorders, and substance abuse. *Medical Clinics of North America, 82,* 359–389.

Frankl, V. (1959). *Man's search for meaning.* New York: Beacon Press.

Freedman, M. P., Smith, K. W., Freeman, S. A., McElroy, S. L., Kmetz, G. E., Wright, R., et al. (2002). The impact of reproductive events on the course of bipolar disorder in women. *Journal of Clinical Psychiatry, 63,* 284–287.

Freud, A., & Furst, S. (Eds). (1967). Comments on trauma: Psychic trauma. In *Psychic trauma.* New York: Basic Books.

Gay, C., Lee, K., & Lee S. (2004). Sleep patterns and fatigue in new mothers and fathers. *Biological Research for Nursing, 5*(4), 311–318.

Gaynes, B. N., Gavin, N., Meltzer-Brody, S., Lohr, K. N., Swinson, T., Gartlehner, G., et al. (2005). Perinatal depression: Prevalence, screening accuracy, and screening outcomes. *Evidence Report Technology Assessment, 119,* 1–8.

Gilman, C. P. (1892). The yellow wallpaper. First published by Small & Maynard, Boston, MA. Retrieved January 2, 2008, from http://www.library.csi.cuny.edu/dept/history/lavender/wallpaper.html

Gjerdingen, D. K., Froberg, D. G., & Fontaine, P. (1991). The effects of social support on women's health during pregnancy, labor and delivery and the postpartum period. *Family Medicine, 23,* 370–375.

Goldsmith, M. (2007). Postpartum depression screening by family nurse practitioners. *Journal of the American Academy of Nurse Practitioners, 19*(6), 321–327.

Gotlib, I. H., Whiffen, V. E., Mount, J. H., Milne, K., & Cordy, N. I. (1989). Prevalence rates and demographic characteristics associated with depression in pregnancy and the postpartum. *Journal of Consulting and Clinical Psychology, 57,* 269–274.

Gregoire, A. J., Kumar, B., Everitt, B., Henderson, A. F., & Studd, J. W. (1996). Transdermal estrogen for treatment of severe postnatal depression. *Lancet, 347,* 930–933.

Grote, N., & Bledsoe, S. (2007). Predicting postpartum depressive symptoms in new mothers: The role of optimism and stress frequency during pregnancy. *Health & Social Work, 32*(2), 107–118.

Grover, S., Avasthi, A., & Sharma, Y. (2006). Psychotropics in pregnancy: Weighing the risks. *Indian Journal of Medical Research, 123,* 497–512.

Hamilton, J. A. (1989). Postpartum psychiatric syndromes. *Psychiatric Clinics of North America, 12*(1), 89–103.

Harlow, H. (1958). The nature of love. *American Psychologist, 13,* 673–685.

Hawley, L., Ho, M., Zuroff, D., & Blatt, S. (2006). The relationship of perfectionism, depression, and therapeutic alliance during treatment for depression: Latent difference score analysis. *Journal of Consulting and Clinical Psycholgy, 74*(5), 930–942.

Hedlund, J., & Vieweg, B. (1979). The Hamilton rating scale for depression. *The Journal of Operational Psychiatry, 10*(2), 149–165.

Hendrick, V. (2003). Alternative treatments for postpartum depression. *Psychiatric Times, 20*(8), 50–51.

Heneghan, A. M., Mercer, M. B., & Deleone, N. L. (2004). Will mothers discuss parenting stress and depressive symptoms with their child's pediatrician? *Pediatrics, 113,* 460–467.

Hiscock, H., & Wake, M. (2001). Infant sleep problems and postnatal depression: A community-based study. *Pediatrics, 107*(6), 1317–1322.

Hiscock, H., & Wake, M. (2002). Randomized controlled trial of behavioral infant sleep intervention to improve infant sleep and maternal mood. *British Medical Journal, 324,* 1062–1065.

Holden, J. M., Sagovsky, R., & Cox, J. L. (1989). Counseling in a general practice setting: A controlled study of health visitor intervention in treatment of postnatal depression. *British Medical Journal, 298*(6668), 223–226.

Hughes, P. M., Turton, P., & Evans, C. D. (1999). Stillbirth as risk factor for depression and anxiety in the subsequent pregnancy: A cohort study. *British Medical Journal, 318*(7200), 1721–1724.

Jenike, M. A. (2004). Obsessive–compulsive disorder. *New England Journal of Medicine, 350,* 259–265.

Jennings, K. D., Ross, S., Popper, S., & Elmore, M. (1999). Thoughts of harming infants in depressed and nondepressed mothers. *Journal of Affective Disorders, 54,* 21–28.

Jones, I., & Craddock, N. (2001). Familiarity of the Puerperal trigger in bipolar disorder: Results of a family study. *American Journal of Psychiatry, 158,* 913–917.

Jones, I. (2005). Bipolar disorder and childbirth: The importance of recognizing risk. *The British Journal of Psychiatry, 186,* 453–454.

Kendall-Tackett, K. (1994). Postpartum rituals and the prevention of postpartum depression: A cross-cultural perspective. *Newsletter of the Boston Institute for the Development of Infants and Parents, 13*(1), 3–6.

Kennedy, H., Beck, C., & Driscoll, J. (2002). A light in the fog: Caring for women with postpartum depression. *Journal of Midwifery and Women's Health, 47*(5), 318–330.

Kleiman, K. (1999). The Postpartum Stress Center risk assessment during pregnancy. Retrieved January 18, 2008, from www.postpartumstress.com

Kleiman, K. (2001). *The postpartum husband: Practical solutions for living with postpartum depression.* Philadelphia: Xlibris.

Kleiman, K. (2005). *What am I thinking: Having another baby after postpartum depression.* Philadelphia: Xlibris.

Kleiman, K., & Raskin, V. (1994). *This isn't what I expected: Overcoming postpartum depression.* New York: Bantam Books.

Klerman, G. L., Weissman, M. M., Rounsaville, B. J., & Chevron, E. (1995). *Interpersonal psychotherapy of depression.* Lanham, MD: Jason Aronson.

Knops, G. G. (1993). Postpartum mood disorders. A startling contrast to the joy of birth. *Postgraduate Medicine, 93,* 103–104, 109–110, 113–116.

Kroenke, K., Spitzer, R., & Williams, J. (2001). The PHQ-9: Validity of a brief depression severity measure. *Journal of General Internal Medicine, 16*(9), 606–613.

Kumar, R. (1994). Postnatal mental illness: A transcultural perspective. *Social Psychiatry and Psychiatric Epidemiology, 29*(6), 250–264.

Kumar, R., & Robson, K. M. (1984). A prospective study of emotional disorders in childbearing women. *British Journal of Medicine, 144,* 35–47.

Lamberg, L. (1999). Safety of antidepressant use in pregnancy and nursing women. *Journal of American Medical Association, 282*(3), 222–223.

Lark, S. (1993). *Anxiety & stress self help book: Effective solutions for nervous tension, emotional distress, anxiety, & panic.* Berkeley, CA: Celestial Arts.

Larsen, K., Schwartz, S. A., Whiteside, S. P., Khandker, M., Moore, K. M., & Abramowitz, J. S. (2006). Thought control strategies used by parents reporting postpartum obsessions. *Journal of Cognitive Psychotherapy, 20*(4), 435–445.

Levinson-Castiel, R., Merlob, P., Linder, N., Sirota, L., & Klinger, G. (2006). Neonatal abstinence syndrome after in utero exposure to selective serotonin reuptake inhibitors in term infants. *Archives of Pediatric and Adolescent Medicine, 160*(2), 173–176.

Liabsuetrakul, T., Vittayanont, A., & Pitanupong, J. (2007). Clinical applications of anxiety, social support, stressors, and self-esteem measured during pregnancy and postpartum for screening postpartum depression in Thai women. *Journal of Obstetrics and Gynecology Research, 33*(3), 333–340.

Lindahl, V., Pearson, J. L., & Colpe, L. (2005). Prevalence of suicidality during pregnancy and the postpartum. *Archives of Women's Mental Health, 8,* 77–87.

Linnon, N. (2003). Postpartum. In Gutkind, L. (Ed.), *Creative Nonfiction, 21,* 102–116.

Little, M. (1993). Margaret Little: Psychotherapy with D. W. W. In Goldman, D. (Ed.) *In one's bones: The clinical genius of Winnicott* (pp. 123–137). London: Jason Aronson, Inc.

Llewellyn, A., Stowe, Z., & Nemcroff, C. (1997). Depression during pregnancy and the puerperium. *Journal of Clinical Psychiatry, 58*(15), 26.

Logsdon, C., Wisner, K., Billings, D., & Shanahan, B. (2006). Raising the awareness of primary care providers about postpartum depression. *Issues in Mental Health Nursing, 27*(1), 59–73.

Lusskin, S., Pundiak, T., & Habib, S. (2007). Perinatal depression: Hiding in plain sight. *The Canadian Journal of Psychiatry, 52*(8), 487–497.

MacLennan, A., Wilson, D., & Taylor, A. (1996). The self-reported prevalence of postnatal depression. *The Australian and New Zealand Journal of Obstetrics and Gynecology, 36,* 313.

Manning, M. (1994). *Undercurrents: A life beneath the surface.* New York: HarperCollins.

Manning, M. (2002). *The common thread: Mothers and daughters: The bond we never outgrow.* New York: HarperCollins.

Marci, C., Ham, J., Moran, E., & Orr, S. (2007). Physiologic correlates of perceived therapist empathy and social–emotional process during psychotherapy. *Journal of Nervous & Mental Disease, 195*(2), 103–111.

Marks, M., & Lovestone, S. (1995). The role of the father in parental postnatal mental health. *British Journal of Medical Psychology, 68,* 157–168.

Martin, J., Hiscock, H., Hardy, P., Davey, B., & Wake, M. (2007). Adverse associations of infant and child sleep problems and parent health: An Australian population study. *Pediatrics, 119*(5), 947–955.

Maslach, C., Schaufel, W., & Leiter, M. (2001). Job burnout. *Annual Review of Psychology, 52*(1), 397.

Matthey, S., Barnett, B., Kavanagh, D. J., & Howie, P. (2001). Validation of the Edinburgh postnatal depression scale for men and comparison of item endorsement with their partners. *Journal of Affective Disorders, 64*(2–3), 175–184.

Mazzeo, S. (2006). Associations among postpartum depression, eating disorders and perfectionism in a population-based sample of adult women. *International Journal of Eating Disorders, 39,* 202–211.

McLearn, K., Minkovitz, C., Strobino, D., Marks, E., & Hou, W. (2006). Maternal depressive symptoms at 2 to 4 months postpartum and early parenting practices. *Archives of Pediatrics and Adolescent Medicine, 160,* 279–284.

Meager, I., & Milgrom, J. (1996). Group treatment for postpartum depression: A pilot study. *Australian and New Zealand Journal of Psychiatry, 30,* 852–860.

Menos, M. D., & Wilson, A. (1998). Affective experiences and levels of self-organization in maternal postpartum depression. *Psychoanalytic Psychology, 15,* 396–419.

Milgrom, J., Martin, P., & Negri, L. (1999). *Treating postnatal depression.* New York: John Wiley & Sons.

Miller, A. (1981). *The drama of the gifted child.* New York: Basic Books.

Miller, L. (2002). Postpartum depression. *Journal of American Medical Association, 287*(6), 762–765.

Misri, S., & Kendrick, K. (2007). Treatment of perinatal mood and anxiety disorders: A review. *Canadian Journal of Psychiatry, 52*(8), 489–498.

Misri, S., & Kostaras, X. (2002). Benefits and risks to mother and infant of drug treatment for postnatal depression. *Drug Safety, 26*(13), 903–911.

Moline, M., Kahn, D., Ross, R., Altshuler, L., & Cohen, L. (2001). Postpartum depression: A guide for patients and families. *Expert Consensus Guideline Series.*

Murray, L. (1992). The impact of postnatal depression on infant development. *Journal of Child Psychology and Psychiatry, 33*(3): 543–561.

Murray, L., & Cooper, P. (1997). Effects of postnatal depression on infant development. *Archives of Disease in Childhood, 77,* 99–101.

Murray, L., Cooper, P., Wilson, A., & Romaniuk, H. (2002). Controlled trial of the short- and long-term effect of psychological treatment of postpartum depression. *British Journal of Psychiatry, 182,* 420–427.

National Institutes of Health (NIH) National Center for Complementary and Alternative Medicine. (2008). St. John's Wort and depression. Retrieved January 31, 2008, from http://nccam.nih.gov/health/stjohnswort/sjwataglance.htm

Nemets, B., Stahl, Z., & Belmaker, R. H. (2002). Addition of omega-3 fatty acid to maintenance medication treatment for recurrent unipolar depressive disorder. *American Journal of Psychiatry, 159*(3), 477–479.

Neugebauer, R., Kline, J., Shrout, P., Skodol, A., O'Connor, P., Geller, P. A., et al. (1997). Major depressive disorder in the 6 months after miscarriage. *Journal of American Medical Association, 277,* 383–388.

Nonacs, R. (2006). *A deeper shade of blue.* New York: Simon & Schuster.

Nonacs, R., Viguera, A., Cohen, L., Reminick, A., & Harlow, B. (n.d.). Risk for recurrent depression during the postpartum period: A prospective study. Massachusetts General Hospital & Harvard Medical School, Boston, MA. Retrieved January 18, 2008, from http://www.womensmentalhealth.org

Northrup, C. (2005). *Mother–daughter wisdom: Understanding the crucial link between mothers, daughters, and health.* New York: Bantam Dell.

Oakley A. (1980). *Women confined: Towards a sociology of childbirth.* Oxford: Martin Robertson.

Oates, M. (2003). Suicide: The leading cause of maternal death. *British Journal of Psychiatry, 183,* 279–281.

O'Hara, M. W. (1986). Social support, life events, and depression during pregnancy and the puerperium. *Archives of General Psychiatry, 43,* 569–573.

O'Hara, M. W. (1987). Postpartum blues, depression and psychosis: A review. *Journal of Psychosomatic Obstetrics & Gynaecology, 73,* 205–227.

O'Hara, M. W. (1994). Postpartum depression: Identification and measurement in a cross-cultural context. In: Cox, J., Holden, J. editors. *Perinatal Psychiatry: Use and misuse of the Edinburg Postnatal Depression Scale.* London: Gaskell.

O'Hara, M. W. (1995). *Postpartum depression: Causes and consequences.* New York: Springer–Verlag.

O'Hara, M. W., Stuart, S., Gorman, L., & Wenzel, A. (2000). Efficacy of interpersonal psychotherapy for postpartum depression. *Archives of General Psychiatry, 57*(11), 1039–1045.

Oren, D. A., Wisner, K. L., Spinelli, M., Epperson, C. N., Peindl, K. S., Terman, J. S., et al. (2002). An open trial of morning light therapy for treatment of antepartum depression. *American Journal of Psychiatry, 159*(4), 666–669.

Pariser, S. F. (1993). Women and mood disorders: Menarche to menopause. *Annals of Clinical Psychiatry, 5,* 249–254.

Patient Health Questionnaire (PHQ-9). (1999). Pfizer, Inc. Retrieved January 18, 2008, from http://www.nyc.gov/html/doh/downloads/pdf/csi/depressionkit-clin-questionnaire.pdf

Paykel, E. S., Emms, E. M., Fletcher, J., & Rassaby, E. S. (1980). Life events and social support in puerperal depression. *British Journal of Psychiatry, 136,* 339–346.

Pearlstein, T., Zlotnick, C., Battle, C., Stewart, S., O'Hara, M., Price, A., et al. (2006). Patient choice of treatment for postpartum depression: A pilot study. *Archives of Women's Mental Health, 9,* 303–308.

Peet, M., Murphy, B., Shay, J., & Horrobin, D. (1998). Depletion of omega-3 fatty acid levels in red blood cell membranes of depressive patients. *Biological Psychiatry, 43*(5), 315–319.

Peterson, C., Prout, M., & Schwarz, R. (1991). *Post traumatic stress disorder: A clinician's guide.* New York: Plenum Press.

PDR *(Physicians' Desk Reference).* (2006). Montvale, NJ: Thomson Healthcare.

Pitt, B. (1968). "Atypical" depression following childbirth. *British Journal of Psychiatry, 122,* 431–433.

Ramsay, R. (1993). Postnatal depression. *Lancet, 341,* 1358.

Rand, M. (n.d.). Boundaries in a therapeutic relationship. Retrieved January 18, 2008, from http://www.4therapy.com

Rand, M., & Fewster, G. (n.d.). Self, body and boundaries. Retrieved January 18, 2008, from http://www.drrandbodymindtherapy.com/boundaries.html

Reed, P., Sermin, N., Appleby, L., & Faragher, B. (1999). A comparison of clinical response to electroconvulsive therapy in puerperal and nonpuerperal psychoses. *Journal of Affective Disorders, 54,* 255–260.

Romito, P. (1990). Postpartum depression and the experience of motherhood. *Acta Obstetricia et Gynecologica Scandinavica, 69*(154), 7–37.

Rosenthal, R., Muran, C., Pinsker, H., Hellerstein, D., & Winston, A. (1999). Interpersonal change in brief supportive psychotherapy. *Journal of Psychotherapy Practice and Research, 8,* 55–63.

Ross, L., Murray, B., & Steiner, M. (2005). Sleep and perinatal mood disorders: A critical review. *Journal of Psychiatry & Neuroscience, 30*(4), 247–257.

Scheier, M., & Carver, C. (1992). Effects of optimism on psychological and physical well-being: Theoretical overview and empirical update. *Cognitive Therapy and Research, 16,* 201–228.

Schore, A. (1994). *Affect regulation and the origin of the self: The neurobiology of emotional development.* Hillsdale, NJ: Lawrence Erlbaum Associates.

Shapiro, F. (2004). *EMDR: The breakthrough "eye movement" therapy for overcoming anxiety, stress, and trauma.* New York: Basic Books.

Sichel, D., & Driscoll, J. (2000). *Women's moods: What every woman must know about hormones, the brain, and emotional health.* New York: Quill.

Sinclair, D., & Murray, L. (1998). Effects of postnatal depression on children's adjustment to school. *British Journal of Psychiatry, 172,* 58–63.

Sit, D., Wisner K., & Rothschild, A. (2006). Review of postpartum psychosis. *Journal of Women's Health, 15*(4), 352–368.

Small, R., Lumley, J., Yelland, J., & Brown, S. (2007). The performance of the Edinburgh Postnatal Depression Scale in English speaking and non-English speaking populations in Australia. *Social Psychiatry & Psychiatric Epidemiology, 42*(1), 70–78.

Spencer, J., Gonzalez, L., & Barnhart, D. (2001). Medications in the breast-feeding mother. *American Family Physician, 64*(1), 119–127.

Spinelli, M. G. (2004). Maternal infanticide associated with mental illness: Prevention and the promise of saved lives. *American Journal of Psychiatry, 161,* 1548–1557.

Stern, G., & Kruckman, L. (1983). Multidisciplinary perspective on postpartum depression: An anthropological critique. *Social Science and Medicine, 17*(15), 1027–1041.

Stowe, Z. N., & Nemeroff, C. B. (1995). Women at risk for postpartum-onset major depression. *American Journal of Obstetrics and Gynecology, 173*(2), 639–645.

Sue, D., & Sue, D. (2003). *Counseling the counseling diverse: Theory and practice* (4th ed.). New York: John Wiley & Sons.

Sugawara, M., Toda, M. A., Shima, S., Mukai, T., Sakakura, K., & Kitamura, T. (1997). Premenstrual mood changes and maternal mental health in pregnancy and the postpartum period. *Journal of Clinical Psychology, 53*(3), 225–232.

Swigart J. (1991). *The myth of the bad mother.* New York: Avon Books.

Taylor, S. (1983). Adjustment to threatening events. *American Psychologist, 38,* 1161–1173.

Taylor, S., Kemeny, M., Reed, G., Bower, J., & Gruenewald, T. (2000). Psychological resources, positive illusions, and health. *American Psychologist, 55*(1), 99–109.

Taylor, S., Lichtman, R., & Wood, J. (1984). Attributions, beliefs about control, and adjustment to breast cancer. *Journal of Personality and Social Psychology, 46,* 489–502.

Tronick, E. Z. (1989). Emotions and emotional communication in infants. *American Psychologist, 44,* 112–119.

Urato, A. (2006). Concerns regarding antidepressant drug use during pregnancy. *Journal of Psychiatry and Neuroscience, 31*(6), 411.

U.S. Preventive Services Task Force. (2002). Screening for depression: Recommendations and rationale. *Annals of Internal Medicine, 136*(10), 760–764.

Ventura, J., & Stevenson, M. (1986). Relations of mothers' and fathers' reports of infant temperament, parents' psychological functioning, and family characteristics. *Merrill–Palmer Quarterly, 32,* 275–289.

Viorst, J. (1972). *Alexander and the terrible, horrible, no good, very bad day.* New York: Simon & Schuster.

Viorst, J. (1986). *Necessary losses.* New York: Fireside.

Ward, R., & Zamorski, M. (2002). Benefits and risks of psychiatric medications during pregnancy. *American Family Physician, 66*(4), 629–636.

Warner, J. (2005). *Perfect madness.* New York: Riverhead.

Warner, R., Appleby, L., Whitton, A., & Faragher, B. (1996). Demographic and obstetric risk factors for postnatal psychiatric morbidity. *British Journal of Psychiatry, 168*(5), 607–611.

Whiffen, V., & Gotlib, I. (1989). Infants of postpartum depressed mothers: Temperament and cognitive status. *Journal of Abnormal Psychology, 98*, 274–279.

Whitten, A., Appleby, L., & Warner, R. (1996). Maternal thinking and the treatment of postnatal depression. *International Review of Psychiatry, 8*(1), 73–78.

Whooley, M. A., Avins, A. L., Miranda, J., & Browner, W. S. (1997). Case-finding instruments for depression: Two questions are as good as many. *Journal of General Internal Medicine, 12*, 439–445.

Why mothers die (2001). Report on confidential enquiries into maternal deaths in the United Kingdom 1997–1999. London: Royal College of Obstetricians and Gynecologists.

Williams, K., & Koran, L. (1997). Obsessive–compulsive disorder in pregnancy, the puerperium, and the premenstruum. *Journal of Clinical Psychiatry, 58*(7), 330–334.

Winnicott, D. W. (1947). Hate in the countertransference. In D. Goldman (Ed.), *In one's bones: The clinicial genius of Winnicott.* London: Jason Aronson, Inc.

Winnicott, D. W. (1951). Transitional objects and transitional phenomena. In *Playing and reality.* New York: Basic Books, 1971.

Winnicott, D. W. (1953). Transitional objects and transitional phenomena. *International Journal of Psychoanalysis, 34*: 89–97.

Winnicott, D. W. (1956). Primary maternal preoccupation. In *Collected papers: Through pediatrics to psycho-analysis.* New York: Basic Books.

Winnicott, D. W. (1960). Ego distortion in terms of true and false self. In *The maturational processes and the facilitating environment.* New York: International Universities Press.

Winnicott, D. W. (1963). Psychiatric disorders in terms of infantile maturational processes. In *The maturational processes and the facilitating environment.* New York: International Universities Press.

Winnicott, D. W. (1965). *The maturational processes and the facilitating environment.* London: Hogarth Press and the Institute of Psychoanalysis. New York: International Universities Press.

Wisner, K. (2006). *Current issues in perinatal psychiatry.* Retrieved November 2, 2006, from Maternal Depression Retreat, University of Pennsylvania (seminar).

Wisner, K. (2007). *Perinatal depression: Diagnosis, treatment & family impact.* November 15, 2007 (audio conference).

Wisner, K., Parry, B., & Piontek, C. (2002). Clinical practice: Postpartum depression. *New England Journal of Medicine, 347*(3), 194–199.

Wisner, K. L., Gelenberg, A. J., Leonard, H., & Zarin, D. (1999). Frank E. Pharmacologic treatment of depression during pregnancy. *Journal of the American Medical Association, 282*, 1264–1269.

Wisner, K. L., Peindl, K. S., & Hanusa, B. H. (1996). Effects of childbearing on the natural history of panic disorder with comorbid mood disorder. *Journal of Affective Disorder, 16*, 3173–3180.

Wisner, K. L., Perel, J. M., Peindl, K. S., Hanusa, B. H., Findling, R. L., & Rapport, D. (2001). Prevention of recurrent postpartum depression: A randomized clinical trial. *Journal of Clinical Psychiatry, 62*(2), 82–86.

Wisner, K. L., & Wheeler R. N. (1994). Prevention of recurrent postpartum major depression. *Hospital Community Psychiatry, 45*, 1191–1196.

Wisner, K. L., Zarin, D. A., Holmboe, E. S., Appelbaum, P. S., Gelenberg, A. J., Leonard, H. L., et al. (2000). Risk-benefit decision making for treatment of depression during pregnancy. *American Journal of Psychiatry, 157,* 1933–1940.

Wolf, N. (1991). *The beauty myth.* New York: HarperCollins.

Yexley, M. J. (2007). Treating postpartum depression with hypnosis: Addressing specific symptoms presented by the client. *American Journal of Clinical Hypnosis, 49*(3), 219–223.

Yonkers, K. & Chantilis, S. (1995). Recognition of depression in obstetric/gynecology practices. *American Journal of Obstetrics & Gynecology, 173*(2), 632–638.

Zelkowitz, P., & Milet, T. (1997). Stress and support as related to postpartum paternal mental health and perceptions of the infant. *Infant Mental Health Journal, 18*(4), 424–435.

Zlotnick, C., Johnson, S., Miller, I., Pearlstein, T., & Howard, M. (2001). Postpartum depression in women receiving public assistance: Pilot study of an interpersonal-therapy oriented group intervention. *American Journal of Psychiatry, 158*(4), 638–640.

Index

H